# FLANNERY O'CONNOR: HER LIFE, LIBRARY AND BOOK REVIEWS

BY

LORINE M. GETZ

# FLANNERY O'CONNOR:
# HER LIFE,
# LIBRARY AND BOOK REVIEWS

BY

LORINE M. GETZ

THE EDWIN MELLEN PRESS
NEW YORK AND TORONTO

Lorine M. Getz


Studies in Women and Religion, Volume Five

The Edwin Mellen Press
New York and Toronto


ISBN 0-88946-997-0

Studies in Women and Religion ISBN 0-88946-549-5
Library of Congress Cataloging Number 80-82800
Printed in the United States of America

*To my Mother and Father*

PREFACE

Flannery O'Connor (1925-1964), America's greatest post-World War II short story writer, uniquely represents the convergence of Roman Catholicism and the American South. Her significance as an artist arises from this convergence. No other writer has so keenly grasped the artistic possibilities present within this combination, and no other has so intensely depicted them. Creatively combining religious motifs she found in the Protestant fundamentalism of her region, with its emphasis on an apocalyptic and avenging God, and in her own Roman Catholicism, with its emphasis on the transforming, sacramental presence of God, within the mundane particularity of everyday concerns, O'Connor explores the essential Christian questions. Her short stories and novels depict characters and events in ways which illuminate, in strange settings of alienation and chaos, the relationship between God and humanity described as the "action of grace."

To date, most scholarly examinations of O'Connor's literary and religious significance have been limited to analyses of her fiction works. Recently, a few critics have sought to examine her non-fiction writings and her intellectual interests in order to understand better O'Connor's worldview. However, these studies have not adequately achieved their goal, largely because they were written without access to the full range of source materials which illuminate O'Connor's religio-cultural background. Only now are these materials becoming publicly available. Within the past decade, two volumes of O'Connor's papers have been published. In 1970, Robert and Sally Fitzgerald edited some of O'Connor's essays

in *Mystery and Manners*; in 1979, Sally Fitzgerald published
a volume of O'Connor's personal letters entitled *The Habit
of Being*. As more primary data and source materials become
accessible, scholars are gaining a greater awareness of both
the Catholic and Southern aspects of Flannery O'Connor's intellectual heritage in which can be found the roots of her
literary genius.

Two additional sources for understanding O'Connor's literary and religious environment have until now been unavailable:
her personal library holdings and her book reviews. As an avid
and eclectic reader, O'Connor accumulated a diversified library.
The nature of her collection, the annotations and inscriptions
within some volumes, and their personal and professional interest for O'Connor suggest lines for further inquiry into her specific intellectual pursuits and their textual sources. More
directly, O'Connor's book reviews, which span nearly the last
decade of her life, provide a means by which to discern her reactions to popular religious and literary writings of her time
and her judgment of them. The library holdings and the book
reviews, valuable sources of insight into O'Connor's intellectual interests and milieu, are presented in this book.

The contents of the volume have been organized to provide some understanding of Flannery O'Connor's personal and
historical uniqueness. Part One discusses her life and
works, situating O'Connor in her Southern and Catholic heri-
tages, and tracing certain fundamental themes which emerge
from these roots in her writings. A chronology of her life
and works completes this section. Part Two presents a description of her personal library holdings followed by a complete
list of works in the Flannery O'Connor Collection now housed
at Georgia College in her hometown in Milledgeville. Inscriptions within these volumes are given and the presence of annotations is indicated. Part Three describes Flannery O'Connor's work as a book critic, presents the texts of her

published reviews and lists all of her known reviews, published and unpublished.

This study of Flannery O'Connor from the perspective of her intellectual activities, including her collected holdings and book reviews, provides further primary material for the continued exploration of the life and works of this twentieth century American literary artist.

I wish to thank Mrs. Regina Cline O'Connor, mother of Flannery O'Connor, for her personal interest and her many kindnesses during the preparation of this study. Sally Fitzgerald, editor of *The Habit of Being* and co-editor of *Mystery and Manners*, read and edited Part I, adding and clarifying biographical detail. Gerald Becham, curator of the Flannery O'Connor Collection, provided invaluable assistance during my research at Georgia College and updated my work to reflect the most recent acquisitions in the collection. Leo Zuber, for many years O'Connor's book review editor, generously supplied otherwise unavailable information.

Permission to use material from the Flannery O'Connor Collection has been granted by Robert Fitzgerald, O'Connor's literary executor and co-editor of *Mystery and Manners*. Permission to copy O'Connor's book reviews was granted by the editors of *The American Scholar*, *The Catholic Week*, *The Bulletin*, and *The Southern Cross*.

Lorine M. Getz

Cleveland, Ohio
May 1980

CONTENTS

PART ONE

FLANNERY O'CONNOR'S LITERARY BIOGRAPHY

## LIFE AND WORKS

Authors differ as to the degree and manner in which
their lives are reflected in their works.  For some, writing
is essentially an autobiographical exercise, and the author's
own life is the ground and the subject of his or her writing:
Thomas Wolfe's *Look Homeward, Angel,* Sylvia Plath's *The Bell
Jar* and James Joyce's *A Portrait of the Artist* are examples.
Other artists write, and insist that their works be read,
without reference to their public or private lives.  Holding
that "the novel is a work of art, and therefore not a facet
of the author's personality,"[1] Caroline Gordon cites the
following example taken from contemporary American fiction:

> Sherwood Anderson's personality was, indeed, engaging
> and he had attending moods of exaltation and despair
> (like many of us), but he was also a considerable art-
> ist.  His work is certainly uneven. . . . but he has
> left short stories behind him which are well-nigh flaw-
> less, and they are not "facets of his personality," but
> works of art complete in themselves.  "I Want to Know
> Why," "I'm a Fool," "The Triumph of the Egg" are contri-
> butions to literature, not autobiography.[2]

Flannery O'Connor's corpus stands somewhere between these
extremes.  Her stories can stand on their own, presupposing
no knowledge of her background or life experience.  Indeed,
because of the difficulties which presently bar access to her
private papers and letters,[3] biographical material is meager

---

[1]Gordon, *How to Read a Novel,* p. 15.

[2]Gordon, pp. 15-16.

[3]Regina Cline O'Connor, the writer's mother, has collected many of her letters.  Some of these letters, recently
made available to Sally Fitzgerald, have been edited and

and often unreliable.  Her family is wary of giving out information, and friends' memories have become hazy and sometimes even contradictory.  It will be some time before all
the evidence is made public so that a reliable biography can
be written.  As with any study of contemporary figures where
all the data are not available, judgments must be tentative
and suggestions or speculations must be weighed against what
evidence there is.[4]  There is sometimes no other recourse,
even for the scholar, than to read her stories as if they
were created *ex nihilo*, and Flannery O'Connor's stories have
survived the test easily.

On the other hand, despite the difficulty resulting from
this lack of precise biographical data, we know that Flannery
O'Connor's work is related to her life, arising out of a
fusion of her southern American setting and a style of Roman
Catholicism which was peculiarly her own.  Her Baldwin County,
Georgia, provincialism was manifest in her style and theology.
She was quite aware of this.  Robert Drake, one of her critics, notes her remark to him that "if she went to Japan and
lived for twenty years and then tried to write a story about
the Japanese, the characters would all talk like Herman Tal-
madge."[5]  Her personal religious views colored her fiction
just as deeply.  She claimed that she was

> no disbeliever in spiritual purpose and no vague be-
> liever.  I see from the standpoint of Christian Orthodoxy.

---

published under the title *The Habit of Being: Letters of Flannery O'Connor*, 1979.

[4]Opposite types of excesses can be seen by contrasting
Hendin, *The World of Flannery O'Connor*, where O'Connor's
tendency toward an isolate lifestyle is so drawn as to stereo-
type her as a social outcast, her religious preoccupation dismissed, with Martin, *The True Country: Themes in the Fiction
of Flannery O'Connor*, which disregards her uniqueness and regards her merely as another spokesperson for Christian
orthodoxy.

[5]Drake, *Flannery O'Connor: A Critical Essay*, p. 11.

This means that for me the meaning of life is centered
in our Redemption by Christ and what I see in the world
I see in its relation to that. I don't think that this
is a position that can be taken halfway or that is particularly easy in these times to make transparent in
fiction.[6]

The following sketch of O'Connor's life will focus upon
three aspects of her development: her roots in the Catholic
and Southern tradition, her literary apprenticeship amid
Northern artistic leaders and contemporary intellectual currents, and the achievement of her artistic maturity based
upon the integration of her regional materials and theological concerns.

## Catholic and Southern Roots

Flannery O'Connor was born on March 25th, 1925, in Savannah, Georgia, and died on August 3rd, 1964, in Milledgeville,
Georgia. Between these dates she traveled briefly to other
parts of the United States, spent her apprenticeship in Iowa,
New York and Connecticut, and made a pilgrimage to Europe. It
would not be incorrect to say, however, that spiritually and
emotionally she was never very many miles from her Georgia
roots.

### Savannah

Until her thirteenth year, O'Connor lived in Savannah,
Georgia's oldest center of learning and culture. From its
beginnings as the seat of England's crown colony, Savannah
was industrial, mercantile and non-agrarian. It was, unlike
most of the South, first settled by Episcopalians and Lutherans as well as by Baptists and Methodists.[7] Although

---

[6] Robert and Sally Fitzgerald, eds., *Mystery and Manners*, p. 32.

[7] In 1733, James Oglethorpe, accompanied by Dr. Henry
Herbert, a clergyman of the Church of England, landed at
Yamacraw Bluff and claimed the territory of Georgia for Eng-
land. Although Lutherans and Methodists arrived in 1734 and

Catholics were excluded in Georgia's charter,[8] in 1794 Savannah welcomed Catholic refugees from the massacres of Santo Domingo.[9] Catholic settlers also came to Savannah from Maryland. By 1820, the church in Savannah was a recognized part of the Catholic see of Baltimore. In 1850, Georgia was made a distinct diocese, with its bishop residing in Savannah.[10]

Surrounded here by a well-established and growing Catholic environment, Flannery O'Connor grew up in the O'Connor family home which stands on the city square opposite the historic Cathedral of Saint John the Baptist, built in 1874.[11] She attended St. Vincent Grade School, staffed by the Sisters of Saint Joseph. The distinctively parochial images, events and expressions occasionally found in her later fiction are no doubt recollections and reminiscences of her childhood experiences. In her story, "A Temple of the Holy Ghost," for example, two students from a girls' convent school attempt to apply literally the religious language of the convent to the secular milieu which they visit as weekend guests. "All weekend the two girls were calling each other Temple One and Temple Two . . ."[12] To entertain some local teenage boys,

---

1736 respectively, Georgia became a royal province in 1795 and the Church of England was named the official church.

[8]Harden, *A History of Savannah and Southern Georgia*, p. 496.

[9]Georgia Department of Agriculture, *Georgia, Historical and Industrial*, p. 412. First colonized by the Spanish, Haiti was then ruled by the French for nearly a hundred years. On May 6, 1794, led by Toussaint L'Ouverture, mulatto and Negro Haitians revolted against the French. Slaves were freed; whites not killed were forced to flee.

[10]Georgia Dept. of Agriculture, p. 413.

[11]Harden, *History of Savannah*, p. 496.

[12]"A Temple of the Holy Ghost," *The Complete Stories of Flannery O'Connor*, p. 236. All references to short stories will be from this volume.

the girls "began to sing with their convent-trained voices:
'Tantum Ergo Sacramentum . . .'"[13]  The influence of O'Connor's
early Catholic background on her writings is not limited to
these parochial images, however.  Her concern with the supernatural meaning of human life pervades her fiction.  The extent to which her early Catholic setting and the deeper experiences of faith influenced her is only gradually becoming
evident to scholars as new biographical data become available.

It is difficult to determine the extent to which the
O'Connor family participated in the intellectual and cultural
life of Savannah, a city long recognized for its emphasis on
public access to substantial library holdings and institutions
of learning.  Some critics have sought to establish in these
early cultural surroundings and in her relationship with her
father the groundwork for O'Connor's literary pursuits.

Sally Fitzgerald, a long-time friend and one-time house-
mate, asserts that as a child Flannery O'Connor delighted her
father with original pieces of verse which she would place
under his napkin at table.[14]  Another critic, who bases much
of her argument on the discovery of at least one volume bearing the father's name in the Flannery O'Connor Collection,
tries to establish that Edward O'Connor was a "man with a
penchant for reading and philosophy"[15] by whom his daughter

---

[13]*Complete Stories*, p. 241.

[14]Sally Fitzgerald, unpublished lecture, Flannery O'Connor Symposium, Georgia College, Milledgeville, Georgia, April 3,
1977.

[15]Feeley, unpublished lecture, Georgia College, July 21,
1975.  The Flannery O'Connor Collection, established in the
Ina Dillard Library of Georgia College in 1971, now contains
many of O'Connor's personal library holdings, manuscripts and
papers.  For further discussion see Part Two.  The collection
includes numerous volumes bearing maternal family names.  At
this time it cannot be established when these volumes were
added to the holdings or by whom.  Before the library holdings
were given to Georgia College, some family members and friends
had access to them.

may well have been encouraged to develop her literary talents.
O'Connor herself, in a letter just published, clarifies this
question of parental influence. She says: "My father wanted
to write but had not the time or money or training or any of
the opportunities I have had. I am never likely to romanticize
him because I carry around most of his faults as well as his
tastes . . . Anyway, whatever I do in the way of writing makes
me extra happy in the thought that it is a fulfillment of what
he wanted to do himself."[16] From this, we note that her father
was an early influence in that he both desired to write himself
and encouraged his daughter, but her development as a writer
came much after her father's death and under the direction of
skilled literary technicians.

During her youth, Flannery O'Connor asserted herself as
a unique individual. Already she displayed a disconcerting
imagination and a capacity for doing the unexpected. She
later recalled her first piece of verse, a product of her
having been ushered into the company of adult visitors to her
home after her mother's advice against expecting a gift: "It's
not the thought, but what they brought."[17] Mary Flannery, as
she had been christened and was called at the time, is remembered as a loner, who, for some inexplicable reason, was known
to have brought her teacher tomatoes in the place of the more
traditional apple.[18] She records that her third-grade teacher
looked askance at her substitution of "St. Cecilia" for "Rover"
in a sentence running "Throw the ball to Rover."[19] She

---

[16]*Habit of Being*, p. 168.

[17]Unpublished fragment, Flannery O'Connor Collection.
This collection of manuscripts and papers is incomplete and
not yet catalogued. Much of the material bears no title,
number or page designation. For a survey of these materials,
see Becham, "The Flannery O'Connor Collection," pp. 66-71.

[18]Interview, Atlanta, Georgia, October 25, 1971. Ano-
nymity requested.

[19]Unpublished fragment, Flannery O'Connor Collection.

identifies herself in an autobiographical piece as "a pigeon-
toed only-child with a receding chin and a you-leave-me-alone-
or-I'll-bite-you complex."[20]

Already herself an unusual child, O'Connor had an early
fascination with things which were out of the ordinary. At
the age of five, she was filmed by Pathé News with her pet
bantam chicken who held the distinction of being able to walk
backwards as well as forwards.[21] In the instance of this news-
reel, as with her later public notice, it was not the publicity, but her own preoccupation with the extraordinary that
motivated her pursuit of the unique. As she notes:

> From that day with the Pathé man I began to collect
> chickens. What had been only a mild interest became
> a passion, a quest. I had to have more and more chick-
> ens. I favored those with one green eye and one orange
> or with overlong necks and crooked combs. I wanted one
> with three legs or three wings but nothing in that line
> turned up . . .[22]

> My quest, whatever it was actually for, ended with pea-
> cocks. Instinct, not knowledge led me to them. I had
> never seen or heard one. Although I had a pen of pheas-
> ants and a pen of quail, a flock of turkeys, seventeen
> geese, a tribe of mallard ducks, three Japanese silky
> bantams, two Polish Crested ones, and several chickens
> of a cross between these last and the Rhode Island Red,
> I felt a lack.[23]

The quest for these birds, which she says was stimulated by
instinct, grew beyond her expectations throughout her life.
In her later short stories O'Connor employs the peacock as a

---

[20]Unpublished fragment, Flannery O'Connor Collection.

[21]*Mystery and Manners*, p. 3.

[22]What did later turn up in her fiction were human beings
of her own design bearing marks of distinction: the one-armed
Mr. Shiftlet, the deaf-mute Lucynell Crater, the mentally re-
tarded child Bishop, the homicidal maniac The Misfit, the her-
maphrodite in a side-show, Joy-Hulga, the Ph.D. with a wooden
leg, and Rufus Johnson, the religious juvenile delinquent with
a club foot.

[23]*Mystery and Manners*, p. 4.

symbol of the transcendent aspects of Christ because of its resplendent beauty and its absolute inutility.[24]

During her first year as a student at Sacred Heart High School, her father's terminal illness abruptly brought to a close the Savannah period of Flannery O'Connor's life, and removed her from its Catholic cosmopolitan environment. Whereas in her earliest days she had been raised in her father's city, surrounded by his family and under his direction, his illness with disseminated lupus effectively removed him from the financial center of the family (he had been in business as a real estate man) and his milieu was displaced for one that, while still Georgian, was less cosmopolitan, more agrarian and culturally Protestant fundamentalist. And it became, for her, matriarchal.

## Milledgeville

In 1938, Flannery O'Connor moved with her parents to her mother's ancestral home in central Georgia. Built in 1820, the Cline House had served as the governor's mansion when Milledgeville was the capital of Georgia. In 1886, Peter Cline, O'Connor's maternal grandfather, purchased the house, establishing it as the Cline family home. From it Peter Cline served as mayor of the town for twenty-two years. In a rare glimpse of life in that house as O'Connor experienced it during her youth, she writes:

> The chief event of the spring when I was growing up was the annual garden club pilgrimage of homes. The various houses in Milledgeville, including our own, were open to the public which trouped through in respectful solemnity to view the past. This was a past which

---

[24]See especially "The Displaced Person," *Complete Stories* pp. 194-235, and her occasional work, "The King of the Birds," *Mystery and Manners*, pp. 3-21. For an extensive and perhaps overextended consideration of O'Connor's use of the symbol see Feeley, *Flannery O'Connor: Voice of the Peacock*.

happened to be in excellent working order and in
which I lived.[25]

Whereas the O'Connor family had been part of the life of
Savannah, the Treanors and the Clines, her mother's family,
were an important part of life in Milledgeville. The Treanor-
Cline stock had been leaders in this part of Georgia since before the days of the American Confederacy. In 1847, before
churches had been established, when there were few Catholics
in central Georgia, the first Mass offered in Milledgeville
was said in the apartment of Hugh Treanor, her great-grand-
father. In 1874, Mrs. Hugh Treanor donated the land on which
the first Catholic church in the town was built. But this is
predominantly a Baptist area. Catholicism did not spread here
as it had grown in Savannah. Although Milledgeville now has
thirty-nine churches, only Sacred Heart Church, the one established in 1874, is Roman Catholic. Catholic schools and other
Catholic institutions have yet to be built here, evidence that
the Irish Catholic settlers, including the Treanor-Cline families, influenced the development of Milledgeville in ways other
than religious.

There is little available data regarding O'Connor's
adaptation to her new life in Milledgeville or to her father's
encroaching death. Whereas her later fiction frequently deals
with themes concerning fear of death, man's struggle against
it and his final acceptance or angry submission, and the loss
of one's home and homesickness, these themes are not always
intermingled and neither is ever portrayed sentimentally. At
any rate, autobiographical data cannot be extrapolated from
the fiction. No stranger to Milledgeville, as she had often
summered there with her cousins, Flannery O'Connor was nonetheless unaccustomed to the focus of social life that was her
inheritance in this town. Once the capital of Georgia, Milledgeville had decreased in importance as Georgia developed.

---

[25]Unpublished manuscript, Flannery O'Connor Collection.

The established customs, values and sensibilities of white
Southern society, now beginning to be challenged in other
parts of the South, remained intact in this rural town.  Although frequently placed at or near the center of social func-
tions, O'Connor remained the shy, reserved girl of her early
childhood.  She retired whenever possible from the attention
of others, preferring the company of a pet chicken for whom
she fashioned an elegant wardrobe.

Since Milledgeville has no Catholic secondary school,
O'Connor was enrolled in Peabody Public High School.  There,
while attending regular classes, she focused her energy on
writing poetry and prose, drawing cartoons and painting.  At
this age, no form of artistic expression was dominant, although
painting was the first laid aside.  She wrote a series of short
books which she labeled "too young for adults and too old for
children."[26]  The subjects of her literary projects varied,
but they were generally centered on daily family life.  Two
of the homemade covers on her earliest books bear the titles:
"My Relitives [sic]," a series of brief comic sketches of aunts
and uncles, and "Don't Tuch [sic]," a kind of personal journal.
Throughout her school years, spelling was hazardous for her.
As she recalls:

> It was a source of some small discomfort to these teach-
> ers that I could add only with the use of my fingers,
> confused history with a foreign language, and put ninety
> percent of my originality into my spelling.  They over-
> looked such matters, however, on the assumption that
> if I ever became a writer, I could rely solely on the
> principles of free creative thought.[27]

Although she had received little encouragement or direction in high school, O'Connor enrolled in the English Department at Georgia College (then known as Georgia State College
for Women) in Milledgeville.  Now determined to gear herself

---

[26]Feeley, unpublished lecture, Georgia College, July 21,
1975.

[27]Unpublished manuscript, Flannery O'Connor Collection.

toward a career either in fiction writing or in cartooning,
she was disappointed to find her undergraduate teachers were
no more interested in aiding a potential artist than they had
been in her progressive, do-it-yourself high school.  Undaun-
ted, she became, during her student years at Georgia College,
the art editor of the student newspaper, *The Colonnade*, the
editor of the literary quarterly, *The Corinthian*, and feature
editor of her senior yearbook.  She seems to have worked
alone, developing her own style according to her view of life
as she was able to portray it.  Disenchanted with the English
department at the College,[28] she changed majors to graduate
with a degree in social science in June of 1945.

During these years, O'Connor had submitted many cartoons[29]
to *The New Yorker*, which encouraged her but never bought any
of her work.  Her artistic future was finally determined when
one of her college teachers did submit some of her *Corinthian*
stories to the Writers' Workshop at the State University of
Iowa.[30]  On the strength of these stories, she was awarded
their Rinehart Fellowship[31] in 1945 by the Workshop's director,

---

[28]Although some present faculty of the English Department
offer other opinions, one official of the College has stated
that College records indicate that to be the reason for O'Connor's change of majors.

[29]Although few of her cartoons seem to have survived, one
of her teachers recalls them as "wonderful, merry" works "pene-
tratingly conceived and skillfully executed" (Meaders, "Flannery O'Connor: 'Literary Witch,'" p. 377).

[30]A description of the course of study at the Writers'
Workshop is given in Hansen, "The Iowa Writers' Workshop,"
p. 315.  The course seeks to "give the creative writer the
tools of literature without stifling his initiative."  On the
M.A. level, to which O'Connor was admitted, the program consists of weekly seminars, a general examination on literature,
and a dissertation described as follows: "[The dissertation]
should be a piece of imaginative writing, a play or novel,
or poem, published under reputable auspices."

[31]Sponsored by the publishing company which later would
hold the first option on her first novel. See *Habit of Being*,
p. 4.

Paul Engle.[32]

## Literary Apprenticeship in the North

This decision to move to Iowa to begin a literary career was not one which O'Connor made lightly. Before leaving home, she and her mother discussed the name by which she would become known as a writer. Reasoning that her double name, Mary Flannery, would be an anomaly outside the South and "Mary O'Connor" on a dust jacket would be a sure way to obscurity, she legally dropped the "Mary" before her name, becoming now for the first time "Flannery O'Connor."[33] This early career confidence was substantiated shortly after her arrival in Iowa as Paul Engle recalls:

> Like Keats, who spoke Cockney but wrote the purest sounds in English, Flannery spoke a dialect beyond instant comprehension but on the page, her prose was imaginative, tough, alive: just like Flannery herself. . . . The stories were quietly filled with insight, shrewd about human weaknesses, hard and compassionate.[34]

Engle notes that as a Workshop Participant O'Connor was shy about reading her own stories aloud. When it was her turn, Engle often read them anonymously to the class for their appraisal. He recalls her sitting at the back of the classroom quietly amid bustling talkers: "The only communicating gesture she would make was an occasional amused and shy smile at something absurd."[35]

---

[32]Engle served as director in Iowa from 1939 until the present. See Wakeman, ed., *World Authors*, p. 1076, for a discussion on Engle's contribution to the Writers' Workshop.

[33]Drake, *Critical Essay*, p. 9.

[34]Giroux, "Introduction," *Complete Stories*, p. vii.

[35]Giroux, p. viii.

Already skilled at fiction writing, Flannery O'Connor became acquainted with established Southern writers who recognized her literary talent. Visiting professors at the Writers' Workshop Andrew Lytle[36] and Robert Penn Warren[37] criticized portions of her work and she rewrote them accordingly. Unlike Engle, Warren too was a Southerner. Like O'Connor, he wrote of Southern life, and he was concerned that the agrarian culture of the South should be preserved against the encroachments of mercantilism and industrialism. In the twenties, Warren and Lytle had been members of the "Fugitive Movement" along with a friend and literary colleague, Allen Tate.[38] Another Southern writer, this time a woman and a convert to Catholicism, who became important in O'Connor's development in this connection, was Caroline Gordon, then the wife of Allen Tate. Gordon, as well known for critical works as for her fiction,[39] had begun her career as an "Agrarian" and

---

[36]Lytle, editor of the *Sewanee Review*, thought O'Connor to be an exceptionally gifted "authentic voice" of Georgia. He was later to publish many of her best stories in his journal. See his article on O'Connor's talent, "Flannery O'Connor: A Tribute."

[37]Although best known for his poetry, Warren is also a novelist, critic and social commentator.

[38]A group of young poets and critics, acutely aware of their Southern heritage, who advocated literary regionalism, concentrating largely on the history and customs of the South in their work which they saw as a continuation of mainstream classical humanism. They understood the poet to be a "fugitive," wanderer or outcast, the one who carries the secret wisdom. Later, four of these writers established a group of twelve scholars from various disciplines who held that the hierarchical society of the early South was preferable to the social disintegration which they saw in the contemporary North and South, and that scientific attitudes and industrialization were responsible for mankind's decay. In 1930, the later group published *I'll Take My Stand*, a declaration of "Agrarian" principles. With Tate, Lytle, and Warren, Donald Davidson and John Crowe Ransom were key figures in both movements.

[39]See Gordon, *How to Read a Novel*; and Gordon and Tate, eds., *The House of Fiction*.

became increasingly taken up with Christian themes and symbols.[40]   The O'Connor-Gordon respect became mutual; the
authors shared ideas, and O'Connor sent manuscripts of stories in progress to Gordon for critique throughout her
career.[41]

Having benefited from the close critiques of several
literary masters, O'Connor's career became confirmed as her
stories began to be accepted for publication.  She sold her
first story, "The Geranium," to *Accent*.  This piece and the
five succeeding stories, "The Barber," "Wildcat," "The Crop,"
"The Turkey," and "The Train," compose a collection entitled
*The Geranium*, which, under Engle's direction, O'Connor submitted as her thesis.[42]   Although structurally weak and not
always clearly focused, these first works[43] nonetheless set
the tone and direction for O'Connor's later stories.  The
manner of life among the various classes and types of people
in rural Georgia and Tennessee, established here as her prin-
cipal concern, will continue to serve as her primary source
and focus throughout her work.

On the basis of  "The Geranium" stories and work which
she planned to incorporate into her novel, *Wise Blood*, and

---

[40]McDowell, *Caroline Gordon*, p. 6.

[41]Gordon, "Heresy in Dixie," p. 266.

[42]The nature and level of achievement required for a
thesis to be accepted at the Writers' Workshop is set forth
in Hansen, "The Iowa Writers' Workshop," p. 315, as follows:
   The only requirements of this culminating piece of imaginative writing are, first, that it illustrates the
   writer's proficiency in technique, his ability to discover and control a mode of expression suited to what he
   has to say; and, secondly, that it illustrates the
   writer's possession of creative energy, the sort of
   energy that distinguishes the really promising young
   author, who writes with a certain authority and seems
   to promise continuous growth.

[43]All included by Engle in *Complete Stories*.

at Engle's recommendation, O'Connor was awarded the Rinehart Iowa prize for a first novel.[44] Then in 1947, at the end of her second year in residence at the Writers' Workshop, she received the Master of Fine Arts degree in the Department of English at the Graduate College of the State University of Iowa. For an additional year she remained at Iowa experimenting with story lines and sharpening her own critical skills under Engle's direction. O'Connor was now ready to work as a professional. According to Engle, "Flannery always had a flexible and objective view of her own writing, constantly revising, and in every case improving. The will to be a writer was adamant; nothing could resist it, not even her own sensibility about her own work. Cut, alter, try again . . ."[45]

Now known in her own right and having prospered in the company of other writers at Iowa, O'Connor was invited to spend the winter of 1948 writing at Yaddo, the Writers' Colony in Saratoga Springs, New York.[46] Founded in 1926 by Katrina Nichols Trask Peabody,[47] a generous and romantic patron of the arts, Yaddo is a five-hundred acre showplace where artists can work unharried by the need to make a living. Accommodation and meals are provided without cost to guests.[48]

---

[44]Giroux, "Introduction," p. viii.

[45]Giroux, pp. vii-viii.

[46]As quoted by Vivante, "Yaddo," pp. 28-29. Elizabeth Ames, the Executive Director of the colony, states: "Yaddo is not for those who are only beginning their work. The only writers, painters, sculptors and composers who are eligible to make application are those who have already published (or exhibited or had performed) work of high artistic merit."

[47]In an article entitled "Yaddo and Substance," Katrina Trask's vision for Yaddo is quoted: "Here will be a perpetual series of house parties—of literary men, literary women, and other artists. . . . At Yaddo they will find the Sacred Fire, and light their torches at its flame" (p. 50).

[48]"Life Visits Yaddo," p. 111.

A strict daily regimen is followed by each artist:

> Yaddo is something like a swank monastery. Most of the
> guests sleep in The Mansion [a fifty-five room Victorian
> Gothic structure in the center of the estate]. Working
> quarters are private studios hidden in near-by groves.
> Breakfast is at 8:15. Box lunches are delivered to the
> studios. Until four, no visiting is permitted, and then
> only with special permission. At dinner, in The Mansion's
> dining room, six tables accommodate the guests [usually
> numbering twenty to thirty per season], who are shifted
> frequently to freshen conversation, and prevent the for-
> mation of cliques. Coffee is served in the main parlor,
> where guests are expected to be interesting, but not to
> read manuscripts. Around ten, when Mrs. Ames retires,
> guests are expected to go to bed, too, not to slip off
> to Saratoga for a beer.

> Monastic also is Mrs. Ames' talent for smelling out in-
> cipient romances, nipping them with subtle but insistent
> notes.[49]

O'Connor worked well at Yaddo. The lifestyle seems to
have been in keeping with her own propensities. Although
little is known of her work habits and lifestyle during earlier periods, the regimen of Yaddo was similar to that established through her own choice both in Connecticut and in
Milledgeville.

Like Yaddo inhabitants before her, including Eudora
Welty, Carson McCullers, Bernard Malamud and Katherine Anne
Porter, Flannery O'Connor benefited not only from the strict
and isolate work routine, but also from the literary contacts
she made. In June, 1948, she sought a literary agent. Elizabeth McKee, taking an interest in the promising young writer,
placed her story, "The Capture,"[50] with *Mademoiselle,* and from
that time on served as her agent.

O'Connor's stories now began to appear with some regular-
ity. She published "The Woman on the Stairs"[51] in *Tomorrow* and

---

[49]"Yaddo and Substance," p. 50.

[50]Retitled from "The Turkey" in the thesis.

[51]Later retitled "A Stroke of Good Fortune."

both "The Heart of the Park" and "The Peeler" in *Partisan Review*.[52]  All of these stories, except "The Woman on the Stairs," were reworked to become part of her novel in progress, *Wise Blood*.  While continuing work on the novel, she met Robert Lowell, who was at Yaddo working on some poetry. Through him she was introduced to Robert Giroux, who was later to become her editor,[53] and to Robert and Sally Fitzgerald.

Venturing more directly into the social literary world she had entered briefly at Yaddo, O'Connor took an apartment on the upper West Side in New York.  According to Gordon, she had decided to live in New York, to write a novel and to make it on her own in the literary world.[54]  This dream, however, was quickly abandoned in favor of a life of relative isolation, similar to the style of her earilier life at home to which she would eventually return.

In 1949, at the invitation of the Catholic poet Robert Fitzgerald and his wife Sally, O'Connor moved in with them as a paying guest on their Ridgefield, Connecticut, farm.  At the time, the Fitzgeralds had two children and were expecting a third.  Sally cared for the children and maintained the daily household regime, freeing Flannery to spend her days in concentration on her novel.  Robert was at that time teaching English and Classics at Sarah Lawrence College,[55] commuting by car from Ridgefield.

There O'Connor lived without luxury in an austere study-bedroom apart from the family in what Robert Fitzgerald describes as their "house of stone and timber set in a wilderness

---

[52]See the Chronology for a complete list of publications by date.

[53]Giroux, "Introduction," p. viii.

[54]Gordon, "Heresy in Dixie," p. 264.

[55]Murphy, ed., *Contemporary Poets of the English Language*, p. 376-377.

of laurel and oak."[56]  She maintained a severe daily schedule.
After attending Mass with one of the parents alternately, and
sharing breakfast with them, she retired to her attic quarters
to work on *Wise Blood*.  Except for lunch with the Fitzgeralds
and a half-mile walk through the woods for the mail, she took
no break from her work.  Her evenings were spent in conversation with the couple.  Although at that time she had no plans
to return to the South to live, O'Connor's tales and remem-
brances were filled with her hometown and its surrounding
countryside, much like her fiction, as Robert Fitzgerald recalls.  He remembers too that the interior life "interested"
her, but that her work took precedence.[57]

These three Catholics were well aware of the post-war
premise that perhaps there exists nothing beyond the immediate present.  Although existentialism[58] and its concept
of "angst" were provocative to the Fitzgeralds, all this was
even more challenging to O'Connor.  Her unsystematic manuscript with its multiplicity of Southern characters and settings began to shift in detail and direction, revealing the
extent to which O'Connor herself was becoming concerned with
the ideas of existentialism.  As she revealed in a letter to
Elizabeth McKee: "I don't have my novel outlined and I have
to write to discover what I am doing. . . . I don't know
so well what I think until I see what I say; then I have to
say it over again."[59]

---

[56]Fitzgerald, "Introduction," *Everything That Rises Must Converge*, p. xiii.

[57]Fitzgerald, p. xiv.

[58]The term here is used broadly to encompass the thought
of philosophers, including Sartre, Heidegger and Kierkegaard,
who stress one's intense awareness of freedom and the contin-
gency of human existence.

[59]Giroux, "Introduction," p. ix.

Her prospectus for *Wise Blood*, written in 1948, states her original direction:

> The principle [sic] character, an illiterate Tennes-
> seean, has lost his home through the breakdown of a
> country community. Home in this instance, stands not
> only for the place and family, but for some absolute
> belief which would give him sanctuary in the modern
> world. All he has retained of the evangelical reli-
> gion of his mother is a sense of sin and a need for
> religion. . . . This sense of sin is the only key he
> has to finding a sanctuary and he begins unconsciously
> to search for God through sin.[60]

As she wrote, discovering her own ideas and absorbing new ones, the manuscript grew to well over a thousand pages. In-defatigable, she rewrote and refined the piece, gradually bringing it around to a serious parody on existentialism. Hazel Motes, her main character, finally emerges as a young man who has lost his childhood faith while in the army, and sets off to the city to "preach the Church without Christ, the church peaceful and satisfied."[61] Placing his faith in material reality, Hazel says: "I'm a member and preacher to the church where the blind don't see and the lame don't walk and what's dead stays that way. Ask me about that church and I'll tell you it's the church that the blood of Jesus don't foul with Redemption."[62]

As a writer, Flannery O'Connor was already accustomed to formulating in her stories the quest for truth. She was also by circumstance and personal practice a Catholic. However, given her strong dissatisfaction with the superficial, she resisted taking refuge in the more simplistic aspects of tra-ditional religion. Feeling no need to shun the secular world, she eagerly explored the philosophy held by the milieu in

---

[60]"Plans for Work: Prospectus for Publishers," Flannery O'Connor Collection.

[61]*Wise Blood*, in *Three by Flannery O'Connor*, p. 78.

[62]*Wise Blood*, p. 60.

which she lived and wrote.  The setting for her quest was
ideal.  As Robert Fitzgerald notes:

> Now, our country family in 1949 and 1950 believed on
> excellent grounds that beyond the immediate there was
> practically everything, like the stars over Taulkinham[63]
> —the past, the future, and the Creator thereof.  But
> the horror of recent human predicaments had not been
> lost on us.  Flannery felt that an artist who was a
> Catholic should face all the truth down to the worst
> of it.[64]

But facing all the truth, especially in the form of a growing
novel of over a thousand pages, was too monumental a task.
In order to consolidate her material, re-establish her direction and clarify her artistic purpose, she began more carefully to limit her sources and narrow her design.  Of her
later stories, Fitzgerald correctly observes that

> it is evident that the writer . . . restricted her hori-
> zontal range; a pasture scene and a fortress wall of
> pine woods reappear like a signature in story after
> story.  The same is true of her social range and range
> of idiom.  But these restrictions, like the humility of
> her style, are all deceptive.  The true range of the
> stories is vertical . . .[65]

Thus, for O'Connor, provincialism and restricted information
became the condition for realizing a greater range of ambition

While she was clarifying objectives, restricting sources
and ordering materials, her novel came increasingly to reflect
the direction her career was taking.  As early as 1948, her
publisher, Holt, Rinehart and Company, who had awarded the
novel a prize and expected to publish it, began to question
her changing approach.  Concerned that the consistent narrow-
ing of the vision and the developing angularity of the work
that later became her hallmark would alienate readers, the
publisher wrote accusing her of nurturing a kind of aloneness
and intentionally writing out of her own experiences only,

---

[63]The name of the city Hazel Motes visits in *Wise Blood*.

[64]Fitzgerald, "Introduction," p. xxvi.

[65]Fitzgerald, p. xxxii.

consciously limiting even these.  Clear about the necessity
and deliberateness of her direction, O'Connor replied:

> I feel that whatever virtues the novel may have are
> very much connected with the limitations you mention.
> I am not writing a conventional novel, and I think that
> the quality of the novel I write will derive precisely
> from the peculiarity or aloneness, if you will, of the
> experience I write from. . . . In short, I am amenable
> to criticism but only within the sphere of what I am
> trying to do; I will not pretend to do otherwise.[66]

When the novel that had taken her from Iowa to Taulkin-
ham was finished, it had taken a direction that was hers, but
not that of her publisher.  When subsequent submission of additional chapters of *Wise Blood* did not allay the publisher's
doubts, she was released from her original contract.  When
this occurred, in October, 1950, publisher Robert Giroux offered a contract for the novel.  It saw publication by Giroux
in 1952, and O'Connor was able to maintain her ideal as a
writer which she had earlier stated in her prospectus for the
work:

> My ultimate purpose as an artist is to produce work
> which will have a human meaning and be of high literary
> calibre.  I cannot determine the significance of its
> presumable contribution to art.  Every work of art is
> an experiment in form in the sense that form is the
> result of a particular material handled by a particular
> person, and in this sense, every work of art adds to
> and alters the tradition; but I believe it must be seen
> from a distance and in the company of its kind before
> its significance can be determined.[67]

The particular material she could handle was that of
rural Georgia and the particular person was a Roman Catholic
Southern agrarian, generally unconventional, who was not writing conventional novels and who knew that the peculiarity of
her experience was her strength.  Even while living in the
North, fascinated with the New York intellectual set,[68]

---

[66]Giroux, "Introduction," p. x.

[67]"Plans for Work," Flannery O'Connor Collection.

[68]Gordon, "Heresy in Dixie," p. 264.

O'Connor had discovered that her Southern background was the
bedrock on which to build her work.  In part this may have
been a relative inadaptability, but in the development of
her literary career, her Baldwin County, Georgia, provincialism became her mark.  For O'Connor as an individual and
as an artist, it was the locale and milieu of the South that
provided in symbol and fact her center of focus.

The further strength of her art is grounded in her religious perspective.  Fascinated from the first by the universal
questions regarding the meaning of life and death, O'Connor
increasingly capitalizes on her singular position as a Roman
Catholic commentator-in-art on the Protestant fundamentalism
of the "Bible Belt" South.  The juxtaposition of these two
such dissimilar styles of Christian belief sets O'Connor's
work apart from Southern literary tradition.  She skillfully
constructs the collision of these two world-views in the
fabric of her stories as "an experiment in form" to reveal
deeper human meaning.

That period from 1945 until 1952, during which O'Connor
was absent from the South, living and writing among prominent
literary figures, was a time of great growth during which she
found her style, established her angle of vision, and claimed
her literary domain.

### Artistic Maturity

Within a year and a half of her move to the Fitzgeralds'
Connecticut farm, just as she had begun to relish the taste
of literary success, O'Connor's career was abruptly interrup-
ted when she developed an incurable disease.  It brought her
near the point of death and when finally controlled required
her permanent return to the South as a semi-invalid in the
custodial care of her mother.  O'Connor's denouement may be
viewed from several perspectives: the impact of the imposi-
tion of radical limits, both in terms of location and physical
health, on her work as a writer; her subsequent focus on

Christian theology and Catholic lay spirituality; and the fuller evolution of her talents in fiction writing. During these last fourteen years of her life, while engaged in a mortal struggle against lupus erythematosus, a correlative of arthritis, Flannery O'Connor came to her full stature as an individual, an artist and a literary theologian.

It was in December, 1950, that she was stricken. While she was traveling to Georgia by train for the Christmas holidays, the disease suddenly grew worse. She was hospitalized in Atlanta where her condition was diagnosed as an advanced attack of lupus. She was thought to be dying. This critical condition was treated and ameliorated with blood transfusions and massive injections of ACTH, a drug still in experimental stages. The ravages of lupus, complicated by her reactions to its treatment, took their toll on the young woman.[69] When she was released from the hospital in the summer of 1951, her condition was stabilized, but she was so weakened that she could no longer climb stairs. Her return to work in the North was impossible.

Some aspects of this enforced return to her native Georgia and its literary, religious, social and familial traditions were propitious for O'Connor's writing career. Although the time and circumstances of her re-entry into the Southern milieu had been determined by the onslaught of disease, she had earlier recognized the Piedmont region to be the source of her most fruitful imaginings. With the drafting of *Wise Blood* while she was still in Connecticut, O'Connor had already begun to claim in her fiction the heritage of her own provincialism by restricting her materials to that

---

[69]Lupus causes the body to produce antibodies that attack its own tissues, affecting the blood and joints. Early in her remission, cortisone proved a more effective and less violent treatment. However, the disease, its treatment, or both caused the deterioration of her hip bones so that she was forced to use a cane and later crutches for mobility.

area with which she was familiar and which she was skilled in depicting.[70]

Spiritually she had never been far from her homeland. While in Iowa and New York, O'Connor had come under the influence of the Agrarians, whose literary credo provided her with a matrix of Southern views and values which she began to explore in her fiction.[71] Nor had she rejected her religious heritage. One critic suggests that she had undergone some sort of religious conversion between the completion of her thesis stories in Iowa and her work on *Wise Blood*.[72] But indications of her religious interests do appear in the thesis stories, as we have noted. While working in the North, she maintained contact with Catholic literary colleagues, including Robert Lowell, Allen Tate, Caroline Gordon, and the Fitzgeralds. Robert Fitzgerald remarks that while in Connecticut O'Connor attended daily Mass and was interested in the development of interior life. But, because she was engaged in launching her writing career, she did not then possess the time to indulge in its active pursuit.[73] These indications would suggest that she had not broken significantly with her Catholic heritage, but that she required time to integrate her religious beliefs and experiences with her art. Her thirteen years as a convalescent would provide this opportunity.

---

[70]O'Connor recognized that provincialism was not without its dangers for the Southern writer: "In almost every hamlet you'll find at least one old lady writing epics in Negro dialect and probably two or three old gentlemen who have impossible historical novels on the way. The woods are full of regional writers, and it is the great horror of every serious Southern writer that he will become one of them" (*Mystery and Manners*, p. 29).

[71]The significance of Agrarianism for her work will be discussed later.

[72]Martin, *True Country*, p. 9.

[73]Sessions, "A Correspondence," p. 209.

Her move to Georgia thus reinforced directions that she had already chosen. O'Connor herself remarks that her return to her own region was fortuitous because "that balance between principle and fact, judgment and observation, which is so necessary to maintain if fiction is to be true" is imperiled when the imagination, easily corrupted by theory, operates in isolation.[74] In addition, as we have noted, the environment which Flannery O'Connor had chosen for herself even while in the North was a rural, isolate setting where her disciplined personal schedule enabled her to concentrate her energy on her stories. It was in precisely this same kind of setting that she would live in Georgia. Her enforced physical limitation and relocation seems thus to have coincided with and confirmed the restrictions inherent in the style, material and direction of her art and appropriate to the mode of her personal life.[75]

Andalusia, a one-hundred-fifty-year-old dairy farm near Milledgeville which Regina O'Connor had inherited from a brother, was chosen for its physical adaptability and idyllic setting as O'Connor's permanent home. There, in the company of her mother and her Uncle Louis, she would enjoy a first floor suite with easy access to a screened-in porch. The scene from the front porch included a sweeping view of the countryside and furnished her with the setting for many fictional encounters between the divine and the human in her later stories. One critic, speaking of his visit to O'Connor in her reclaimed environment, noted: "All around us I saw the materials of her fiction, the South she used: the leathery

---

[74]*Mystery and Manners*, pp. 53-54.

[75]Critics generally agree that the illness did not radically change the direction of her life. Hendin adds: "Its horror was that it prevented her life from changing at all. . . . Her illness seems only to have reinforced and cemented an isolation that had always existed . . ." (Hendin, *World of O'Connor*, p. 9).

country people, the hired hands, the mythical elderly ladies
we met in town, the dirt roads, the pick-up trucks, Dr. Pepper
signs, pentecostal churches. Most central of all was her
mother . . ."[76]

Even while in the North, O'Connor had been in daily
contact with her mother.[77] On Flannery's return home, Regina
became a primary and important presence in her daughter's life
Taking their cues from O'Connor's fictional matriarchies and
from Milledgeville gossip, critics have variously portrayed
the mother-daughter alliance. The actual nature of their
relationship and its influence on O'Connor's fiction is difficult to assess, but her concern for the family as the basic
unit of society, in both her private and creative worlds,
marks her as a traditional Southerner in this regard.

The two women established a clear division of labor
within the household at Andalusia. "You run the farm and
I'll run the writing," Regina once quoted her daughter.[78]
Regina managed the house, the farm and the finances. She
guarded her daughter's limited strength, provided for her
daily needs and assured that she was essentially free to work.
As the writer's reputation grew, Regina handled the schedule
of visitors as well. The radically simple lifestyle of a
semi-invalid daughter proved productive for O'Connor the artist.[79] She wrote undisturbed in the mornings, broke for a
leisurely lunch with her mother, eaten at the elegant old
Sanford House restaurant in town when her health and the weather permitted, and then spent the rest of the day alone, reading, writing letters, painting or resting. Occasionally she

---

[76]Gilman, "On Flannery O'Connor," p. 26.

[77]Sessions, "A Correspondence," p. 209.

[78]Shannon, "The World of Flannery O'Connor," p. 9.

[79]Despite her physical condition, she was prolific during
this time. See Chronology, especially 1952-1955.

entertained guests who called or met with a local literary group to exchange and criticize original stories.[80]

Like Milledgeville and the surrounding area, Andalusia was a remnant of the Old South.[81] The social order and manners of the post-bellum South prevailed.[82] Most of the farm labor was provided by white tenants and black workers who occupied cottages scattered in clumps of trees at the periphery of the farm. One of the dairy supervisors at Andalusia was a capable Polish war refugee, a "displaced person," as this category of refugee was popularly called. The Pole provided the shell of the character of Mr. Guizac, a curious hybrid of medieval European Catholicism and American technology. He constitutes O'Connor's most distinct Christ figure.[83]

Blacks, unlettered and seemingly as enduring as the landscape, played an integral role in the conduct of daily life on the O'Connor farm. Jack and Louise Hill and Shot, their boarder, lived in a weathered shack just behind and to the left of the main house. Under the dairyman's or Regina's direction, they did the hard labor on the farm. O'Connor came

---

[80]O'Connor conducted these Wednesday evening sessions on the porch at Andalusia. At her urging, the participants also read and discussed Henry James' *What Maisie Knew*, as an example of what she thought to be an excellent development of a child's character, and Bernanos' *The Diary of a Country Priest* (Mary Barbara Tate, Interview, Milledgeville, Georgia, June 23, 1975).

[81]The term "Old South" will be used throughout as it has been defined by the Agrarians in *I'll Take My Stand*, to designate the ideal society having an agrarian economy, employing the manners and social arts of eighteenth century Europe and supporting a stable democratic society based on the natural, non-scientific person.

[82]For O'Connor's catalogue of human types based on the order of the Old South, see "Revelation," p. 508.

[83]See "The Displaced Person," pp. 194-235.

to know these Blacks well and, somewhat out of character for
the times, she understood many of the injustices done to them
by her society.  She never tried to write from their perspective, however, because she was "never able to understand how
they think."[84]  Nor did she indicate concern for their social,
economic or political plight in her works.

Whereas O'Connor was regarded with fondness from a respectful distance by the farm's black inhabitants, her acceptance by the townspeople seems mixed.  Her friend, Louise
Abbot, remembers her as somewhat overshadowed by her mother's
presence in Milledgeville.  "I don't remember seeing much
indication that her townspeople noticed her very much or
thought of her except as Regina Cline O'Connor's daughter,
Mary Flannery, who had some stories published.  I am sure that
this is the way she wanted it."[85]  Meaders, on the other hand,
recalls that the Cline family and their associates were gentee
people, proud of their proper heritage.  "How then, as one elderly lady exclaimed, did [Mary] Flannery O'Connor even hear
all the ugly words she wrote into her books—much less learn
what they meant."[86]

That her stories were an embarrassment, if not an anomaly
to her relatives and their friends did not escape O'Connor's
notice.  She wrote to the Fitzgeralds on separate occasions:
"My kinfolks think I am a commercial writer now and really
they are very proud of me.  My Uncle Louis is always bringing
a message from somebody at the King Hdw. Co., who has read

---

[84]Unpublished manuscript, Flannery O'Connor Collection
(Gabriel, in her thesis story, "Wildcat," is her only black
protagonist.  Her handling of this character is a case in
point.)

[85]Abbot, "Remembering Flannery O'Connor," p. 11.

[86]Meaders, "Literary Witch," p. 379.  In keeping with
the point made above, and at the suggestion of Sally Fitzgerald that Meaders' omission of "Mary" gives an inauthentic
reading, I have added it.

*Wise Blood*. The last was: ask her why she don't write about some nice people. Louis says, I told them you wrote what *paid*."[87] and "My current literary assignment (from Regina) is to write an introduction for Cousin Katie 'so she won't be shocked,' to be *pasted* on the inside of her book. This piece has to be in the tone of the *Sacred Heart Messenger* and carry the burden of contemporary critical thought. I keep putting it off."[88]

Not unlike her own family and friends, many of O'Connor's early readers and critics, unprepared for her style, were confused and angered by her unsympathetic use of familiar Southern motifs and figures.[89] Claiming that her use of her region, when combined with her own vision of reality, produced a type of fiction uniquely her own, O'Connor stated:

> Today each writer speaks for himself . . . for even if there are no genuine schools in American letters today, there is always some critic who has just invented one and is ready to put you into it. . . . I have found that no matter for what purpose peculiar to your special dramatic needs you use the Southern scene, you are still thought by the general reader to be writing about the South and are judged by the fidelity your fiction has to typical Southern life.

---

[87]Fitzgerald, "Introduction," p. xxi, italics hers. The irony in Louis Cline's comment was apparent to O'Connor, who was singularly uninfluenced by commercialism throughout her career, a stance she had established in her refusal to alter the text of *Wise Blood* to suit her first publisher.

[88]Fitzgerald, p. xix, italics hers. The book was a copy of *Wise Blood*, intended as a gift.

[89]This genre, generally known as the grotesque, is used by many Southern writers. It is characterized by a preoccupation with the irrational, the abnormal and the bizarre. While it depicts the fearful, unpredictable and awesome aspects of life, it nevertheless recognizes the moral nature of the universe. For a detailed description of the "grotesque" in literature, see William O'Connor, *The Grotesque: An American Genre, and other Essays*, especially pp. 4-18; and Thomson, *The Grotesque*. We will return to a more detailed discussion of Flannery O'Connor's use of the grotesque later in this section.

I am always having it pointed out to me that life in
Georgia is not at all the way I picture it . . .[90]

Often creating shockingly misshapen or grotesque characters whose rural Southern identities and concerns cannot be
mistaken, O'Connor maintained that she did not intend to
write about the South *per se*, but rather that she employed
the particular milieu with which she was intimately familiar
and in which she found that point of convergence between the
particular and the universal, unique to her vision, to reveal
the truth about the human condition.

> As a fiction writer who is a Southerner, I use the idiom
> and the manners of the country I know, but I don't con-
> sider that I write *about* the South.  So far as I am con-
> cerned as a novelist, a bomb on Hiroshima affects my
> judgment of life in rural Georgia, and this is not the
> result of taking a relative view and judging one thing
> by another, but of taking an absolute view and judging
> all things together; for a view taken in light of the
> absolute will include a good deal more than one taken
> merely in the light provided by a house-to-house
> survey.[91]

Her personal reservations regarding the categorization
of her works[92] notwithstanding, O'Connor's corpus clearly
bears the marks of Southern literary roots: the consistent
use of authentic cadences of speech, regional settings and
character types spanning the entire social order from back-
woods evangelists to illiterate tramps to pseudo-aristocratic
matrons.  If her approach is unique, her art is nonetheless
part of the Southern literary tradition.  The two characteristics of that tradition which most influenced O'Connor's
work are Agrarianism and grotesquerie.  We will turn our

---

[90]*Mystery and Manners*, pp. 37-38.

[91]*Mystery and Manners*, p. 143, italics hers.

[92]Early excesses range from Malin's simple inclusion
of her work as typical in *New American Gothic* to Bernetta
Quinn's disclaimer that O'Connor's work was at all regional
in favor of a completely universalist reading in *The Added
Dimension: The Art and Mind of Flannery O'Connor*.

attention here to a description of each of these, giving
examples of their importance in her fiction.

The manner in which O'Connor made use of both Agrarian
and grotesque motifs can be clarified by distinguishing in
her works between matter and meaning. The matter, or "physical substance," of her stories consists in the particular
landscape, characters, concerns and body of manners of her
native Piedmont territory, while the meaning refers to "some
deep lesson" or universal truth which she seeks to convey
through her literature.[93] While much of the "matter" of her
fiction reflects both the Agrarian concerns[94] of such Fugitive[95] writers as Robert Penn Warren, John Crowe Ransom and
Allen Tate, and the grotesque subjects of Carson McCullers
and Erskine Caldwell, O'Connor herself tends to underestimate
these aspects of her art as merely the means she uses to attain
her own "end," namely the "meaning" or true vision of reality
which she intends to embody. Nonetheless, for a full understanding of Flannery O'Connor's contribution, neither Agrarianism nor grotesquerie may be lightly dismissed.

The Agrarian movement, initiated in the 1920's by a group
of Southern writers who feared that the prevailing American
way of scientific and economic progress would transform the
rural South into an "undistinguished replica of the usual
American industrial complex"[96] and pleaded rather for the
"recognition of the greater authenticity and promise of a
Southern culture that was conservative, agrarian and human-

---

[93]Holman, "Her Rue with a Difference," pp. 73-74.

[94]Agrarian influence was first noted by Duhamel, "The
Novelist as Prophet," pp. 88-107.

[95]"Agrarian" and "Fugitive" are used interchangeably
here since the notions of these three writers dominated both
movements.

[96]Twelve Southerners, "Introduction: A Statement of
Principles," *I'll Take My Stand*, p. xxi.

istic,"[97] first captured Flannery O'Connor's attention through
her personal acquaintances with several of its founders: Robert Penn Warren and Andrew Lytle, her occasional teachers and
critics at the Iowa Writers' Workshop; and Allen Tate, then
the husband of her life-time friend and critic from New York,
Caroline Gordon. That a novice writer in an alien environment should examine a more familiar philosophical and literary
position is not unusual. Holman suggests:

> Almost all artists feel a hunger for meaning, a need for
> structure, and a rage for order in existence, and believe
> that the human spirit should never calmly surrender its
> endless search for order. Twentieth-century writers con-
> fronted with the spectacle of the mechanized culture of
> America have taken many different roads to many different
> regions of the spirit. . . . The Southerner, predisposed
> to look backwards as a result of his concern with the
> past, has tended to impose a desire for a social struc-
> ture that reflects moral principles and he has tried to
> see in the past of his region at least the shadowy out-
> lines of a viable and admirable moral-social world.[98]

O'Connor shared with the Agrarians their scorn for ur-
banization, industrialism, scientism in education and materialistic progressivism. Like them, she recognized that while
the reality of daily life in the Old South was less than
ideal,[99] the experience, heritage and values of the Old South
should provide for both the North and the South a critical
humanizing corrective to the popular notion of limitless progress and directionless development. To this, although not
all the Agrarians would concur, Warren and Tate would add that
industrialized humanity by definition also urbanized and therefore secularized stands in desperate need of spiritualization;
and Flannery O'Connor would agree with them. Whether Southern
society possesses the religious basis for such a spiritualiza-

---

[97]Duhamel, "The Novelist as Prophet," p. 88.

[98]Holman, "Her Rue with a Difference," pp. 77-79.

[99]Mullins, "Flannery O'Connor: An Interview," pp. 33-34.

tion is an issue on which O'Connor offers the lone positive reponse.

Throughout the entire corpus of her mature works, beginning with *A Good Man Is Hard to Find* (although traces are found in the earlier *Wise Blood*), O'Connor uses Agrarian concepts and values as the matrix from which to develop tension in her stories. In some instances, O'Connor reiterates the Agrarian position. An example is her hostile treatment of characters defined by their adherence to modern principles gained through scientific or rationalistic education: Joy-Hulga Hopewell, the Ph.D. with a wooden leg and matching nihilistic philosophy,[100] Sheppard, the City Recreation director and part-time counselor at the Reformatory who tries to save a young delinquent with criminal tendencies through simple psychology and his interest in astronomy,[101] and Rayber, the deaf school teacher whose reliance on science alone prevents him from recognizing natural life.[102]

In a few instances Agrarian values are comically disparaged, as in the description of General Sash, the one-hundred-four-year-old Civil War veteran who

> had not actually been a general in that war. He had probably been a foot soldier; he didn't remember the war at all. . . . He didn't remember the Spanish-American war in which he had lost a son; he didn't even remember the son. He hadn't any use for history because he never expected to meet it again. To his mind history was connected with processions and life with parades and he liked parades.[103]

---

[100]"Good Country People," *Complete Stories*, pp. 271-291.

[101]"The Lame Shall Enter First," *Complete Stories*, pp. 445-482.

[102]*The Violent Bear It Away*, in *Three By Flannery O'Connor*, pp. 305-447.

[103]"A Late Encounter with the Enemy," *Complete Stories*, pp. 135-136.

The traditional Southern insistence on the maintenance
of social order, the reality of the socio-economic decline of
the South, and the struggle of uprooted individuals to regain
some sense of honor and "place" are Agrarian themes which
frequently appear in O'Connor's stories. In perhaps her most
explicit exposé of these concerns, "Everything That Rises
Must Converge,"[104] she uses the uprooted state of a pseudo-
aristocrat in the context of social upheaval amid changing
race relations in the South to reveal her own position,
namely that mankind's experience of estrangement exists on
two levels of reality: the historical and the essential.
Here O'Connor departs radically from the Fugitive Movement's
naturalistic philosophy of human existence.

In this story, Julian's mother initiates the alienation
theme with her statement: "With the world in the mess it's
in, it's a wonder we can enjoy anything. I tell you, the bottom rail is on the top. Of course, if you know who you are,
you can go anywhere. . . . I can be gracious to anybody. I
know who I am."[105] Julian, the college-educated, pseudo-
intellectual son, replies: "They [the Blacks, specifically
here] don't give a damn for your graciousness. Knowing who
you are is good for one generation only. You haven't the
foggiest idea where you stand now or who you are."[106] Following a violent confrontation between his mother and a black
woman[107] over money offered to the black woman's son, Julian,

---

[104] In *Complete Stories,* pp. 405-420.

[105] Everything That Rises," p. 407.

[106] "Everything That Rises," p. 407.

[107] Neither the Agrarians nor O'Connor attempt to deal with
black issues. With the early exception of Gabriel in "The Wild
cat," O'Connor did not attempt to delineate black experience.
In her stories, two types of Blacks are caricatured: the rural
Black, a moral innocent even when he is defined as an expert
chicken thief like Rabie ("The Geranium," p. 5) and the city
Black who, like Julian's mother's double, having been assimi-

who now feels justified by the turn of events, tries to impose
upon his stricken mother the reality of her fallen position:

> "Don't think that was just an uppity Negro woman. That
> was the whole colored race which will no longer take
> your condescending pennies. That was your black
> double. . . . What all this means," he said, "is that
> the old world is gone. The old manners are obsolete
> and your graciousness is not worth a damn. . . . From
> now on you've got to live in a new world and face a
> few realities for a change. Buck up," he said, "it
> won't kill you."[108]

The tension between the traditional parent who relies on
the established social hierarchy and its accompanying body of
manners for a sense of identity and propriety and the college
graduate son who naively and spitefully condemns the ways of
the older generation in the light of progressive social ideas
focuses attention on a theme central to contemporary Southern
literature. O'Connor has remained within the limits of possibility in her material. On the literal level, the story
works. However, whereas the Fugitives, while championing
the cause of the mother, would be willing to accept moderate
and gradual social adjustment as inevitable, Flannery O'Connor substantiates neither position and rejects compromise.

With her powerful, ironic conclusion, O'Connor chal-
lenges her readers to venture beyond the humanistic solutions
offered by social probability or human sentiment, either
Agrarian or progressive. Through an unexpected turn of
events, "the bottom rail is on the top" for Julian and for
the unsuspecting reader who may have identified with the
position of either the mother or the son. While Julian is
delivering his abrasive speech to his mother concerning the
reality of her situation and her potential ability to adapt
without significant personal cost, she has suffered a stroke

---

lated into white culture, is no less mediocre than city
Whites.

[108]"Everything That Rises," p. 419.

and died.  Leaving the now confused and motherless Julian to
reorder his universe, the reader is compelled to move beyond
questions related to the potential demise of the Old South,
the changing mores between Whites and Blacks, the communication gap between generations and the value of contemporary
education to the more ultimate questions concerning the nature
of reality, one's true identity and the meaning of life in
death.

Here, at the junction of the temporal and the eternal,
the particular and the universal, O'Connor's work completely
diverges from the philosophy of the Agrarians.  Able to agree
with their contention that religious belief is a critical
element in human existence, especially in relation to the
history and future of the South, she rejects both their reading of the religious history of the region and their recommendation to return to Deism as the most acceptable religious
stance for a culture which seeks to be both agrarian and contemporary.  Blaming what they take to be the South's tragic
loss of the Civil War, from which they maintain it has never
recovered, on the fact that the South did not have enough
faith in its own kind of God, Tate states:

> The South could blindly return to an older secular
> polity [feudal agrarianism], but the world was too
> much with it, and it could not create its appropriate
> religion [medieval Roman Catholicism].

> There were two results of this anomalous position . . .
> The South, as a political atmosphere formed by the
> eighteenth century, did not realize its genius in time,
> but continued to defend itself on the political terms
> of the North; and thus, waiting too long, it let its
> powerful rival gain the ascendancy.  Its religious
> impulse was inarticulate simply because it tried to
> encompass its destiny within the terms of Protestant-
> ism, in origin, a non-agrarian and trading religion;
> hardly a religion at all, but a result of secular am-
> bition.  The Southern politicians could merely quote
> Scripture to defend slavery, the while they defended
> their society as a whole with the catch-words of
> eighteenth century politics. . . .

> Because the South never created a fitting religion, the
> social structure of the South began grievously to break
> down two generations after the Civil War; for the social
> structure depends on the economic structure, and economic
> conviction is the secular image of religion.  No nation
> is ever simply and unequivocally beaten in war; nor was
> the South.  But the South shows signs of defeat, and
> this is due to its lack of a religion which would make
> her special secular system the inevitable and permanently
> valuable one.[109]

The Agrarians dismissed Christianity as an appropriate relig-

ious base in either of its historical forms: Roman Catholicism,

which would have been the happy companion in structure and

form to the feudal economy, but which the Southerners could

not assimilate, and which hence played no significant role in

the establishment of the South; and Protestantism, which was

seen to be essentially a product of an urban industrial and

commercial ideology.  Like the South itself, before it became

devoutly orthodox and literal in its use of Protestant Chris-

tianity, the Agrarians were inclined to support "Jeffersonian

liberalism of the Deistic type."[110]

O'Connor, less concerned than the Agrarians to reconstruct

the religious and social realities of the South's past, seeks

rather to interpret its present socio-religious milieu and to

expose the possible directions in its future.  As she inter-

prets the evidence, the South has been primed for conversion.

It is precisely the remembered loss of the Civil War and the

exaggerated, literal Judaeo-Christian mythos of the region,

unique to the South in their confluence, which give the changing

life of the Southern people a potential direction and hermeneu-

tic.

Reflecting on the continuing importance of the war experi-

ence, but reversing the Agrarians' interpretation of it in the

light of her Christian vision, O'Connor said, "we have had our

---

[109]Tate, "Remarks on the Southern religion," p. 173.

[110]Owsley, "The Irrepressible Conflict," p. 81.

Fall. We have gone into the modern world with an inburnt
knowledge of human limitations and with a sense of mystery
which could not have developed in our first state of innocence—as it has not sufficiently developed in the rest of
our country. . . . Behind our history, deepening it at every
point, has been another history."[111]  In some cultures, knowledge of the Scriptures is reserved to the wealthy or educated
in the South the Bible is quoted by even the poor and illiterate. Even facile and unreflective knowledge of Bible stories
and symbols provides the Southern "everyman" with a rich
mythic texture on which to fashion the fabric of his life.

Having discussed the Agrarian influence and "matter" in
Flannery O'Connor's art, we now turn our attention to her use
of the grotesque. There has been much discussion among critics which suggests that O'Connor belongs to the school of the
Southern grotesque, which readily employs comic, yet terrifying actions, exaggerated situations and abnormal characters.[1]
O'Connor's own grotesque descriptions include rapes, murders,
drownings, arson, and thefts; a preacher who carries "Jesus
like a stinger in his head," a valise which looks "like the
head of a hippopotamus," a city which rises "like a cluster
of warts," and a young man's heart which begins "to grip him
like a little ape clutching the bars of its cage", a Ph.D.
with a wooden leg, a juvenile delinquent with a club foot,
and an "idiot" child.

This kind of emphasis on the deformed and the bizarre is
typical of the genre known as the "grotesque," which is frequently found in Southern literature. Among the characteristics of true grotesque are the following:

> . . . that the sharp division between tragedy and comedy
> has broken down; that the sublime sometimes lurks behind
> weirdly distorted images; and that the literature of the

---

[111]*Mystery and Manners*, p. 59.

[112]For a detailed discussion of O'Connor's use of the
grotesque, see Muller, *Nightmares and Visions: Flannery
O'Connor and the Catholic Grotesque*.

grotesque is in reaction against the sometimes bland
surfaces of bourgeois customs and habits.[113]

Though this genre is not the only way used in literature
to depict the alienation of modern society, it is one way of
creating images of a world out of human control, and it is a
particularly prevalent way. The South has been the source of
especially heavy emphasis on the genre:

> Perhaps the South has produced more than its share of
> the grotesque. The writers are easily listed: Erskine
> Caldwell, William Faulkner, Robert Penn Warren, Eudora
> Welty, Carson McCullers, Flannery O'Connor, Truman Capote
> and Tennessee Williams. Some of the reasons are clear
> enough; the old agricultural system depleted the land and
> poverty breeds absurdity;[114] in many cases people were
> living with a code that was no longer applicable, and
> this meant a detachment from reality and loss of vitality.
> But there are reasons beyond these. The grotesque has
> been seen everywhere in American life and fiction, and
> beyond them.[115]

The grotesque, then, depicts the essential estrangement of
humankind from its humanity, especially prevalent in the
changing social order of the South (a theme emphasized by the
Agrarians, as we have seen), but also found wherever writers
wish to create literary images in fiction of human alienation.

While acknowledging that she deliberately employs elements of the grotesque, including irony, violence and caricature, O'Connor rejects the facile labeling of her art as grotesque.[116] She insists that her use of the grotesque differs
from that of other Southern writers, such as Carson McCullers,

---

[113]William Van O'Connor, *The Grotesque*, p. 5.

[114]It is interesting to note that while the Agrarians
saw the old agricultural order as the source of harmony and
humanization, it is seen here as a source of poverty leading
to modern dehumanization and estrangement.

[115]William Van O'Connor, *The Grotesque*, p. 6. See also
Louise Gossett, *Violence in Recent Southern Fiction*.

[116]"Some aspects of the Grotesque in Southern Fiction,"
*Mystery and Manners*, especially p. 44.

in so far as it is based on her religious understanding of
human life.  Believing that the present historical condition
of humanity is a distortion of what the human being is meant
to be, she insists that her use of the grotesque is not so
much a literary technique as a statement of reality as she
understands it.  Furthermore, she finds modern individuals
not only unconscious of their essential flaw but also committed to the belief that they possess the scientific and rationa
capabilities to create their own future.

Her grotesque images thus serve two purposes.[117]  First,
they portray ordinary people as the freaks that they are.
Her freaks are figures of everyone's essential displacement
and fallen state.  Second, they draw attention to the futility
of human actions to remedy the situation.  O'Connor caricature
humanity's depraved condition and exaggerates the divine means
which must be exercised by God to reach mankind.  Using a
literary style akin to the cartoon, she seeks to make a seriou
statement through the comic means of exaggeration and emphasis
As one critic succinctly notes, "The swift stroke, the telling
detail—these quickly sketch the significant features of [her]
subject."[118]  Her flat characters are examples, vehicles whose
attitudes and actions personify their spiritual alienation.
Rarely interested in society, economy, history or human rela-
tionships in themselves, O'Connor prefers to depict humans in
relation to spiritual events and realities.  Her characters,
usually confirmed in pride and egoism, generally experience
some type of violence which forces them toward some illumina-
tion or revelation concerning their sinfulness, ignorance and
dependency.

The grotesque itself is an ambiguous genre.  Freaks may
be essentially evil, but appear to be good and suffer finally

---

[117]"Some Aspects of the Grotesque," *Mystery and Manners*,
p. 45.

[118]Walters, *Flannery O'Connor*, p. 15.

to be unmasked through violent events; or they may appear to
be diseased or displaced until through some violence they are
shown to be either saved or well on the way to salvation.[119]
There is no adequate explanation for her characters' actions
except in relation to God or the devil. As one critic has
noted, the sociology of poverty and the psychology of fear
may help to interpret actions, but they are unable to reach
the central drama which O'Connor portrays, namely humanity's
depraved state and willful flight from God's mercy, and God's
unrelenting pursuit.[120] In many instances, God's grace which
pursues, encounters and endeavors to correct appears as divine
wrath. Such a radical portrayal of the grace-event has led
some critics to accuse O'Connor of being unchristian or even
in league with the devil.[121]

Now incomplete and prone to evil (a position radically
different from the Agrarian principle of natural goodness),[122]
mankind nonetheless can achieve its potential wholeness through
the free acceptance of grace. Using the literary techniques
of the grotesque, with its emphasis on distortion, caricature,
melodrama and fusion of the human with mechanical or animal
images, O'Connor sought to reveal humanity's essential estrangement from itself and the ground of meaning. Clarifying her
position that the South is not unique in its sinful state, she
stated unequivocally: "We are all grotesque and I don't think

---

[119]See Orvell, *The Invisible Parade: The Fiction of Flannery O'Connor*, p. 44.

[120]Louise Gossett, "The Test by Fire: Flannery O'Connor," p. 76.

[121]See, for example, Hawkes, "Flannery O'Connor's Devil"; and O'Brien, "The Un-Christianity of Flannery O'Connor."

[122]In her first published collection of short stories, O'Connor reveals and explores the fallen condition of man. She once referred to the collection, *A Good Man Is Hard to Find,* as "nine stories about original sin" (Fitzgerald, "Introduction," p. xxii.)

the Southerner is any more grotesque than anyone else; but
his social situation demands more of him than that elsewhere
in this country."[123]  Relying heavily on her region's primitive Protestant fundamentalist understanding of mankind for
her context, she exploited the potential for grotesquerie
that her environment afforded her fiction.

The technique of the grotesque, although frequently mis-
read by O'Connor's early critics as evidence that her work is
essentially misbegotton Gothic unable to reach Hawthorne's or
Poe's level of suspense of horror,[124] is in her writings essentially a comic form in which she was able to execute the
reality of her tragic vision of life in conjunction with her
style of the verbal cartoon.  By combining the horrible with
the ludicrous, she established a detached aesthetic position
which is both amusing and devastating:

> Essentially the grotesque in literature is a method of
> investigating certain metaphysical problems through
> fictive constructions.  In other words, the grotesque
> projects a world vision that is framed by distinct
> techniques: in the best grotesque art, vision and
> technique must function congruently.  The vision itself
> presents existence as deprived of meaning.  All traces
> of natural order are willfully subverted so as to pro-
> duce an alienated world, a world in which man, sensing
> the radical discontinuity of things, is estranged from
> his environment.  This division between man and his
> environment is what actually produces the grotesque or
> the absurd, wherein man discovers that in a universe
> which is disjointed and senseless, which is contradic-
> tory in every aspect, he is something less than what
> he should be.[125]

To critics disoriented by the grotesque elements in her
stories, Flannery O'Connor defended her use of the unfamiliar
genre: "To be able to recognize a freak, you have to have
some concept of the whole man, and in the South the general

---

[123]Mullins, "Interview," pp. 33-34.

[124]See especially Malin, *New American Gothic*, pp. 7-10.

[125]Muller, *Nightmares and Visions*, p. 5.

conception of man is still, in the main theological. . . . I
think it is safe to say that while the South is hardly Christ-
centered, it is most certainly Christ-haunted."[126]

In order to understand the full implications of her
statement, it is necessary to recall that her particular region of the South is far from the fertile gulf-coast of the
Deep South and the cosmopolitan Southern cities where Protestantism has either taken a liberal, naturalistic direction or
has been assimilated with financial and cultural concerns,
thus becoming more middle class and respectable. "It [the
Piedmont region] is a land wracked by disease peculiar to
poverty, by a vicious sharecropper system, by little education, and a superstitious, intense, pietistic, but non-theo-
logical religious passion."[127] The inhabitants of the region,
mainly Scotch-Irish in background, are a "harsh, impetuous
people, with a deep sense of integrity, a tendency to make
their own laws, and to worship God with individual and singular fervor."[128] Because the Piedmont believers have neither
the institutional protection of a developed ritual and sacra-
mentality nor individual sophistication to shield them in
their confrontation with the numinous, their religious quest
has taken the form of a highly individualized, fanatical
struggle against a personalized evil spirit. O'Connor uti-
lized this puritanical religionism in her fiction:

> The fanaticism and torment that characterizes the
> emotion-torn, apocalyptic primitive Protestantism
> of the back-country South, with its revivals, evan-
> gelicals, testimonies, visions, prophets and halluci-
> nations, became in her fiction the unlettered, naive
> search for spiritual existence in a world grown com-
> placent and materialistic. Her sympathies lie not
> with the prosperous, well-adjusted and comfortable mid-
> dleclass churches, but with those who stand outside

---

[126]*Mystery and Manners*, p. 44.

[127]Holman, "Her Rue with a Difference," p. 75.

[128]Rubin, "Flannery O'Connor and the Bible Belt,"
p. 53.

the respectable community, refuse to accept its accom-
modations and compromises, and preach the fire and the
plague.[129]

O'Connor's preoccupation with and respect for the primitive fundamentalist's intense spiritual quest deepens in
juxtaposition to the growth of her own Catholicism during the
final phase of her work.  Her return to the seat of Protestant evangelism in the South, possibly coupled with her own
personal requirements for a more intensified inquiry into the
spiritual life, continued a direction that had been present
in nascent form even in her thesis stories[130] and which was
to dominate her mature works.  The unique religious vision
which Flannery O'Connor presents flows from the convergence
of the fierce Christian fundamentalism of her environment and
her own style of Roman Catholic orthodoxy.

In her use both of Agrarianism and of the grotesque,
O'Connor transcends the purely secular and literal levels of
meaning.  Her recourse to Agrarian principles is not for the
purpose of re-establishing the traditional agrarian South und
deistic religion.  Rather, she attempts to demonstrate how th
Civil War was of a positive value in revealing to the South i
Fall and its need for Redemption.  Similarly, her use of the
grotesque moves beyond its possibilities as a mere literary
genre to suggest the spiritual alienation of mankind from a
God whose grace alone can redeem it and return it to its orig
nal order.

O'Connor's illness, which had caused her to return to
the South, confined her there.  Just as she had easily accept

---

[129]Rubin, "Flannery O'Connor and the Bible Belt," p. 53.

[130]"The Geranium" and "The Turkey" are among the earlies
examples of her literary treatment of religious themes.  It i
interesting to note that during her literary career she rewrote her first complete story, "The Geranium," three times,
entitled it successively "Exile in the East," "Coming Home"
and "Judgement Day."

her return home, so too she saw her illness as a personal event confirming symbols (the grotesque, mankind's need for Redemption, the saving action of grace, etc.) which were already preoccupying her attention as an artist. However, unlike her profitable utilization of the surrounding region's fundamentalism and provincialism, her relationship to her own physical diminishment and its effect on her work are more difficult to assess.

Flannery O'Connor said very little publicly of her condition. Her few recorded references to her illness have appeared until now primarily in quotations from her letters to the Fitzgeralds included in Robert Fitzgerald's "Introduction" to *Everything That Rises Must Converge*, which was not published until after O'Connor's death. In every instance she appears lighthearted and almost sportive about her condition. On separate occasions, she wrote: ". . . I am doing fairly well these days, though I am practically baldheaded on top and have a watermelon face . . ." and "I am walking with a cane these days which gives me a great air of distinction. . . . I now feel that it makes very little difference what you call it. As the niggers say, I have the misery."[131] Once when asked how she wrote so capably in her condition, O'Connor quipped: "I type with my hands, not my feet."[132]

> In all that cheerful patter you miss entirely the sense of suffering that must have been its ultimate source. The country diction is oddly mute about the anguish of a woman feeling the slow violence of disease. It is in fact so inexpressive of anything humanly true that its silence becomes eloquent. What that silence says no one can know for sure.[133]

---

[131]Fitzgerald, "Introduction," pp. xxi-xxii.

[132]Turner, "Visit to Flannery O'Connor Proves a Novel Experience," p. 2-G.

[133]Hendin, *World of O'Connor*, p. 11.

Not only silence, but denial is in evidence in her comment to Meaders that: "There has been no interesting or noble
struggle. The only thing I wrestle with is the language and
a certain poverty of means in handling it, but this is merely
what you have to do to write at all."[134]  The only hint of
something deeper, something more, perhaps indicating that
O'Connor may have seen the "slow violence of disease" as a
potential means of redemption, is found in her response to a
friend's temporary affliction with an ear infection.  Abbot
initiated the discussion by stating that she was suspicious
that much of the so-called "spiritual suffering" had a natural
explanation.  "Her answer to this, most unsatisfactory to me,
was that you could save your soul through inner ear trouble.
Wasn't it Dostoevsky, she asked, who worked out his salvation
through his epilepsy?"[135]  Even this comment can be read as
flippant or perhaps masochistic.  Critics of her fiction
struggle with this same kind of apparent coldness, lack of
compassion and detachment in her stories, for example, the
accounts of the death of the child in "The River"[136] and the
Grandmother in "A Good Man Is Hard to Find."[137]  In the latter
tale, after killing the old woman, the Misfit reflects: "She
would have been a good woman, if there had been somebody there
to shoot her every minute of her life. . . . It's no real
pleasure in life."[138]

Fictional characters, displaying physical disfigurements
of every description, never receive sympathetic treatment from
O'Connor, nor do they desire it.  Fourteen-year-old Rufus

[134]Meaders, "Literary Witch," p. 379.
[135]Abbot, "Remembering O'Connor," p. 13.
[136]*Complete Stories*, pp. 173-174.
[137]*Complete Stories*, pp. 131-132.
[138]*Complete Stories*, p. 143.

Johnson, who has a club foot and a criminal record, declares:
"I lie and steal because I'm good at it. My foot don't have
a thing to do with it!"[139] He interprets his affliction as
a spiritual mark: "The lame shall enter [the Kingdom of
Christ] first! The halt'll be gathered together. When I
get ready to be saved, Jesus'll save me . . . ."[140] In O'Connor's salvation economy, of course, affliction does not guar-
antee sanctity; that is always a matter of free choice, as
Johnson is quite aware. Joy-Hulga, for example, is unaware
that her spiritual life is as hollow as her wooden leg.[141]

Perhaps O'Connor most nearly reveals her personal position regarding illness, disease and disfigurement in her
"Introduction" to *A Memoir of Mary Ann*:

> The creative action of the Christian's life is to pre-
> pare his death in Christ. It is a continuous action in
> which this world's goods are utilized to the fullest,
> both positive gifts and what Père Teilhard de Chardin
> calls "passive diminishments."[142]

She points out that Mary Ann, a child born with a cancer of
the face, also possessed the ability not merely to endure her
fate, but to build upon it. That a child was required to
bear a fatal disfigurement appears an evil turn of events.
But for O'Connor, every man bears the same mark of finitude.
Furthermore, the apparent face of evil may in fact yield an
unexpected boon.

> Most of us have learned to be dispassionate about evil,
> to look it in the face and find, as often as not, our
> own grinning reflections with which we do not argue,

---

[139]"The Lame Shall Enter First," *Complete Stories*,
p. 480.

[140]"The Lame Shall Enter First," p. 480.

[141]See "Good Country People," pp. 243-261.

[142]Dominican Sisters of Our Lady of Perpetual Help Cancer
Home, *A Memoir of Mary Ann*, Flannery O'Connor, ed., p. 17.
Also published as *The Death of a Child*. Introduction pub-
lished separately as "The Mystery of Suffering."

but good is another matter. Few have stared at that
long enough to accept the fact that its face too is
grotesque, that in us the good is something under con-
struction. The modes of evil usually receive worthy
expression. The modes of good have to be satisfied
with a cliché or a smoothing down that will soften
their real look. When we look into the face of good,
we are liable to see a face like Mary Ann's, full of
promise.[143]

For O'Connor, those who bear a more obvious sign also
possess the key to the truth of the human condition. Here
Abbot's personal reflection seems to add clarity:

There was something terrifying in Flannery. There were
those who sensed this and misnamed it—or so I believe.
They called it coldness or cruelty. They described it
as a deficiency in love or compassion, head overbalanc-
ing heart. I think we simply did not know how to take
her, especially in a society where affection and pity
can be passed out as easily as finger sandwiches at a
party and are apt to be about as substantial. I felt
the terror long before I had a glimmer of what caused
it. I think part of it was the utter seriousness with
which she took my difficulties, the extent to which I
sensed she was willing to go to help, the terror of
being, in her eyes, "always valuable and always responsible."[144] It was, too, the terror of encountering
humility and charity of such depth and such a fierce
and faithful holding on to the truth.[145]

The depth of O'Connor's commitment to her quest for
truth and her knowledge of mankind's ultimate responsibility
was manifest amid the comedy of her fiction. Thomas Merton
recognized in her stories the same honest, but humble, focus
on human nature which Abbot had detected. Robert Giroux

---

[143]*Memoir of Mary Ann*, p. 20.

[144]Abbot does not note her source, but the full quotatio
appears in Lockridge, "An Afternoon with Flannery O'Connor,"
p. 39. "I can accept the universe as it is—I don't have to
make up my own sense of values. I can apply to a judgment
higher than my own—I'm not limited to what I personally feel
or think. And I have a sense of personal responsibility; I
believe that a person is always valuable and always responsible."

[145]Abbot, "Remembering O'Connor," p. 13.

served as editor to both O'Connor and Merton. He was given
a private edition of *Prometheus: A Meditation* by Merton to
deliver to O'Connor as a token of his interest and admiration.
Giroux recalls that both writers possessed "a highly developed
sense of comedy, deep faith, great intelligence. The aura
of aloneness surrounding each of them was not an accident.
It was their métier, in which they refined and deepened their
very different talents in a short span of time."[146] Thomas
Merton eulogized O'Connor after her death in 1964, in *Raids
on the Unspeakable*:

> She respected all her people by searching for some sense
> in them, searching for truth, searching to the end and
> then suspending judgment. To have condemned them on
> moral grounds would have been to connive with their own
> crafty arts and their own demonic imagination. It would
> have meant getting tangled up with them in the same
> machinery of unreality and contempt. The only way to
> be saved was to stay out of it, not to think, not to
> speak, just to record the slow, sweet, ridiculous ver-
> balizing of Southern furies, working their way through
> their charmingly lazy hell.
>
> That is why when I read Flannery I don't think of Heming-
> way, or Katherine Anne Porter, or Sartre, but rather of
> someone like Sophocles. What more can be said of a
> writer? I write her name with honor, for all the truth
> and all the craft with which she shows man's fall and
> his dishonor.[147]

Although not all critics, literary or religious, would
assent to such lavish praise of O'Connor's art, her fiction
began to gain professional recognition as early as 1953. In
that year and the one following, she was awarded a *Kenyon
Review* Fellowship. In 1954, "The Life You Save May Be Your
Own" won for her the first of many O. Henry Awards for prize
stories.[148] Harcourt, Brace and Company published her first

---

[146]Giroux, "Introduction," p. xiii.

[147]Merton, "Flannery O'Connor: A Prose Elegy," *Raids on
the Unspeakable*, 41-42.

[148]See Chronology for a complete list of prize stories
and awards.

collection of short stories, entitled *A Good Man Is Hard to
Find*, in 1955.  Growing public interest in her fiction,
coupled with her keen wit and wry humor, made O'Connor an
increasingly popular lecturer.  Accepting as her health permitted invitations from Georgian and other Southern colleges,
Roman Catholic institutions, such as the University of Notre
Dame, and even local high schools, she spoke on a wide variety
of topics related to creative writing, Southern regionalism
and the relationship between art and belief.  Often using the
same basic core of insights and ideas, she reworked and al-
tered her lectures continually, aiming both for greater clarity
and more specific relevance to a particular audience.  The ex-
tant manuscripts of these lectures have been edited by Robert
and Sally Fitzgerald and were issued posthumously in 1970.[149]

As her literary acumen began to reveal the depth of her
spiritual roots, O'Connor was sought out by the review editor
of the newspaper published by the Catholic Diocese of Georgia
to write book reviews on contemporary religious thought from
the perspective of a Catholic lay person.  She wrote well over
a hundred reviews of works of fiction, literary criticism,
philosophy, psychology and a wide range of theological topics.
More than seventy of these reviews were published at regular
intervals between 1956 and 1964, the year of her death.
Copies of O'Connor's submitted reviews, published and unpublished, as well as portions of her annotated literary holdings have recently become accessible to the public.  These
rich new resources, when studied in relation to her complete
fiction corpus and her occasional prose, promise to shed further light on her own spiritual and theological journey.

Flannery O'Connor's work was temporarily halted in 1958
when she was prevailed upon by a cousin to travel with Regina

---

[149]*Mystery and Manners: The Occasional Prose of Flannery
O'Connor*.  The original manuscripts form part of the Flannery
O'Connor Collection.

to Lourdes and then on to Rome for an audience with the Pope. According to Fitzgerald's account, "Flannery dreaded the possibility of a miracle at Lourdes, and she forced herself to the piety of the bath for her mother's sake and Cousin Katie's . . ."[150] Her urgent desire to be spared a cure seems to indicate that she had met her disease, accepted its limitations and used these to further the development of her spirit as well as her art. She was spared the miracle and went on to Rome where she was most impressed with Pope Pius XII "who received her with interest and gave her a special blessing."[151]

Returning home, and exempted from further intrusions, O'Connor set herself to the final tasks of her life and career. Supported by a generous Ford Foundation grant in 1959, she completed her second novel, *The Violent Bear It Away*, which was published in 1960, and completed the manuscript for a second collection of short stories, *Everything That Rises Must Converge*, which was published posthumously in 1965. She began to sketch plans for a third novel, tentatively entitled *Why Do the Heathen Rage?*[152] By this time her stories had become well-defined vehicles for public access to her particular religious vision. These mature writings witness her development of a rich intellectual and contemplative life and provide for scholars a carefully delineated exposé of O'Connor's understanding of the religious nature of the world.

---

[150]Fitzgerald, "Introduction," p. xiv.

[151]Fitzgerald, p. xxiv.

[152]She published a brief selection from the planned novel in *Esquire*, 60 (July, 1963), pp. 60-61. However, Burns holds that she actually began this work sometime between 1954 and 1957, and that all of its usable material is encompassed within the stories in *Everything That Rises Must Converge* (Burns, "How Wide Did 'The Heathen' Range?" pp. 25-41).

Her contribution to literature began to be recognized
by the academic world. She was awarded two honorary degrees:
Doctor of Letters of St. Mary's College, Notre Dame, in 1962,
and a similar degree in 1963 from Smith College. Two final
first prize O. Henry Awards were given in 1963 to "Everything
That Rises Must Converge" and in 1964 to "Revelation."

Although her health began to deteriorate in late 1963,
O'Connor continued her writing. The necessity of abdominal
surgery in the spring of 1964 caused a major setback in her
general condition. Commenting to Caroline Gordon, who visite
her in the hospital, she said: "The doctor says I can't do
any work. But he says it's all right for me to write a little fiction."[153] Keeping a notebook under her pillow, she
wrote "whenever they aren't doing anything to me."[154] Her
final stories, "Parker's Back" and "Judgement Day," completed
just prior to her death, have been included with "Revelation"
in the second collection of her short stories.[155] With most
of her intended work completed, Flannery O'Connor died in a
coma on August 3, 1964.

In addition to *Everything That Rises Must Converge* and
*Mystery and Manners,* her posthumous publications include one
final story, "Parker's Back," published by *Esquire* in April,
1965, and a final collection, *The Complete Stories of Flanner*
*O'Connor,* published in 1971. This volume, which includes all
of her stories and an introduction and memoir by her editor,
Robert Giroux, received the National Book Award. *The Habit*
*of Being,* a selection of O'Connor's letters edited by Sally
Fitzgerald, was published in 1979.

---

[153]Gordon, "Heresy in Dixie," p. 265.

[154]Gordon, p. 265.

[155]*Complete Stories,* pp. 510-530, 488-509, and 531-
550.

*   *   *

In this First Section we have charted the life and works of Flannery O'Connor. We have especially noted how her fiction is related to her response to the influence of her societal, familial, religious and literary milieu. Section Two will examine O'Connor's personal library holdings to determine the literary and religious spectrum against which she developed as an intellectual and critic, especially during her mature period of fiction and prose writing at Andalusia. From a description of the extent of the holdings, their most significant characteristics and their known usage, we will seek to assess O'Connor's sources and sensitivities.

CHRONOLOGY OF THE LIFE AND WORKS
OF FLANNERY O'CONNOR

In addition to the significant events in the life of
Flannery O'Connor, this list includes her known publications
and posthumous collations of her work. Within the entries
of the given year, the personal events appear first, followed by publications and awards. Fiction publications are
listed first, then essays and book reviews.

1925    Born Mary Flannery O'Connor on March 25th in Savannah,
        Georgia; only child of Edward Francis O'Connor
        and Regina Cline O'Connor.

1930    Appeared in Pathé News Film with pet Bantam chicken
        that walked forwards and backwards.

1931    Enrolled in parochial school, Savannah.

1938    Moved with family to Milledgeville, Georgia; father ill
        with disseminated lupus.
        Enrolled in Peabody High School, Milledgeville.

1941    Father died of lupus, February 1st.

1942    Graduated from Peabody High School.
        Enrolled in Georgia State College for Women, Milledge-
        ville (now known as Georgia College).[1]
        Served as editor of the literary quarterly, *The Corin-
        thian,* and art editor of the student newspaper,
        *The Colonnade.*

1945    Served as feature editor of senior year book.
        Graduated from Georgia State College for Women with a
        B.A. in Social Science.
        Dropped "Mary" from name.
        Enrolled in Writers' Workshop, State University of
        Iowa (now the University of Iowa).

---

[1]By beginning her college education in the summer term
and continuing her studies year-round, she was able to obtain
her degree in three years.

1946    Published first short story:
        "The Geranium," *Accent*.[2]
        Flannery O'Connor Collection established at Ina Dillard
            Russell Library, Georgia College.[3]

1947    Began work on her first novel, *Wise Blood*.
        Received Master of Fine Arts degree from the State
            University of Iowa.

1948    Resided at Yaddo, a writers' colony in Saratoga Springs,
            New York.
        Engaged Elizabeth McKee as her literary agent.
        Published short stories:
            "The Train," *Sewanee Review*.
            "The Capture," *Mademoiselle* (earlier titled "The
                Turkey").

1949    Stayed briefly in a New York City apartment house.
        Returned to Milledgeville for an extended visit from
            March to September.
        Moved to the Connecticut  farm of Robert and Sally Fitz-
            gerald in September.
        Published short stories:
            "The Heart of the Park," *Partisan Review*.
            "The Woman on the Stairs," *Tomorrow* (later retitled
                "A Stroke of Good Fortune").
            "The Peeler," *Partisan Review*.

1950    Hospitalized in Atlanta in December with first major
            attack of lupus.

1951    Moved permanently to Andalusia farm, Milledgeville.

1952    Published first novel:
            *Wise Blood*.
        Published short story:
            "Enoch and the Gorilla," *New World Writing*.

1953    Published short stories:
            "A Good Man is Hard to Find,"  *The Berkeley Book
                of Modern Writing*.

---

[2]Full bibliographical information for the published fiction is given in the Bibliography.  Publication information
for the book reviews, in so far as it is available, is given
in Part Three.  O'Connor's essays are edited and reprinted
by Sally and Robert Fitzgerald in *Mystery and Manners*.

[3]The early collection consisted of fiction pieces from
her high school and college days.  As her stories appeared in
print, copies were added to the collection along with newspaper interviews and articles.

"The Life You Save May Be Your Own," *Kenyon Review*
"The River," *Sewanee Review.*
"A Late Encounter with the Enemy," *Harper's Bazaar*
Received the *Kenyon Review* Fellowship in Fiction.

1954    Published short stories:
        "A Circle in the Fire," *Kenyon Review.*
        "A Temple of the Holy Ghost," *Harper's Bazaar.*
        "The Displaced Person," *Sewanee Review.*
        Reappointed Kenyon Fellow.
        Received O. Henry Award, second prize, for "The Life
        You Save May Be Your Own."

1955    Published first collection of short stories:
        *A Good Man Is Hard to Find.*
        Published short stories:
        "The Artifical Nigger," *Kenyon Review.*
        "Good Country People," *Harper's Bazaar.*
        "You Can't Be Any Poorer Than Dead," *New World
        Writing.*
        Received O. Henry Award, second prize, *The Best America
        Short Stories of 1955,* for "A Circle in the Fire."

1956    Began a series of lecture trips to colleges and univer-
        sities.
        Published short story:
        "Greenleaf," *Kenyon Review.*
        Published first book reviews:
        *The Malefactors,* by Caroline Gordon.
        *The Presence of Grace,* by J. F. Powers.
        *Two Portraits of St. Thérèse of Lisieux,* by
        Etienne Robo.
        *Humble Powers,* by Paul Horgan.
        *Letters from Baron von Hügel to a Niece,* by
        Friedrich von Hügel.
        *Beyond the Dreams of Avarice,* by Russell Kirk.
        *The Catholic Companion to the Bible,* by Ralph
        L. Woods, ed.
        *Meditations before Mass,* by Romano Guardini.
        Received O. Henry Award, *The Best American Short Storie
        of 1956,* for "The Artificial Nigger."

1957    Published short story:
        "A View of the Woods," *Partisan Review.*
        Published first essays:
        "The Church and the Fiction Writer," *America.*
        "The Fiction Writer and His Country," *The Living
        Novel.*
        Reviewed:
        *The Metamorphic Tradition in Modern Poetry,* by
        Bernetta Quinn.
        *Writings,* by Edith Stein.
        *Criticism and Censorship,* by Walter F. Kerr.

> Received National Institute of Arts and Letters grant.
> Received O. Henry Award, first prize, *The Best American Short Stories of 1957,* for "Greenleaf."

1958 Traveled to Lourdes and Rome with mother; audience with Pope Pius XII.
> Published short story:
> "The Enduring Chill," *Harper's Bazaar.*
> Reviewed:
> *The Transgressor,* by Julian Green.
> *Patterns in Comparative Religion,* by Mircea Eliade.
> *American Classics Reconsidered,* by Harold C. Gardiner, ed.
> *Israel and Revelation,* by Eric Voeglin.
> *Late Dawn,* by Elizabeth Vandon.
> Received O. Henry Award, *The Best American Short Stories of 1958,* for "A View of the Woods."

1959 Published essay:
> "Replies to Two Questions," *Esprit.*
> Reviewed:
> *Freud and Religion,* by Gregory Zilboorg.
> *Temporal and Eternal,* by Charles Péguy.
> *Harry Vernon at Prep,* by Franc Smith.
> Received a grant from the Ford Foundation.

1960 Published second novel:
> *The Violent Bear It Away.*
> Published short story:
> "The Comforts of Home," *Kenyon Review.*
> Reviewed:
> *Jesus Christus: Meditations,* by Romano Guardini.
> *Mary, Mother of Faith,* by Josef Weiger.
> *The Pyx,* by John Buell.
> *Sister Clare,* by Loretta Burrough.
> *God's Frontier,* by J. L. M. Descalzo.
> *The Modernity of St. Augustine,* by Jean Guitton.
> *The Christian Message and Myth,* by L. Malavez.
> *Christ and Apollo,* by William F. Lynch.
> *The Son of Man,* by François Mauriac.
> *The Science of the Cross,* by Edith Stein.
> *Beat on a Damask Drum,* by T. K. Martin.
> *Pierre Teilhard de Chardin,* by Nicolas Corte.
> *Soul and Psyche,* by Victor White.
> *Christian Initiation,* by Louis Bouyer.
> *Modern Catholic Thinkers,* by A. Robert Caponigri, ed.

1961 Published short stories:
> "Everything That Rises Must Converge," *New World Writing.*
> "The Partridge Festival," *Critic.*

Published Essays:
  "Living with a Peacock," *Holiday* (later retitled
    "The King of the Birds").
  "The Novelist and Free Will," *Fresco*.
Edited:
  *Death of a Child* (later retitled *Memoir of Mary
    Ann*). Introduction by Flannery O'Connor also
    published separately under the title "The
    Mystery of Suffering."
Reviewed:
  *The Divine Milieu*, by Pierre Teilhard de Chardin.
  *The Life of St. Catherine of Siena*, by Raymond
    of Capua.
  *The Cardinal Stritch Story*, by Marie Cecilia
    Buehrle.
  *Leo XIII: A Light from Heaven*, by William J.
    Kiefer.
  *Cross Currents* (quarterly).
  *The Conversion of Augustine*, by Romano Guardini.
  *The Critic* (quarterly).
  *Stop Pushing!* by Dan Herr.
  *Life's Long Journey*, by Kenneth Macfarlane Walker.
  *Selected Letters of Stephen Vincent Benét*, by
    Charles Fenton, ed.
  *The Resurrection*, by F. X. Durrwell.
  *Themes of the Bible*, by Jacques Guillet.
  *The Mediaeval Mystics of England*, by Eric Col-
    ledge, ed.
  *Freedom, Grace and Destiny*, by Romano Guardini.
  *The Range of Reason*, by Jacques Maritain.
  *The Bible and the Ancient Near East*, by G. E.
    Wright.
  *The Old Testament and Modern Study*, by H. H.
    Rowley, ed.
  *The Novelist and the Passion Story*, by F. W.
    Dillistone.
  *Teilhard de Chardin*, by Oliver A. Rabut.
  *The Phenomenon of Man*, by Pierre Teilhard de Chardi
1962 Published short story:
  "The Lame Shall Enter First," *Sewanee Review*.
Reviewed:
  *Conversations with Cassandra*, by Sister M.
    Madeleva.
  *Christian Faith and Man's Religion*, by Marc C.
    Ebersole.
  *Christianity Divided*, by Daniel J. Callahan, Heiko
    A. Oberman and Daniel J. O'Hanlon, eds.
  *Evidence of Satan in the Modern World*, by Léon
    Cristiani.
  *The Georgia Review* (quarterly).
  *The Conscience of Israel*, by Bruce Vawter.
  *The Victorian Vision*, by Margaret M. Maison.

*Toward the Knowledge of God,* by Claude Tresmontant.
*The Cardinal Spellman Story,* by Robert I. Gannon.
*The Council, Reform and Reunion,* by Hans Küng.
*The Integrating Mind,* by William F. Lynch.
*Mystics of Our Times,* by Hilda Graef.
*The Catholic in America,* by Peter J. Rahill.
Second printing of *Wise Blood* with "Introduction" by
    Flannery O'Connor.
Received honorary Doctor of Letters, St. Mary's College,
    Notre Dame.

1963  Published short story:
    "Why Do the Heathen Rage?" *Esquire.*
  Published essays:
    "Fiction Is a Subject with a History; It Should Be
      Taught That Way," *The Georgia Bulletin.*
    "The Regional Writer," *Esprit.*
  Reviewed:
    *The Bible: Word of God in Words of Men,* by Jean
      Levie.
    *Frontiers in American Catholicism,* by Walter J.
      Ong.
    *New Men for New Times,* by Beatrice Avalos.
    *Seeds of Hope in the Modern World,* by Barry
      Ulanov.
    *The Wide World, My Parish,* by Yves Congar.
    *Letters from a Traveler,* by Pierre Teilhard de
      Chardin.
    *Saint Vincent de Paul,* by M. V. Woodgate.
    *The Holiness of Vincent de Paul,* by Jacques
      Delarue.
    *St. Vincent de Paul,* by Leonard von Matt and
      Louis Cognet.
    *What is the Bible?* by Henri Daniel-Rops.
    *Faith, Reason and the Gospels,* by John J.
      Heaney, ed.
    *Image of America,* by Norman Foerster.
    *The Modern God,* by Gustave Weigel.
    *Evangelical Theology,* by Karl Barth.
    *Morte d'Urban,* by J. F. Powers.
  Received Honorary Doctor of Letters, Smith College.
  Received O. Henry Award, first prize, *Prize Stories of
    1963,* for "Everything That Rises Must Converge."

1964  Underwent abdominal surgery in Spring; lupus reactivated.
  Published short story:
    "Revelation," *Sewanee Review.*
  Published essay:
    "The Role of the Catholic Novelist," *Greyfriar.*
  Reviewed:
    *The Kingdom of God,* by Louis J. Putz, ed.
    *Prince of Democracy,* by Arline Boucher and
      John Tehan.

Printing of *Three by Flannery O'Connor* (contains *Wise
  Blood*, *A Good Man Is Hard to Find* and *The Violent
  Bear It Away*).
Died August 3rd at hospital in Milledgeville.

## Posthumous Publications,
## Collations and Awards

1965   Publication of second collection of short stories:
          *Everything That Rises Must Converge.*
       Publication of "Parker's Back," *Esquire.*
       Publication of essay:
          "Some Aspects of the Grotesque in Southern
          Fiction," *Cluster Review.*
       O. Henry Award, first prize, *Prize Stories of 1965,*
          to "Revelation."

1966   National Catholic Book Award to *Everything That Rises
          Must Converge.*

1970   Publication of *Mystery and Manners: The Occasional
          Prose of Flannery O'Connor*, by Sally and Robert
             Fitzgerald, eds.
       Publication of "Wildcat," *North American Review.*
             "The Barber," *Atlantic.*
       Manuscripts added to the Flannery O'Connor Collection
          by Regina Cline O'Connor.

1971   Publication of *The Complete Stories of Flannery O'Con-
          nor*, by Robert Giroux, ed.; National Book Award.
       Publication of "The Crop," *Mademoiselle.*
       Establishment of the Flannery O'Connor Memorial Room at
          the Ina Dillard Russell Library, Georgia College.

1974   Substantial portion of personal library holdings given
          to Georgia College by Regina Cline O'Connor.

1979   Publication of *The Habit of Being: Letters of Flannery
          O'Connor*, by Sally Fitzgerald, ed.

PART TWO
FLANNERY O'CONNOR'S PERSONAL LIBRARY

AN INTRODUCTION TO FLANNERY O'CONNOR'S PERSONAL LIBRARY

More than six hundred volumes of Flannery O'Connor's personal library, all but a few collected during her final thirteen years at Andalusia, are now housed in the Flannery O'Connor Collection at Georgia College.[1] These volumes reflect O'Connor's personal and professional interests, both religious and literary, as well as the contemporary Catholic and Southern milieu in which she lived and wrote.

The collection is approximately two-thirds religious works (Christian classics, theology, scripture, ecumenical and world religion, and psychology of religion) and one-third literary works (Greek classics in translation, literary theory and criticism, poetry and fiction). Religious authors whose works most often appear in the holdings include Augustine, Thomas Aquinas, John Henry Newman, Jacques Maritain, Teilhard de Chardin, Romano Guardini, and Martin D'Arcy. Predominant literary authors include Nathaniel Hawthorne, Henry James, T. S. Eliot, Joseph Conrad, William Faulkner, François Mauriac and Katherine Anne Porter. Most of these authors were popular either among Catholic or Southern intellectuals of the fifties and early sixties. They bear special relationship to O'Connor's life and works in that she was uniquely part of both the Catholic and the Southern renaissances which occurred separately in the first half of the twentieth century.

Many of the volumes in the collection bear inscriptions, page references or annotations. Approximately one hundred

---

[1]An alphabetical listing of the complete holdings at Georgia College is found following this Introduction.

and fifty books bear the inscription "Flannery O'Connor" in her hand. Some of these inscriptions include the date.[2] Fewer than ten inscriptions indicate, either by date or through the inclusion of "Mary" before her name, volumes acquired prior to her mature period at Andalusia.[3] O'Connor seems to have followed no rule as to which books she inscribed. Her name, occasionally followed by the date, appears on the flyleaf in both fiction and non-fiction works. Inscriptions appear more frequently, but not exclusively, in books which she did not review. Some heavily annotated volumes bear no inscription, while some, otherwise unmarked, are inscribed. Certainly no case can be made that she inscribed those books most important to her.

Annotations in the form of lists appear on the dust jackets of both fiction and non-fiction works.[4] Although dust jacket markings occur infrequently in fiction books, they are, wherever they do appear, lists of other books which O'Connor associated with the work in question. In non-fiction works, the dust jacket markings are most frequently lists of page numbers for referral within that volume. Often these

---

[2]All inscriptions are given following the entry in the List of Flannery O'Connor's Personal Library Holdings. A few inscriptions indicate original holdings of another family member, often a Cline or Treanor. See, for example, Adams, Henry, *The Education of Henry Adams*, and England, John, *Works*. Some books received as literary awards and gifts from friends or other authors can also be detected by their inscriptions. See, for examples, Bellamann, Katherine, *A Poet Passed This Way*, and Buber, Martin, *Eclipse of God*.

[3]Among these early acquisitions are the only annotated fiction works in the collection: Dante's *The Divine Comedy* and Joyce's *Dubliners*. The interlinear nature of the notations and the fact that she did not mark the text of any other fiction book in the library indicates that she may have used these works as college texts.

[4]All dust jacket markings are listed after the entry in the List of Library Holdings.

pages are the sources for quoted material used in her book
reviews or important textual annotations.

Of the one hundred and thirty-one known book reviews,
only ninety of the titles appear in the collection.[5] Copies
of four of the seventeen reviewed fiction works are included:
Caroline Gordon's *The Malefactors*, François Mauriac's *Lines
of Life* and *The Son of God*, and J. F. Powers' *Morte d'Urban*.
As is true of all the fiction works acquired during her mature
period, these volumes are not marked or annotated. Of the
eighty-six non-fiction review books found in the collection,
nine have textual annotations and dust jacket markings, seventeen have only dust jacket markings, seven have only textual
markings and fifty-two contain no markings of any kind. In
general markings and annotations in review books correspond
to materials and quotations used by O'Connor in the reviews.[6]

The only published work to date which examines O'Connor's
annotated library holdings is Feeley's *Flannery O'Connor: The
Voice of the Peacock*.[7] Although problematic in its style and
method, Feeley's work does provide an overview of O'Connor's
holdings and reproduces many of O'Connor's annotations within
key texts. Proceeding in a meditative, non-critical style,
Feeley has sought to weave a single tapestry from the complex
notational materials and from O'Connor's own writings. Though
an interesting exercise, Feeley's work invalidly attempts to
establish a direct correlation between what O'Connor read and
what she wrote. Employing a circular methodology, Feeley uses
O'Connor's fiction as a framework for the annotated material
and then applies selected quotations from this material to

---

[5]No copies of reviewed periodicals or pamphlets appear
in the collection. Missing fiction and non-fiction books may
have been loaned or lost.

[6]For further discussion see Part Three, An Introduction
to Flannery O'Connor's Book Reviews.

[7]Published in 1972.

explicate the fiction.  Seeking to include as much data as
possible, she attempts to incorporate some aspect of each of
O'Connor's stories into a set of annotations or titles in the
library.  Feeley does not approach the library critically,
nor does she fully evaluate her findings against either the
full range of O'Connor's fiction or her complete library
holdings.  Whereas she exaggerates the neo-Thomistic aspects
of both the fiction and the collection, she neglects the
Southern and grotesque.  In his review of this work, Frederick Asals notes:

> Inescapably what Sister Kathleen [Feeley] brings are
> her own preoccupations as a Catholic, and while she can
> hardly be faulted for that, it is somewhat disappoint-
> ing at this date that the Flannery O'Connor that emerges
> from *Voice of the Peacock* is once more the figure of
> simple (if well read) Christian piety, all tensions
> gone.  For here again is the "spiritualized" O'Connor
> ("her illness both debilitated the flesh and forged the
> spirit that was Flannery O'Connor's.  Her fiction is
> the product of that spirit . . ."), that defender of
> the Faith dedicated to flailing out at modern heresies
> from her rock of Truth--hardly the complex woman who
> repeatedly insisted, "We write with the whole person-
> ality."[8]

In her treatment of Flannery O'Connor, Feeley has erred
on the side of misapplied charity.  O'Connor is a complex
writer and an eclectic reader.  She thought and wrote at the
crossroads of Catholicism and Southern literature during a
period when both these cultural forces were experiencing rebirth.  Central to an understanding of the significance of
O'Connor's contribution is an awareness of the conscious tension between these contrasting milieus.

---

[8]Asals, "Review of Kathleen Feeley's *Flannery O'Connor:
Voice of the Peacock*," p. 63.

Holdings Related to the Catholic Renaissance

Flannery O'Connor's mature period from 1951 to 1964 coincides with the last decade of the Catholic Intellectual Renaissance in Europe and with the birth of Catholic intellectualism in North America.[9] The roots of the Catholic intellectual awakening in Europe can be traced to the sustained influence of Modernism which, though condemned as a heresy in 1907, nonetheless raised questions related to the consciousness of the age which Church scholars reflected later in their theological teachings. The coming of age of the American Catholic Church can be dated from the 1908 papal constitution, "Sapienti consilio," which withdrew the mission status of the American Church and placed it on an equal basis with the established churches of Europe. The cross-cultural experiences of American and European Catholics during the Second World War and the 1943 encyclical "Divino afflante Spiritu" concerning the application of scientific principles to the critique of Scripture further enhanced the intellectual dialogue within the Catholic church and drew Catholic thinkers into dialogue with their Protestant and secular counterparts. This growth of scholarship and intellectual activity continued both in Europe and in the United States, culminating in the Second Vatican Council in 1964.

Aspects of Modernism, an ideology which had challenged the authority of the Church and sought to revolutionize Catholic doctrine through its evolutionary, naturalistic philosophy and historio-critical method, gradually "humanized" even official doctrine including: respect for Biblical criticism, an understanding of the growth and development of dogma, the validity of the historical method, an acceptance

---

[9]For further discussion see, for example, Ellis, *American Catholicism*, pp. 124-254, and Hitchcock, "Postmortem on a Rebirth," pp. 211-225.

of evolutionary biological theory, a more humanized mode of
Church authority, an appreciation of spiritual anthropology,
a return to traditional Christian sources, a deeper understan
ing of the relationship of the social sciences to revealed
truth, a stress on the place of the laity in the Church, and
a move from parochialism toward ecumenism.[10]

Not unlike other American Catholics, Flannery O'Connor
was primarily attracted to the works of Catholic Renaissance
thinkers in Europe.  Though certainly not herself a modernist
she avidly read near-modernists, including von Hügel and Newman.[11]  Her volumes of von Hügel are among the most heavily
annotated of her holdings, and she frequently quoted both
Newman and von Hügel in her letters and lectures.  She respected Newman's intellectual acumen and his ability to defen
the Faith against the attacks of non-believers.[12]  Her major
marking in his *Apologia Pro Vita Sua* is Newman's statement
that the Church permits nothing to stand between God and man:

> Only this I know, and did not know then, that the Catho-
> lic Church allows no image of any sort, material or im-
> material, no dogmatic symbol, no rite, no sacrament, no
> Saint, not even the Blessed Virgin herself, to come be-
> tween the soul and its Creator.  It is face to face,
> "solus cum solo," in all matters between man and his
> God.  He alone creates; He alone has redeemed; before
> His awful eyes we go in death; in the vision of His
> eternal beatitude.[13]

---

[10]For further discussion of Modernism, see Heaney, "Modernism," pp. 991-995.

[11]Newman defended the Modernists' position of the development of dogma and the value of experience in contrast to
merely notional knowledge; von Hügel concurred with the Modernist position on the value of Biblical criticism and exegesis.  Both of these scholars managed to remain within the
Church and their modernizing tendencies gradually influenced
the official teaching in these matters.

[12]See, for example, *The Habit of Being*, p. 477.

[13]John Henry Newman, *Apologia Pro Vita Sua*, p. 203,
O'Connor Collection.

This statement, somewhat atypical for Newman, reflects O'Connor's own view of the starkness of the confrontation between God and humanity. She frequently employs variations of Newman's phrase "before His [God's] awful eyes" in her fiction works.[14]

O'Connor's markings in von Hügel's *Letters from Baron von Hügel to a Niece* reflect a similar interest. Throughout the text, she has underlined references to the "cost" of belief in Christ.[15] Though the human price is substantial, O'Connor's markings indicate agreement with von Hügel's statement that only through such devastating experience can mankind be freed from its more terrible earthly existence.[16] These annotations give some insight into O'Connor's worldview. Though she respected both Newman and von Hügel for their clarity of vision and their intellectual honesty, she did not share their more "humanizing" approach to the Christian life. Though both thinkers moderate these more stark statements of the awesomeness of God and the misery of much of the human condition with equal emphasis on the mercy and love of God and the goodness of earthly life, O'Connor takes note only of the most absolute statements, revealing her own tendency toward a Jansenistic interpretation of reality. Her numerous markings in C. S. Lewis' *The Problem of Pain* further suggest the extent to which she examined the relationship between the pain of human existence resulting from sin and God's perfect love which demands total self-abnegation.

Catholic Renaissance writers rejected the blatant religious skepticism of the Modernists, but took up the human-

---

[14]See, for example, "Parker's Back," especially pp. 522 and 527.

[15]On pp. 64-65, for example, "costingly," "gently costly," "Deeply, costingly," are underlined throughout the text.

[16]" . . . the full, truly free, beauty of Christ above completely liberates us from this miserable bondage" (von Hügel, *Letters*, p. 65, O'Connor Collection).

izing elements of the movement.  They sought to employ modern
scientific methods to conduct a systematic, rational investi-
gation of both tradition and contemporary experience in their
search for truth.  Leaders of this rebirth of Christian rationalism include the Maritains, Gilson, Bloy, Péguy, and
Marcel.  O'Connor read all of them.  She wrote positive reviews of Maritain's *The Range of Reason*, Gilson's *Reason and
Revelation in the Middle Ages* and *Painting and Reality*, and
Péguy's *Temporal and Eternal*.[17]  In her review of *The Range
of Reason*, O'Connor calls Maritain "one of the major voices
in modern philosophy to reassert the primacy of reason."[18]
She further notes in the review that unlike Enlightenment
philosophers, Maritain respects the value of revelation and
holds it in proper relation to reason.  O'Connor respected
the attempts made by such writers as Maritain, Marcel and
Gilson to develop a Christian aesthetic by which contemporary
artistry might be evaluated.  She quotes them frequently in
her essays and lectures on the relationship between literature and belief.[19]  She also read historians of culture including Ong, Berenson, D'Arcy, Dawson, Chesterton, Weigel
and Lynch.

Interested in Biblical study and contemporary understand
ing of the Scriptures, O'Connor collected works on the Bible
throughout her mature period.  Her earliest acquisitions are
two volumes of Knox in 1949, two years before she moved to
Andalusia.  Her interest continued through the next decade.
She reviewed at least thirteen works on Biblical scholarship
and read in addition *A Study of Hebrew Thought* by Tresmontant
*Understanding Biblical Research* by Luis Alonso Schökel and

---

[17]Of these, only O'Connor's review of Maritain's *The
Range of Reason* was published.

[18]See Part Three, Book Review 46.

[19]See *Mystery and Manners*, especially "Catholic Novelists
and Their Readers," pp. 169-190.

*The Bible in Current Catholic Thought* by McKenzie.[20] Despite
the number of reviews which she wrote on the topic, O'Connor's
collection of Scripture-related works is nearly unmarked.
Only two works, one of which she reviewed, are annotated.
The style of annotation in both volumes is similar. Under-
lines are used for emphasis within the text and important passages are marked in the margin. In Tresmontant's *A Study of
Hebrew Thought*, for which no review has been found, O'Connor
marked throughout the text statements concerning the flesh-
spirit distinction in the Hebrew Scriptures. Marked passages
include:

> No matter how paradoxical it appears to our secretly
> Manichean habits, the Hebrew has a sense and a love of
> the carnal because he has a sense of the spiritual and
> perceives the presence of the spiritual within the car-
> nal. The carnal is desirable because of the intelli-
> gible mystery with which it is filled. Meaning lies
> just beneath the skin. The Hebrew is carnal because
> he knows what it is to be barred through the sensible.[21]

> The flesh-spirit dialectics is proper to the Bible and
> must not be confused with the body-soul dialectics of
> the Greeks. . . . The opposition of flesh to spirit is
> an opposition between two orders. *Flesh*, as we have
> seen, is man's *index of frailty*, that frailty that comes
> of being made of dust. The *spirit* is man's *participa-
> tion in the supernatural order.*[22]

This distinction would appear to be of professional as well
as personal interest to O'Connor inasmuch as it relates not
only to her own questions, but also to her creative arts of
employing the sensible to define and depict spiritual significance.

---

[20] Known unpublished reviews of Scripture works include
Bruns, *Hear His Voice Today*; McKenzie, *The Two-Edged Sword*;
and Vawter, *A Path through Genesis*. Texts of published reviews are found in Part Three.

[21] Tresmontant, *A Study of the Hebrew Bible*, p. 103,
O'Connor Collection.

[22] Tresmontant, *A Study*, p. 108, O'Connor Collection, emphasis O'Connor's.

In Vawter's *The Consciousness of Israel*, O'Connor has
marked a series of statements defining and describing the
Old Testament prophets.  She employs these same passages
in her review, praising Vawter for enabling readers to understand the prophetic element in the Old Testament.[23]  The role
and call of the prophet was also of artistic interest to
O'Connor whose own prophets are not unlike those described
by Vawter's account of the pre-exilic prophets.

Reflecting the concern of the age for tradition and the
classics, O'Connor's holdings include primary works of Christian saints and mystics.  She read both Thomas Aquinas and
Augustine in translation, as well as commentators on these
key figures.  Although O'Connor often refers to Thomas and
even calls herself a Thomist, her copies of Augustine are
more marked and show signs of wear.  Her annotated copies of
Guardini further indicate her interest in Augustinian theology.  She also read Teresa of Avila's *The Interior Castle*,
Catherine of Genoa's *Treatise on Purgatory* and *The Dialogue*,
and Catherine of Siena's *The Dialogue of the Seraphic Virgin*.  In addition to Underhill's *Mysticism*, O'Connor read a
wide range of the lives of Christian mystics including
Meister Eckhart and John of the Cross.  Her holdings also
include numerous histories of the Christian tradition, from
the early Church through the Protestant Reformation.

Protestant Christianity interested O'Connor.  She read
both histories of the Reformation and major contemporary Protestant theologians including Barth and Buber.  An examination of these volumes indicates that O'Connor read them thoroughly.  Her copy of Barth's *Evangelical Theology* is among
the most carefully annotated in the collection.  O'Connor
reiterates Barth's definition of "evangelical" theology as
that theology which treats of the God of the Gospel.[24]  She

---

[23]See Part Three, Book Review 55.

[24]See Part Three, Book Review 70.

compares Barth's evaluation of human activity in the light of God's transcendence to Thomas' vision that his work, *The Summa Theologica*, was "all straw." This comparison is also written in the margin of her copy of *Evangelical Theology*.[25] O'Connor responded to the orthodoxy in Barth's work and found "little or nothing in this book that the Catholic cannot recognize as his own."[26]

In addition to her interest in ecumenism (in the best sense of the term, for O'Connor had little sympathy for the sentimental or liberalizing aspects of the ecumenical movement), O'Connor was interested in the study of world religions and their interface with Catholicism. Her library includes a copy of de Lubac's *Aspects of Buddhism* and several books on Zen. Her interest in religious phenomena and human experience is apparent in her annotations of Eliade's *Patterns in Comparative Religion* and William James' *The Varieties of Religious Experience*. Numerous other works of social scientists and spiritual anthropologists who analyzed human experience in relation to Christianity and other world religions and who attempted to bridge the gap between traditional theology and the emerging social sciences are found in the collection. Scientist and priest Pierre Teilhard de Chardin is one such scholar whom O'Connor read with enthusiasm. In her reviews, she hails him as a prophet whose work may restore the sense of expectation which has disappeared from modern religion.[27] The works of psychologists, including Freud, Jung and Neumann, were important to O'Connor for their insight into human drives and responses. She was particularly interested in dreams and their religious significance. Her *Douay*

---

[25] Barth, *Evangelical Theology*, p. 137, O'Connor Collection.

[26] Book Review 70.

[27] O'Connor wrote numerous reviews of Teilhard and his commentators. See especially Book Review 33, *The Divine Milieu*.

*Bible* contains numerous annotations in the sections which
recount prophetic dreams.  In her lecture "Catholic Novelists," O'Connor speaks of the relationship between dreams
and revelations.[28]  On the relationship between psychology
and religious experience, O'Connor read and reviewed
Mounier's *The Character of Man*, Hostie's *Religion and the
Psychology of Jung*, and White's *Soul and Psyche*.

O'Connor's holdings include numerous literary works
which can be classified as religious in their worldview.
Among the Catholic Renaissance writers represented are
Europeans: Bernanos, Mauriac, and Waugh; and Americans:
Powers, Gordon and Lowell.  Anglo-Catholics T. S. Eliot and
C. S. Lewis are well-represented in the collection.  Works
by Russian orthodox writers, especially Dostoevsky, abound.
There are a few other scattered religious works, including
Kazantzakis' *The Odyssey* and Weil's *Waiting for God*.  None
of these are annotated.  O'Connor wrote reviews of novels by
Gordon, Mauriac, Waugh and Powers.[29]  In each review, she
stresses the "Catholic" elements within the work.

The O'Connor library holdings related to the Catholic
Intellectual Renaissance are representative of the movement.
Very few of the volumes precede the dates of the movement's
height in the fifties and early sixties.[30]  The holdings are
eclectic and heavily European.  They include major works of
Biblical criticism, Christian history and philosophy, traditional Christian sources, ecumenism, religion and the social sciences, and Christian literature.  Although there are

---

[28]*Mystery and Manners*, see especially pp. 179-182.

[29]O'Connor's review of Waugh's *The Ordeal of Gilbert
Pinfold* remains unpublished.  For published reviews on the
others see Book Reviews 1, 26 and 71.

[30]Nearly all the works before 1951 are either college
text books or family holdings.  O'Connor died during Vatican
II, which marks the culmination of the Catholic Intellectual
Movement.

a few volumes on the newly emerging laity, including de Smedt's
*The Priesthood of the Faithful,* and a few books on ecclesiology,
there is little in the collection reflecting the Church's emphasis on morals,[31] Christian education, liturgy or the Sacraments.

## Holdings Related to the Southern Literary Renaissance

Beginning in 1930 with the Agrarian movements and continuing beyond the death of Flannery O'Connor in 1964, the American South experienced a rebirth which produced nearly twenty
writers who drew national or international attention.[32]  The
Agrarian movement began in response to Mencken's observation
in 1917 that the South was a cultural wasteland and in reaction to the social decay of the region.  The initial achievements of the Agrarians were heightened and developed as a result of World War II, which had brought Southerners into contact with other Americans and Europeans and fostered the industrialization of the South.

Leading literary artists of the movement included William
Faulkner, Katherine Anne Porter, William Styron, Carson McCullers and Flannery O'Connor.  In addition to this increased
literary production of recognized quality, the central marks
of the Southern renaissance were an increased interest in
history and the development of new critical theory.  The
Agrarians provided a new traditionalist worldview and a realistic theory of art which served as directives for younger
artists.  Central members of this group whose influence continued to shape Southern literature after the end of the
Agrarian movement include John Crowe Ransom, Robert Penn Warren and Allen Tate.  Their attempt to discover human dignity
amid societal disarray and the decline of moral and religious

---

[31]The single volume on moral theology is Heribert
Jone's pocket manual.

[32]For further discussion see Bradbury, *Renaissance in
the South.*

values led to the rejection of the Romantic view of mankind's
perfectibility and the adoption of a classic view which
stressed the tragic human flaw.  Many artists rejected the
Protestantism of the region in favor of Catholicism with its
developed symbols and sacraments.  The writings of Catholic
Europeans, especially Flaubert, Mauriac and Bernanos, and
Orthodox Russians, especially Dostoyevsky, were examined for
their expressions of religious integrity.  Symbolic "natural-
ism" was accepted as the most authentic mode of expression and
emphasis was placed on art as an expression of truth.  New
critics developed a highly intensive, analytic approach to
texts.  They supported the belief that a work is autonomous
and should be judged on its merits without reference to its
author: the test of a work is its artistic unity and its ultimate effect.

Flaubert, Williams James and their successors, Conrad,
Chekhov and Joyce, became models for the Renaissance writers.
They looked to historians such as C. Vann Woodward and literary critics such as Allen Tate and Cleanth Brooks for schol
arship and clarity of expression.  The works of regionalists,
especially Sherwood Anderson and Ring Lardner, were valued
for their ability to recreate regional dialect and to express
local color.  Several American expatriots, including T. S.
Eliot, James Joyce, Ernest Hemingway and Ezra Pound, who had
fled the American scene for the European cultural and intellectual milieu, were studied for their realism, historical
consciousness and naturalistic symbolism.  Southern Renaissanc
writers gave attention to world classics, especially Greek
tragedies.

The Renaissance writers undertook their search of the
past both for historical insight and for literary forms.  The
works on which they focused reveal interest not unlike that
reflected in the holdings of the Flannery O'Connor Collection

O'Connor's holdings are eclectic, revealing both her
wide-ranging interests and the nature of the literary movemer

of which she was a part. In addition to standard sources such as dictionaries, she has selections of classics in translation, including works by Sophocles, Plato, Aristotle, Aristophanes, Homer, and Horace. Many of the translations were done by Robert Fitzgerald, a fellow Catholic and personal friend of O'Connor's. She also owned copies of *The Complete Greek Tragedies*, Herodotus' *Histories*, *The Complete Works of Tacitus*, and Dante's *Divine Comedy*. She held scattered copies of modern classics, including three volumes of Dickens, Swift's *Gulliver's Travels*, Melville's *Moby Dick* and Hawthorne's *The House of the Seven Gables*, *The Marble Faun* and *The Scarlet Letter*.

O'Connor collected numerous histories, mostly on the American South. These include Bonner's *The Georgia Story*, Cash's *The Mind of the South*, Simkins' *The Everlasting South*, Longstreet's *Georgia Scenes*, and Woodward's *The Burden of Southern History* and *Origins of the New South*. She also owned Toynbee's *A Study of History*, Dawson's *The Dynamics of World History* and de Tocqueville's *Democracy in America*.

General works on literature and volumes of literary criticism abound. Included in the general holdings are Cassill's *Writing Fiction*, Strunk's *Elements of Style*, Richards' *Practical Criticism*, and Chase's *The American Novel and Its Tradition*. Her collection of criticism includes works by Cleanth Brooks, Robert Penn Warren, Allen Tate and Caroline Gordon, the key critics of the Southern Renaissance movement. She collected critical essays by Eliot, Crane and James.

The fiction collection includes novels and collections of short stories by a wide range of American, European and Russian authors. Writers represented in novel and short story form include Dostoyevsky, Hawthorne, Gordon and Porter. Other short story collections of note include Kafka's *Selected Stories*, Dinesen's *Seven Gothic Tales*, Lardner's *The Collected Short Stories*, Mann's *Death in Venice, and Seven Other Tales*, Welty's *The Bride of the Innisfallen, and Other*

*Stories*, and Updike's *The Same Door*. Most noteworthy among
the novels are extensive holdings of works by individual
authors. O'Connor owned at least eleven novels by Mauriac,
ten by Conrad (including two copies of *Nostromo*), six by
Faulkner, four each by William James and Wyndham Lewis, and
three each by Hawthorne, Waugh, Gogol, Jones and Porter.
Isolated volumes of interest include West's *The Day of the
Locust*, Mansfield's *The Garden Party*, Ford's *The Good Soldier*, Gordon's *The Malefactors* and Powers' *Morte d'Urban*.
Of these, she reviewed only two novels by Mauriac, *The Son
of Man* and *Lines of Life*, Powers' *Morte d'Urban* and Gordon's
*The Malefactors*.

O'Connor's holdings include various anthologies of poetry
and the collected poetry of several authors significant to the
Southern Renaissance. Among these are T. S. Eliot's *Collected
Poems*, *Four Quartets*, and *The Waste Land*, Robert Lowell's
*Imitations*, *Life Studies*, *Lord Weary's Castle* and *The Mills
of the Kavanaughs*, and Katherine Anne Porter's *The Old Order*.
The collection includes a few volumes of plays: three by
Eliot, and one each by Ibsen, Molière and Turgenev.

The library includes a few commentaries on specific literary artists or works. There are one each on Henry James,
Joseph Conrad and James Joyce, and two on Nathaniel Hawthorne
Caroline Gordon's book on Ford's *A Good Soldier* is the only
critique of a single work.

Only four volumes in the collection related to the South
ern Literary Renaissance are annotated. These are Mauriac's
*Mémoires Intérieurs*, James' *Notebooks*, Fuller's *Man in Modern
Fiction* and Tate's *A Southern Vanguard*. The marking in Mauria
is a two-page section on *The Scarlet Letter* in which he state
that, for him, the great value of the work lies in its abilit
to expose to the believer they mystery of evil. O'Connor's
markings indicate her concurrence with Mauriac's judgment.
In James, she especially notes the phrase ". . . the theoret-

ical must be drenched with the actual."[33] She also emphasizes James' conviction, which he states in conjunction with his novel, *What Maisie Knew*, that "the *scenic* method is my absolute, my imperative, my only salvation."[34] All of the markings in Fuller relate to the uniqueness, imperfection and responsibility which are based on the freedom experienced by each individual. The markings in Tate concern the changing moral order in the South, the necessity of formality in manners for one's personal survival, and the danger of moral fervor and good intentions as a substitute for depth perception and patient interaction.

In general, O'Connor's library holdings related to the Southern Literary Renaissance are representative of the multiple tenets of the movement. The collection includes works of general interest concerning Southern and literary history, selected classics, ancient and modern, and the fiction and theory works of major writers of the Southern Literary Renaissance movement.

* * *

An examination of the two general categories of O'Connor's personal library reveals significant parallels. Examined in sections related to the two milieus of which she was a part, the collection reveals a basic structure. The sections on the Catholic Renaissance and on the Southern Renaissance each contain approximately thirty classic texts (the religious works are primarily those of the saints and Church fathers, and the literary works are primarily those of the early Greeks), some historical materials related to the development of each, poetry and prose essays, related materials, and representative fiction works. The over-balance

---

[33]James, *The Notebooks*, p. xii, O'Connor Collection.

[34]James, *The Notebooks*, p. xviii, O'Connor Collection, italics his.

of religious works in the collection may well be directly
related to the work as a book reviewer for the Catholic press
which O'Connor undertook during her last years.  Copies of
review books were sent to O'Connor and in many instances they
remained part of her holdings.

LIST OF FLANNERY O'CONNOR'S PERSONAL LIBRARY HOLDINGS

It is impossible at this time to determine Flannery
O'Connor's complete holdings. Books were added to and de-
leted from her library both during her life and after her
death. However, substantial portions of her library, given
to Georgia College over the course of five years by Regina
Cline O'Connor, are now housed at the College's Ina Dillard
Russell Library. The following list, based on my personal
research and updated by curator Gerald Becham, includes all
the volumes found at the present time in the Flannery O'Connor
Collection.

This revised list completes and corrects the early partial list published by Kathleen Feeley[1] and Virginia Wray's
unpublished list found in the collection. Discrepancies between these early lists and the present one are due in some
measure to the fact that Feeley had only limited access to
the library at Andalusia and published her work before the
books were collected and moved to Georgia College. She lists
only selected volumes, but even these entries do not correspond
completely (titles, publication data, etc.) to the holdings
now in the collection. Wray's work, a shelf list based on
what was thought to be O'Connor's book order[2] and used as a
reference tool in the collection previous to its being catalogued, is incomplete and contains some incorrect publication
data. The present listing offers greater accuracy, since

---

[1]Feeley, pp. 188-191.

[2]According to Becham, more recent information indicates
that one of O'Connor's cousins worked in the Andalusia library
to organize it in a more systematic way after O'Connor's death.

it is based on a systematic examination of the actual volumes
housed in the complete collection to date.

A few volumes, two of which are included in Feeley's
list, are not now found in the collection. These two items
are added in a supplementary list. They may be among the few
volumes not given to the Georgia College Library. In additio
to the volumes withheld by O'Connor's family, other works
known to have been in her possession are not among the holdings.[3] Flannery O'Connor reviewed books which are not now
in the library.[4] Doubtless other volumes were loaned, lost
or given away.

At least two volumes now included in the collection
probably are not Flannery O'Connor's. One, a United States
Department of Agriculture publication on water, may well have
been acquired by her mother or uncle in conjunction with the
farm's operation. Another, *American Catholic Who's Who, 1964
and 1965*, which contains an article on O'Connor published
after her death in 1964, was given to her family.

The following is an alphabetical list of all the volumes
now housed in the Flannery O'Connor Collection. Additional
relevant data, including recognized review books, inscribed
volumes and annotated texts are given after the publication
data. "Ins." indicates the name "Flannery O'Connor" written in her own hand; where a date follows the inscription,
I have added the given date (Ins., August, 1961); where the

---

[3] A copy of Jacques Maritain, *Art and Scholasticism,* annotated by O'Connor, is currently held by Sally Fitzgerald.
The copy now in the collection is a replacement provided
O'Connor by Fitzgerald who had mislaid the original (Sally
Fitzgerald, "The Habit of Being," p. 14). Robert Giroux
notes that he gave O'Connor an autographed copy of *Prometheus: A Meditation* from Thomas Merton (Giroux, "Introduction, p. xiv). This volumes is not among the items in the
collection.

[4] A complete list of O'Connor's published and unpublished
reviews is found in Part Three. "Coll." after an entry indicates that the review book remains in the Flannery O'Connor
Collection.

inscription is something other, I list it as it appears
(Ins.: To Flannery from . . .). "Annot." after an entry
indicates that O'Connor annotated the volume. "Dj." followed by page numbers indicates markings which appear on the
book's dust jacket. Known review books are indicated by
"Rev." after the item. It is possible that additional review copies remain undetected either because O'Connor did
not complete the review or because her review has been lost.
Cross references are given where necessary to facilitate
the correlation of this list with the catalogue entries found
in the Flannery O'Connor Collection at Georgia College.

*Acts of Violence.* See Kozlenko, William, ed.

Adam, Karl. *The Christ of Faith: The Christology of the
Church.* Trans. Joyce Crick. New York [c. 1957]. Rev.

--------. *The Son of God.* Trans. Philip Hereford. New
York, 1960.

Adams, Henry. *The Education of Henry Adams: An Autobiography*
(1907). New York, 1931. Ins.: E. F. O'Connor [Flannery
O'Connor's father].

--------. *Mont-Saint-Michel and Chartres* (c. 1905). Garden
City, N.Y., 1959. Bookmarker, p. 18.

Allen, Frederick Lewis. *A Register of the Papers of Frederick
Lewis Allen in the Library of Congress.* Washington,
1958.

Alonso Schökel, Luis. *Understanding Biblical Research.* Trans.
Peter J. McCord. New York, 1963. Ins., 1963.

Alter, Karl J[oseph]. *The Mind of an Archbishop: A Study of
Man's Essential Relationship to God, Church, Country, and
Fellow Man.* Patterson, N.J., 1960.

*The American Benedictine Review,* 14, No. 2 (June, 1963).

*The American Catholic Who's Who, 1964 and 1965.* Grosse Pointe,
Mich., 1965.

Amis, Kingsley. *Lucky Jim: A Novel.* New York, 1964. Ins.

Anderson, Sherwood. *Winesburg, Ohio: A Group of Tales of Ohio
Small Town Life.* New York, 1947. Ins., 1960.

Aristophanes. *The Birds.* Trans. Dudley Fitts. New York,
1957.

--------. *The Frogs.* Trans. Dudley Fitts. New York, 1955.

Aristotle. *On Man in the Universe: Metaphysics, Parts of Animals, Ethics, Politics, Poetics.* Ed. Louise Ropes Loomis. New York, 1943. Ins.: M. F. O'Connor, 1943 [previous to dropping "Mary"].

Augustine. *The Confessions.* Trans. Edward B. Pusey. New York, 1952. Nameplate: Miss Viola Berry, 419 Sinclair Avenue, N.E. Atlanta, Georgia. Annot.

--------. *Nine Sermons of St. Augustine on the Psalms.* Trans. Edmund Hill. New York, 1959. Ins., 1959.

Avalos, Beatrice. *New Men for New Times: A Christian Philosophy of Education.* New York, 1962. Rev.

Babbitt, Irving. *Rousseau and Romanticism.* 2nd ed. New York, 1955.

Babel, Isaak [Emmanuilovich]. *Collected Stories.* Ed. and trans. Walter Morison. New York, 1960.

Barnett, Lincoln [Kinnear]. *The Universe and Dr. Einstein.* 2nd rev. ed. New York, 1960. Ins.: Flannery--Pax Tecum! Roslyn.

Barrows, Herbert, et al. *An Introduction to Literature in Four Parts.* Ed. Gordon N. Ray. Boston, 1959. (Contains her "The Displaced Person").

Barth, Karl. *Evangelical Theology: An Introduction.* Trans. Grover Foley. New York, 1963. Annot. Rev.

Baruch, Bernard M[annes]. *Baruch: The Public Years.* New York, 1960.

Beach, Joseph W[arren]. *The Twentieth Century Novel: Studies in Technique.* New York, 1932.

Bedford, Sybille. *A Legacy.* New York, 1957.

Beerbohm, Max. *Max's Nineties: Drawings, 1892-1899.* Philadelphia, 1958.

--------. *Seven Men, and Two Others.* New York, 1959.

--------. *Zuleika Dobson: Or, an Oxford Love Story.* New York, 1926.

Béguin, Albert. *Léon Bloy: A Study in Impatience.* Trans. Edith M. Riley. New York, 1947.

Bellamann, Katherine. *A Poet Passed This Way.* Mill Valley, Cal., 1958. Ins.: Henry H. Bellamann Special Award presented to--Flannery O'Connor to recognize unusual artistic talent. April, 1964.

Berenson, Bernhard. *Aesthetics and History in the Visual Arts.* Garden City, N.Y., 1953.

Bergson, Henri [Louis]. *The Creative Mind.* Trans. Mabelle Andison. New York, 1946.

--------. *The Two Sources of Morality and Religion*. Trans.
Ashley Audra and Cloudesley Brereton. Garden City,
N.Y., 1935; rpt. 1954.

--------. *The World of Dreams*. Trans. Wade Baskin. New
York, 1958.

Bernanos, Georges. *The Diary of a Country Priest*. Trans.
Pamela Morris. Garden City, N.Y., 1960. (2 copies).
Ins. copy 1: For Flannery O'Connor on Valentine's Day,
my love, Roslyn. (We've just been studying this in
Fiction--thought you might like it, too.)

--------. *Joy*. Trans. Louise Varese. New York, 1946. Ins.

--------. *The Last Essays*. Trans. Joan and Barry Ulanov.
Chicago, 1955.

*The Best American Short Stories*. See Foley, Martha, and David
Burnett.

*The Bestiary*. See White, T[erence] H[anburt], ed.

Beyle, Marie Henri (Stendhal). *The Charterhouse of Parma*.
Trans. C. K. Scott-Moncrieff. Garden City, N.Y., 1953.

--------. *The Red and the Black*. Trans. C. K. Scott Mon-
crieff. New York, 1926. Ins.

*Bible, The Holy*. Douay Version. London, 1957. Ins., 1959.
Dj.: No 12:8. Annot.

*Bible, The Holy*. New Testament. Trans. R[onald] A[rbuthnott]
Knox. New York, 1948. Ins., 1949. On memo sheet enclosed: I Cor. iii 16; I Cor. vi 19; I Cor. ii 10. Annot.

*Bible, The Holy*. Old Testament. 2 vols. Trans. R[onald]
A[rbuthnott] Knox. New York, 1948 and 1950. Ins., 1949
[Vol. I].

Blackmur, R[ichard] P. *Anni Mirabiles, 1921-1925*. Washington,
1956.

Blodgett, Harold [William], ed. *The Story Survey*. Philadelphia, 1939.

Bloy, Léon. *Pilgrim of the Absolute*. Trans. John Coleman and
Harry Lorin Binsse. New York, 1947. Ins., 1947.

Boas, George. *The Limits of Reason*. New York, 1961.

Bock, Frederick. *The Fountains of Regardlessness: Poems*. New
York, 1961.

Bonner, James C[alvin]. *The Georgia Story*. Oklahoma City,
1958. Ins.: For Flannery O'Connor with sincere appreciation. James C. Bonner, Oct. 23, 1958.

Bossuet, James (Jacques) Bénigne. *History of the Variations
of the Protestant Churches*. Vol. I. Boston, n.d. (circa
1870). Ins.: Dct. Cook. 1872. Mrs. H. J. Cook. Albany
Dougherty Co. 2nd flyleaf: Hugh Cline from Mrs. Cook.

Boswell, James. *The Life of Samuel Johnson*. Abridged ed.
    New York, 1952.

Bouyer, Louis. *Christian Initiation*. Trans. J. R. Foster.
    New York, 1960. Rev.

--------. *Newman: His Life and Spirituality*. Trans. J. Lewi
    May. New York, 1960.

--------. *The Roman Socrates: A Portrait of St. Philip Neri*.
    Trans. Michael Day. Westminster, Md., 1958.

--------. *The Spirit and Forms of Protestantism*. Trans.
    A. V. Littledale. Westminster, Md., 1956. Ins., 1957.
    On publisher's slip enclosed: 82, 88, 93, lapidary, Ober
    lin, 193-6. Written on the bottom of the slip; not more
    than 200 words--E. H. [Eileen Hall, the book review
    editor for *The Bulletin*]. Rev.

Bowen, Elizabeth. *The Death of the Heart*. New York, 1955.

--------. *The House in Paris*. New York, 1957.

--------. *Stories by Elizabeth Bowen*. New York, 1959.

Bragdon, Claude [Fayette]. *Merely Players*. New York, 1929.
    Bookplate: Miller's Book Store, Atlanta, Ga.

Brandes, George (Georg Morris Cohen). *William Shakespeare*.
    Trans. William Archer, Mary Morison, and Diana White.
    New York, 1898; rpt. 1936. Ins.: To Monsignor Dodwell
    with love, Jimmy. I'm the loneliest man in Denmark.
    2nd Ins.: With best regards for your understanding and
    inspiration--Nena--. Bookplate: Miller, Inc., Booksel-
    lers, Atlanta, Ga.

Brillet, Gaston. *Prophecy*. Vol. III of his *Meditations on
    the Old Testament*. Trans. Jane Wynne Saul. New York,
    1961.

Brodin, Pierre. *Présences contemporaines: Écrivains Améri-
    cains d'aujourd'hui*. Paris, 1964.

Brooks, Cleanth. *The Hidden God: Studies in Hemingway, Faulk
    ner, Yeats, Eliot, and Warren*. New Haven, 1963. Ins.

--------. *The Well Wrought Urn: Studies in the Structure of
    Poetry*. New York, 1947. Ins.

--------, and Robert Penn Warren, eds. *Understanding Fiction*
    New York, 1959.

--------, eds. *Understanding Poetry: An Anthology for Colleg*
    *Students*. New York, 1938.

Brown, Ashley, and Robert S. Haller, eds. *The Achievement of
    Wallace Stevens*. Philadelphia, 1962.

Brownson, Orestes [Augustus]. *The Brownson Reader*. Ed. Alva
    S. Ryan. New York, 1955. Back cover: 85.

Bruckberger, Raymond Léopold. *Madeleine et Judas.* Summit,
   N.J., 1955.

Bruno [de Jésus-Marie], ed. *Love and Violence.* Trans.
   George Lamb. New York, 1954.

————————. *St. John of the Cross.* Ed. Benedict Zimmerman.
   New York, 1932. Dj.: 91.

————————, ed. *Three Mystics: El Greco, St. John of the Cross,
   and St. Teresa of Avila.* New York, 1949.

Bruns, J. Edgar. *Hear His Voice Today: A Guide to the Content
   and Comprehension of the Bible.* New York, 1963. Rev.

Bryan T[homas] Conn. *Confederate Georgia.* Athens, Ga., 1953.
   Ins.: To Flannery O'Connor with regard, T. Conn Bryan,
   May 16, 1953.

Buber, Martin. *Between Man and Man.* Trans. Ronald Gregor
   Smith. Boston, 1955. Annot.

————————. *Eclipse of God: Studies in the Relation between Religion and Philosophy.* New York, 1958. Ins.: To Flannery O'Connor from Ted Spivey, Nov. 4, 1958. Annot.

Buehrle, Marie Cecilia. *The Cardinal Stritch Story.* Milwaukee, 1959. Rev.

Bulfinch, Thomas. *Bulfinch's Mythology: The Age of Fables,
   The Age of Chivalry, Legends of Charlemagne.* New York,
   1934.

Butler, Alban, ed. *The Lives of the Saints.* Vol. I-IV. Baltimore, 1845. Ins. Vol. II, III and IV: Treanor, Milledgeville, Georgia.

Call, Hughie (Florence). *The Little Kingdom.* New York, 1964.

Callahan, Daniel J., Heiko A. Oberman, and Daniel J. O'Hanlon,
   eds. *Christianity Divided: Protestant and Roman Catholic
   Theological Issues.* New York, 1961. Rev.

Caponigri, A[loysius] Robert, ed. *Modern Catholic Thinkers:
   An Anthology.* New York, 1960. Ins., 1960. Rev.

Capote, Truman. *The Muses Are Heard: An Account.* New York,
   1956. Ins.

Carlyle, Thomas. *Collected Works: Sartor Resartus, On Heroes
   and Hero Worship, and Characteristics.* New York, n.d.

Carritt, E[dgar] F[rederick], ed. *Philosophies of Beauty from
   Socrates to Robert Bridges: Being the Sources of Aesthetic
   Theory.* London, 1931. Ins., Milledgeville, Georgia.

Cash, W[ilber] J[oseph]. *The Mind of the South* (1941). Garden City, N.Y., 1954.

Cassill, R[onald] V[erlin]. *Writing Fiction.* New York, 1962.

--------, Herbert Gold, and James B. Hall. *Fifteen by Three: Short Stories*. New York, 1957.

Catherine of Genoa. *Treatise on Purgatory, and The Dialogue*. Trans. Charlotte Balfour and Helen Douglas Irvine. New York, 1946. Ins., 1948.

Catherine of Siena. *The Dialogue of the Seraphic Virgin*. Trans. Algar Thorold. New York, 1944. Ins., 1949.

*Catholic Mind*, 60, No. 1160 (February, 1962). (Contains her "Mystery of Suffering").

Cecil, David. *Early Victorian Novelists: Essays in Revaluation* (1934). Harmondsworth, Middlesex, 1948.

Cerf, Bennett Alfred, ed. *Great German Short Novels and Stories*. New York [c. 1933].

--------. *Great Modern Short Stories: An Anthology of Twelve Famous Stories and Novelettes*. New York, 1942. Ins.

Cervantes [Saavedra, Miguel de]. *The Adventures of Don Quixo* Trans. J. M. Cohen. Harmondsworth, Middlesex, 1954.

Chaine, J[oseph]. *God's Heralds: A Guide to the Prophets of Israel*. Trans. Brendan McGrath. New York, 1954. Dj.: 123 swallow the book, 157. Rev.

Chase, Richard [Volney]. *The American Novel and Its Traditio* Garden City, N.Y., 1957.

Chekhov, Anton [Pavlovich]. *Great Stories*. Ed. David H. Greene. Trans. Constance Garnett. New York, 1959.

--------. *Selected Stories*. Ed. Lucy M. Cores. New York, 1943.

Cheney, Brainard. *This is Adam: A Novel*. New York, 1958.

Chesterton, G[ilbert] K[eith]. *Lunacy and Letters*. Ed. Dorothy Collins. New York, 1958.

Christ, Frank L., and Gerard E. Sherry, eds. *American Catholicism and the Intellectual Idea*. New York, 1961. Ins. To Miss O'Connor with kindest regards, Gerard Sherry.

*Christianity and Crisis*. See Cowan, Wayne H., ed.

Clayton, John Bell. *The Strangers Were There: Selected Stories*. New York, 1957.

Colette, Sidonie [Gabrielle]. *My Mother's House, and The Vag* bond. Garden City, N.Y., 1955.

Colledge, Eric, ed. *The Mediaeval Mystics of England*. New York, 1961. Rev.

Collins, James [Daniel]. *The Existentialists: A Critical Study*. Chicago, 1952. Ins., 1954.

*The Complete Greek Tragedies.* See Grene, David, and Richmond Lattimore.

Compton-Burnett, Ivy. *Brothers and Sisters: A Novel.* New York, 1956. (2 copies).

————. *A Heritage and Its History.* New York, 1960.

Congar, [George] Yves (Marie Joseph). *The Wide World, My Parish: Salvation and Its Problems.* Trans. Donald Attwater. Baltimore, 1961. Ins., 1962. Dj.: 96, 135, 139. Rev.

Conrad, Joseph. *Almayer's Folly.* New York, 1947.

————. *Lord Jim.* New York, 1931. Ins.

————. *Nostromo.* New York, 1951. (2 copies). Dj. copy 1: Faulkner, *Absalom, Absalom.* Hawthorne, *The Scarlet Letter.* Gardner, *Collected Short Stories.* Melville, *Moby Dick.* K. A. Porter, *Pale Horse, Pale Rider.* Wharton, *The Age of Innocence.* Dj. copy 2: Guy de Maupassant, *Best Short Stories.*

————. *The Portable Conrad.* Ed. Morton Dauwen Zabel. New York, 1947.

————. *The Rescue: A Romance of the Shallows.* Garden City, N.Y., 1960.

————. *The Secret Agent: A Simple Tale.* Garden City, N.Y., 1953.

————. *Under Western Eyes.* New York, 1951. Ins., 1954.

————. *Victory.* New York, 1921. Ins., 1952.

————. *Youth, and Two Other Stories.* New York, 1905.

Conyngham, D[avid] P[ower]. *Lives of the Irish Saints: From St. Patrick down to St. Laurence O'Toole.* New York, 1870. Back cover: Error 51, 107, 109, 114?, 71 (grammatical).

Copleston, F[rederick Charles]. *Aquinas.* Baltimore, 1955.

————. *St. Thomas and Nietzsche.* 2nd ed. London, 1955.

Corte, Nicolas (pseud., i.e. Léon Cristiani). *Pierre Teilhard de Chardin: His Life and Spirit.* Trans. Martin Jarrett-Kerr. New York, 1960. (2 copies). Ins. 1960 [copy 1]. Rev.

Cowan, Wayne H., ed. *Christianity and Crisis.* New York, 1957.

Cowley, Malcolm, ed. *Writers at Work: The Paris Review Interviews.* New York, 1958.

Crane, R[onald] S[almon]. *Critics and Criticism: Essays in Method by R. S. Crane.* Abridged ed. Chicago, 1957.

Crane, Stephen. *Stories and Tales.* Ed. Robert Wooster Stallman. New York, 1958.

Cranston, Ruth (Anne Warwick, pseud.). *The Miracle of Lourdes*
New York, 1957. Back cover: Mo 9-8460.

Crehan, Joseph. *Early Christian Baptism and the Creed: A
Study in Antenicene Theology.* London, 1950.

Cummings, E[dward] E[stlin]. *The Enormous Room.* New York,
1934. Ins., July, 1952. Dj.: Aquinas, *Introduction to
St. Thomas Aquinas.* Balzac, *Père Goriot, and Eugénie
Grandet.* Chaucer, *The Canterbury Tales.* Conrad,
*Nostromo.* Hawthorne, *The Scarlet Letter.* Melville,
*Moby Dick.*

Curtis, Edith Roelker. *A Season in Utopia: The Story of Brook
Farm.* New York, 1961. Ins., 1963.

Daniélou, Jean. *The Dead Sea Scrolls and Primitive Christianity.* Trans. Salvator Attanasio. New York, 1962.

Daniel-Rops, Henri. *Jesus and His Times.* Trans. Ruby Millar.
New York, 1954.

Dante, Alighieri. *The Divine Comedy.* Trans. Carlyle-Wick-
steed. New York, 1932. Ins., 1946. Annot.

D'Arcy, Martin C[yril]. *Communism and Christianity.* Baltimore, 1956.

--------. *The Meaning and Matter of History: A Christian
View.* New York, 1959. Dj.: 114 Toynbee. Annot.

--------. *The Meeting of Love and Knowledge: Perennial Wisdom.* New York, 1957. Dj.: 122, 126, 128, 150. Annot.
Rev.

--------. *The Mind and Heart of Love: Lion and Unicorn, a
Study in Eros and Agape.* New York, 1947. Ins., 1947.

--------. *The Nature of Belief.* New ed. St. Louis, 1958.

Davenport, Basil, ed. *The Portable Roman Reader.* New York,
1951.

Dawson, Christopher [Henry]. *The Dynamics of World History.*
Ed. John J. Mulloy. New York, 1962.

--------. *Progress and Religion.* Garden City, N.Y., 1960.

de la Bedoyere, Michael. *The Archbishop and the Lady: The
Story of Fénelon and Madame Guyon.* New York, 1956.
Dj.: 84, 136, 150-1, 185, 227, 224. Rev.

--------. *The Life of Baron von Hügel.* New York, 1951.

Delarue, Jacques. *The Holiness of Vincent de Paul.* Trans.
Suzanne Chapman. New York, 1960. Rev.

Dickens, Charles. *Great Expectations.* New York, 1956.

--------. *Hard Times.* New York, 1960.

--------. *Oliver Twist.* London, 1950.

Dillistone, F[rederick] W[illiam]. *The Novelist and the Passion Story: A Study of Christ Figures in Faulkner, Mauriac, Melville, Kazantzakis.* New York, 1960. Rev.

Dinesen, Isak (pseud., i.e. Karen Blixen). *Seven Gothic Tales.* New York, 1934. Ins.

Donne, John. *Complete Poetry and Selected Prose.* Ed. Charles M. Coffin. New York, 1952.

Dorrance, Ward, and Thomas Mabry. *The White Hound.* Columbia, Mo., 1959.

Dostoyevsky, Fyodor. *Best Short Stories.* Trans. David Magarshack. New York, 1955.

--------. *Crime and Punishment.* Trans. Constance Garnett, Cleveland, 1947. Ins.

--------. *The Devils (The Possessed).* Trans. David Magarshack. Baltimore, 1953.

Drucker, Peter F[erdinand]. *The New Society: An Anatomy of the Industrial Order.* New York, 1950. Ins., 1955.

Durrell, Lawrence. *Justine.* New York, 1957.

Durrwell, F[rancis] X[avier]. *The Resurrection: A Biblical Study.* Trans. Rosemary Sheed. New York, 1960. Dj.: 54. Rev.

Ebersole, Marc C. *Christian Faith and Man's Religion.* New York, 1961. Rev.

Eckhart, Meister. *Meister Eckhart: A Modern Translation.* Trans. Raymond Bernard Blackney. New York, 1957.

Eichner, Sister Mary Maura. *The Word Is Love.* New York, 1958. Ins.: For Flannery O'Connor who knows in what mysterious ways God speaks this word, Sister Maura.

Eliade, Mircea. *Patterns in Comparative Religion.* Trans. Rosemary Sheed. New York, 1958. Annot. Rev.

--------. *Sacred and Profane Beauty: The Holy in Art.* Trans. Willard R. Trask. New York, 1963. Ins., 1963.

Eliot, George (pseud., i.e. Mary Ann Evans, afterwards Cross). *Best Known Novels.* New York, n.d.

--------. *Middlemarch.* London, 1950. Ins., 1954.

Eliot, T[homas] S[tearns]. *Collected Poems.* New York, 1936. Ins. Flyleaf: highly technical disciplin [sic].

--------. *The Confidential Clerk: A Play.* New York, 1954. Ins., April, 1954.

--------. *The Cultivation of Christmas Trees.* New York, 1956.

--------. *The Elder Statesman: A Play.* New York, 1959. Ins. on card enclosed: With compliments of Robert Giroux. Farrar, Straus and Cudahy, Inc.

--------. *Essays on Elizabethan Drama.* New York, 1956.

--------. *Four Quartets.* New York, 1943. Ins.

--------. *Murder in the Cathedral.* New York, 1935. Ins., 1950.

--------. *On Poetry and Poets: Essays.* New York, 1961.

--------. *The Sacred Wood: Essays on Poetry and Criticism.* 7th ed. New York, 1960.

--------. *The Waste Land, and Other Poems.* New York, 1934.

--------, and George Hoellering. *The Film of Murder in the Cathedral.* New York, 1952. Ins., 1952.

Ellmann, Richard. *James Joyce.* New York, 1959.

England, John. *Works.* Vols. I and V. Baltimore, 1849. Ins.: John Treanor, S.J.

Engle, Paul, ed. *Midland: Twenty Years of Fiction and Poetry Selected from the Writing Workshops of the State University of Iowa.* New York, 1961. Ins., 1961. (Contains her "Artificial Nigger").

Faulkner, William. *Absalom, Absalom!* New York, 1951.

--------. *The Mansion.* New York, 1959.

--------. *Pylon.* New York, 1951.

--------. *Sanctuary, and Requiem for a Nun.* New York, 1954.

--------. *Three Famous Short Novels.* New York, 1958.

--------. *The Unvanquished.* New York, 1952.

Fénelon, François de Salignac de La Mothe. *Letters to Men and Women.* Ed. Derek Stanford. Westminster, Md., 1957. Dj.: 28 on style, 73, 102. Annot. Rev.

Fergusson, Francis. *The Idea of a Theater, A Study of Ten Plays: The Art of Drama in Changing Perspective.* Garden City, N.Y., 1953.

Fielding, Henry. *The Adventures of Joseph Andrews.* New York, 1930.

--------. *The History of Tom Jones, A Foundling.* New York, 1940.

Fitzgerald, Robert. *In the Rose of Time.* Norfolk, Conn., 1956. Ins.: To Flannery O'Connor, in memory of the resurrection of Hazel Motes. Robert Fitzgerald.

Flood, J[oseph] M[ary], ed. *The Mind and Heart of Augustine.* Fresno, Cal., 1960.

Foerster, Norman. *Image of America: Our Literature from Puritanism to the Space Age*. Notre Dame, 1962. Rev.

--------, et al. *Literary Scholarship: Its Aim and Methods*. Chapel Hill, N.C., 1941.

Foley, Martha and David Burnett, eds. *The Best American Short Stories, 1962, and the Yearbook of the American Short Story*. New York, 1962. (Contains her "Everything That Rises Must Converge").

Ford, Ford Madox. *The Good Soldier: A Tale of Passion*. New York, 1951. Ins.: Brown [Illegible first name]. Bookplate: S. Wright, New and Second-Hand Bookseller.

--------. *Joseph Conrad: A Personal Remembrance*. London, 1924.

Forster, E[dward] M[organ]. *Aspects of the Novel*. New York, 1954.

--------. *A Passage to India*. New York, 1924. Ins.

Fowlie, Wallace. *The Spirit of France: Studies in Modern French Literature*. New York, 1945.

Francis de Sales. *Introduction to a Devout Life*. Ed. and trans. Joseph Mary Lelen. New York, 1946.

Fremantle, Ann (Jackson). *A Treasury of Early Christianity*. New York, 1953.

Freud, Sigmund. *The Basic Writings of Sigmund Freud*. Ed. and trans. A. A. Brill. New York, 1938. Ins., 1947.

Fuller, Edmund. *Man in Modern Fiction: Some Minority Opinions on Contemporary American Fiction*. New York, 1958. Annot.

Gannon, Robert I[gnatius]. *The Cardinal Spellman Story*. Garden City, N.Y., 1962. Rev.

Gardiner, Harold C[harles], ed. *American Classics Reconsidered: A Christian Appraisal*. New York, 1958. Ins. Rev.

Gardner, John [Champlin], and Lennis Dunlap. *The Forms of Fiction*. New York, 1962.

Gelin, Albert. *The Key Concepts of the Old Testament*. Trans. George Lamb. New York, 1955.

Gilson, Etienne Henry. *Reason and Revelation in the Middle Ages* (1937). New York, 1961. Rev.

--------. *The Unity of Philosophical Experience* (1937). New York, 1952.

Gleason, Robert W. *The Study of Scripture*. New York, 1962.

--------. *The World to Come*. New York, 1958. Ins., 1959.

Gogol̆, Nikolăi [Vasilevich]. *Dead Souls*. Trans. Andrew R. MacAndrew. New York, 1961.

--------. *Mirgorod.* Trans. David Magarshack. New York, 1962.

--------. *Taras Bulba.* Trans. Jeremiah Curtin. New York, 1888.

Goldbrunner, Josef. *Holiness is Wholeness.* Trans. Stanley Goodman. New York, 1955. Ins., 1955.

Gollancz, Victor. *From Darkness to Light: A Confession of Faith in the Form of an Anthology.* New York, 1956.

Gordon, Caroline. *A Good Soldier: A Key to the Novels of Ford Madox Ford.* Davis, Cal., 1963.

--------. *The Malefactors.* New York, 1956. Rev.

--------. *Old Red, and Other Stories.* New York, 1963.

--------, and Allen Tate. *The House of Fiction: An Anthology of Short Stories.* New York, 1960. Ins., 1960. (Contains her "A Good Man Is Hard to Find").

Graef, Hilda. *Mystics of Our Times.* Garden City, N.Y., 1962 Rev.

Graham, Aelred. *Zen Catholicism: A Suggestion.* New York, 1963. Ins., 1963. Dj.: 17, 18, 32, 39, 45, 56, 84, 108 128, 134, 139, 157, 192. Rev.

Grene, David, and Richmond Lattimore, eds. *The Complete Greek Tragedies: I Aeschylus, II Sophocles, III and IV Euripides.* 4 vols. Chicago, 1959.

Grierson, Herbert [John Clifford]. *Cross-Currents in Seventeenth Century English Literature: The World, the Flesh, and the Spirit, Their Actions and Reactions.* New York, 1958.

Guardini, Romano. *The Conversion of Augustine.* Trans. Elinor C. Briefs. Westminster, Md., 1960. Dj.: 138. Rev.

--------. *The Death of Socrates: An Interpretation of the Platonic Dialogues: Euthyphro, Apology, Crito, and Phaedo.* Trans. Basil Wrighton. New York, 1948. Ins., 1956.

--------. *The Faith and Modern Man.* Trans. Charolotte E. Forsyth. New York, 1952.

--------. *Freedom, Grace and Destiny: Three Chapters in the Interpretation of Existence.* Trans. John Murray. New York, 1961. Dj.: 80-81, 163, 231. Annot. Rev.

--------. *Jesus Christus: Meditations.* Trans. Peter White. Chicago, 1959. Rev.

--------. *The Lord.* Chicago, 1954. Ins., 1954.

--------. *Meditations before Mass.* Trans. Elinor C. Briefs. Westminster, Md., 1956. Dj.: 22, 42, 73, 91, aim-96, 104 f., 160, 180. Annot. Rev.

--------. *Prayer in Practice.* Trans. Leopold of Loewenstein-Wertheim. New York, 1957. Dj.: 126, 148, 162, 167-8. Rev.

--------. *Prayers from Theology.* Trans. Richard Newnham. Freiburg, West Germany, 1959. Ins.

--------. *The Rosary of Our Lady.* Trans. H. von Schuecking. New York, 1955. Dj.: 31, 35, 47, 52. Annot. Rev.

--------. *Sacred Signs.* Trans. Grace Branham. St. Louis, 1956.

Guillet, Jacques. *Themes of the Bible.* Trans. Albert J. LaMothe. Notre Dame, 1960. Rev.

Guitton, Jean. *The Modernity of St. Augustine.* Trans. A. V. Littledale. Baltimore, 1959. Rev.

Guthrie, W[illiam] K[eith] C[hambers]. *The Greeks and Their Gods.* Boston, 1956.

Hawkes, John. *The Beetle Leg.* New York, 1951.

--------. *The Cannibal.* Norfolk, Conn., 1949.

Hawthorne, Nathaniel. *Collected Works: The Scarlet Letter; The House of the Seven Gables; plus The Best of the Twice-Told Tales.* New York, n.d.

--------. *The House of the Seven Gables.* New York, 1951.

--------. *The Marble Faun; or, The Romance of Monte Beni.* New York, 1958.

--------. *The Scarlet Letter.* New York, 1950.

Heaney, John J., ed. *Faith, Reason and the Gospels: A Selection of Modern Thought on Faith and the Gospels.* Westminster, Md., 1962. Rev.

Heidegger, Martin. *Existence and Being* (1927). Chicago, 1949. Ins., 1954.

Heller, Erich. *The Disinherited Mind: Essays in Modern German Literature and Thought.* New York, 1952.

Herberg, Will, ed. *Four Existentialist Theologians: A Reader from the Works of Jacques Maritain, Nicholas Berdyaev, Martin Buber, Paul Tillich.* Garden City, N.Y., 1958.

Herodotus. *The Histories.* Trans. Aubrey de Selincourt. Harmondsworth, Middlesex, 1954.

Hicks, Granville, ed. *The Living Novel: A Symposium.* New York, 1957. (Contains her "The Fiction Writer and his Country").

Hieronymus, Saint.  See Jerome.

Hockett, Homer Carey.  *Political and Social Growth of the*
    *American People.*  3rd ed.  New York, 1943.  Ins.: M. F.
    O'Connor, Milledgeville, Georgia.

Hölderlin, Friedrich.  *Selected Poems.*  Trans. James Blair
    Leishman.  2nd ed.  London, 1954.

Homer.  *The Odyssey.*  Trans. Robert Fitzgerald.  Garden City,
    N.Y., 1961.  Ins.: With love to Flannery and Regina at
    the farm.  April 3, 1961, Robert Fitzgerald.

Hopkins, Gerard Manley.  *Poems and Prose.*  Harmondsworth, Mid-
    dlesex, 1958.

Horace.  *Selected Poems.*  Ed. George F. Whicher.  New York,
    1947.

Hostie, Raymond.  *Religion and the Psychology of Jung.*  Trans.
    G. R. Lamb.  New York, 1957.  Ins., 1957.  Rev.

Hubbell, Jay B[roadus].  *Southern Life in Fiction.*  Athens,
    Ga., 1960.  Ins., 1960.

Hügel, Friedrich von.  *Essays and Addresses on the Philosophy*
    *of Religion* (1921).  2 vols.  London, 1949 and 1951.
    Ins., 1956.  Rev.

--------.  *Letters from Baron Friedrich von Hügel to a Niece*
    (1928).  Ed. Gwendolen Greene.  Chicago, 1955.  Ins.,
    March, 1956.  Dj.: 121, 136.  Annot.  Rev.

--------.  *Some Notes on the Petrine Claims.*  New York, 1930.
    Ins.

Hughes, Philip.  *A Popular History of the Catholic Church*
    (1940).  Garden City, N.Y., 1955.  Stamped: Notre Dame
    Book Shop, Savannah, Georgia.

--------.  *A Popular History of the Reformation.*  Garden
    City, N.Y., 1957.  Rev.

--------.  *The Reformation in England.*  Vol. I.  New York, 19⁵

Hughes, Richard [Arthur Warren].  *A High Wind in Jamaica.*  Nev
    York, 1932.

Hyman, Stanley Edgar.  *The Armed Vision: A Study in the Methoc*
    *of Modern Literary Criticism.*  2nd. ed., abridged.  New
    York, 1955.

Ibsen, Henrik.  *A Doll's House, Ghosts, An Enemy of the Peopl*
    and *The Master Builder.*  New York, 1950.

*An Introduction to Literature.*  See Barrows, Herbert, et al.

Jackson, Holbrook.  *The Eighteen Nineties: A Review of Art an*
    *Ideas at the Close of the Nineteenth Century* (1913).
    Harmondsworth, Middlesex, 1950.

Jackson, James. *The Papers of James Jackson, 1781-1798.* Ed. Lilla M. Hawes. Vol. XI of *Collections of the Georgia Historical Society.* Savannah, 1955.

James, Henry. *The American Scene, together with Three Essays from "Portraits of Places."* Ed. W. H. Auden. New York, 1946. Ins., 1954.

--------. *Daumier, Caricaturist.* Emmaus, Pa., 1954.

--------. *The Future of the Novel: Essays on the Art of Fiction.* New York, 1956.

--------. *Hawthorne.* Garden City, N.Y., 1958.

--------. *Letters.* Ed. Percy Lubbock. Vol. II. New York, 1920. Flyleaf: names crossed out: Minnie Bullock, May K. Yarborough, Beck, Hournoy; not marked: Lucy Cragg, Ida Munro.

--------. *Notebooks.* Ed. F. O. Matthiessen and Kenneth B. Murdock. New York, 1955. Annot.

--------. *The Portrait of a Lady.* New York, 1909.

--------. *What Maisie Knew.* Garden City, N.Y., 1954.

James, William. *Selected Letters.* Ed. Elizabeth Hardwick. New York, 1961.

--------. *The Varieties of Religious Experience: A Study in Human Nature* (1902). New York, 1961. Ins., 1963. Annot.

*Japanese Haiku.* See Yashuda, Kenneth.

Jarrell, Randell. *Poetry and the Age.* New York, 1955.

Jenks, Barbara C. *The Dr. Tom Dooley Story.* South Bend, Ind., 1961.

Jarrett-Kerr, Martin. *Studies in Literature and Belief.* London, 1954. Ins., 1959.

Jerome. *The Satirical Letters.* Trans. Paul Carroll. Chicago, 1956. Back of title page: I like the rule that corrects the emotion. Braque. Annot.

Johnson, Samuel. *Dr. Johnson's Prayers.* Ed. Elton Trueblood. New York, 1947.

--------. *Lives of the English Poets.* Vols. I and II. London, 1953 and 1954.

Jone, Heribert. *Moral Theology.* Trans. Urban Adelman. Rev. ed. Westminster, Md., 1961.

Jones, Alexander. *Unless Some Man Show Me.* New York, 1962. Ins., 1962.

Jones, Madison. *A Buried Land.* New York, 1963. Ins.: For Flannery, with all respects, Madison.

--------. *Forest of the Night.* New York, 1960.

--------. *The Innocent.* New York, 1957.

Journet, Charles. *The Meaning of Grace.* Trans. A. V. Littledale. New York, 1960. Ins., 1960. Dj.: 35. Rev.

--------. *The Wisdom of Faith: An Introduction to Theology.*
Trans. R. F. Smith. Westminster, Md., 1952.

Joyce, James. *Dubliners.* New York, 1926. Ins. Annot.
Back cover: 1. You huntin something--she drawled. You
lost something. Something's on your
mind.
2. Mrs. Eyed him steadily with only a sligh
smirk.
⎧Not (?)
3. ⎨Nabs (?) alright, sugar.

Jung, Carl G[ustav]. *Modern Man in Search of a Soul.* Trans.
W. S. Dell and Cary F. Baynes. New York, 1933. Annot.

--------. *The Undiscovered Self.* Trans. R. F. C. Hall. New
York, 1959. Annot.

Kafka, Franz. *Selected Stories.* Trans. Willa and Edwin Muir
New York, 1952. Ins., 1952.

Kazantzakis, Nikos. *The Odyssey: A Modern Sequel.* Trans.
Kimon Friar. New York, 1958.

Kazin, Alfred. *The Inmost Leaf: A Selection of Essays.* New
York, 1955. Ins., Milledgeville.

Keeler, Clyde E[dgar]. *Land of the Moon-Children: The Primitive San Blas Culture in Flux.* Athens, Ga., 1956. Ins.
For Flannery O'Connor, Clyde Keeler, Dec. 14, 1956.

--------. *Secrets of the Cuna Earthmother: A Comparative Stu*
*of Ancient Religions.* New York, 1960. Ins.: To Flanner
O'Connor with best wishes, Clyde Keeler, Jan. 27, 1960.

Kelly, Bernard. *Metaphysical Background of Analogy: A Paper*
*Read to the Aquinas Society in London in 1957.* London,
1958.

Kenner, Hugh. *Paradox in Chesterton.* London, 1948.

Kerr, Walter F. *Criticism and Censorship.* Milwaukee, 1954.
Ins. Rev.

Kiefer, William J. *Leo XIII: A Light from Heaven.* Milwaukee
1961. Rev.

Kierkegaard, Søren. *Fear and Trembling, and The Sickness unt*
*Death.* Trans. Walter Lowrie. Garden City, N.Y., 1954.

Kirk, Russell. *Beyond the Dreams of Avarice: Essays of a Social Critic.* Chicago, 1956. Dj.: 56, 60, 139, 90. Rev

————————. *The Conservative Mind: From Burke to Santayana.*
Chicago, 1953. Ins., 1954.

Kissane, E[dward] J., ed. *The Word of Life: Essays on the Bible.* Westminster, Md., 1970. Flyleaf: Sister Julia to Flannery O'Connor.

Knox, R[onald] A[rbuthnott]. *Enthusiasm: A Chapter in the History of Religion, with Special Reference to the Seventeenth and Eighteenth Centuries.* London, 1959. Ins., 1961.

————————. *In Soft Garments: A Collection of Oxford Conferences.* 2nd ed. New York, 1953. Dj.: 183. Rev.

————————. *Lightning Meditations.* New York, 1959. Ins.: To Flannery O'Connor with a blessing from Father Paul.

————————. *St. Paul's Gospel.* New York, 1951.

Kozlenko, William, ed. *Acts of Violence.* New York, 1959. (Contains her "A Good Man Is Hard to Find").

Lackman, Max. *The Augsburg Confession and Catholic Unity.* Trans. Walter R. Bouman. New York, 1963. Ins., 1963. Dj.: 14, 18, 24, 26, 29, 32, 40, 74, 77*, 78, 85, 103, 107*, 120, 138. Annot.

Lafayette [Marie Madeleine, comtesse] de. *The Princess of Cleves.* Trans. Nancy Mitford. Binghamton, N.Y., 1951.

Lamb, George, trans. See Bruno [de Jésus-Marie], ed.

Landa, Michel [Lee]. *The Cactus Grove.* Trans. Edward Hyams. London, 1960. (Dj. contains blurb on her *The Violent Bear It Away*).

Lardner, Ring [Gold] [Wilmer]. *The Collected Short Stories.* New York, n.d. Ins., 1953.

Lawler, Justus George. *The Christian Imagination: Studies in Religious Thought.* Westminster, Md., 1955. Annot.

Lawrence, D[avid] H[erbert]. *Studies in Classic American Literature* (1923). Garden City, N.Y., 1951.

Lear, Edward. *Teapots and Quails, and Other New Nonsenses.* Ed. Angus Davidson and Philip Hofer. London, 1954.

Leetham, Claude. *Rosmini: Priest, Philosopher and Patriot.* Baltimore, 1958. Dj.: 108, 127, 137, Jansenism, 142, 152, 266, [272], 319. Rev.

Leeuw, Gerardus van der. *Sacred and Profane Beauty: The Holy in Art.* Trans. David E. Green. New York, 1963.

Lepp, Ignace. *Atheism in Our Time.* Trans. Bernard Murchland. New York, 1963. Ins., 1963.

Leskov, Nikolaĭ [Semenovich]. *Selected Tales.* Trans. David Magarshack. New York, 1961.

Lesser, M. X., and John N. Morris, eds. *Modern Short Stories The Experience of Fiction.* New York, 1962. (Contains her "The Artificial Nigger").

Levie, Jean. *The Bible: Word of God in Words of Men.* Trans. S. H. Treman. New York, 1962. Rev.

Levin, Harry. *The Power of Blackness: Hawthorne, Poe and Melville.* New York, 1960.

Lewis, C[live] S[taples]. *The Case for Christianity.* New York, 1944. Ins.: M. F. O'Connor, Milledgeville, Georgia.

————. *The Problem of Pain* (1940). New York, 1962. On front and back flyleaves: I am the mother of fair love, and of pain, and of knowledge and of holy hope. Ecclea. Annot.

Lewis, Dominic Bevan Wyndham. *Doctor Rabelais.* New York, 1957. Dj.: 147, 51, 129, 253-4.

Lewis, [Percy] Wyndham. *The Demon of Progress in the Arts.* Chicago, 1955.

————. *The Red Priest.* London, 1956. Ins., 1957.

————. *The Revenge for Love.* Chicago, 1952. Ins., 1953.

————. *Self-Condemned.* London, 1954.

*Lives of the Saints.* See Butler, Alban, ed.

Lombardo, Agostino, ed. *Studi americani.* Vol. II. Rome, 1956.

Longstreet, A[ugustus] B[aldwin]. *Georgia Scenes: Characters, Incidents, etc., in the First Half Century of the Republic.* New York, 1957.

*Love and Violence.* See Bruno [de Jésus-Marie], ed.

Lowell, Robert. *Imitations.* New York, 1961.

————. *Life Studies.* New York, 1959.

————. *Lord Weary's Castle.* New York, 1946.

————. *The Mills of the Kavanaughs.* New York, 1951. Ins

Lubac, Henri de. *Aspects of Buddhism.* Trans. George Lamb. New York, 1954.

————. *The Drama of Atheist Humanism.* Trans. Edith M. Riley. Cleveland, 1950; rpt. 1963. Ins., 1963.

————. *Further Paradoxes.* Trans. Ernest Beaumont. Westminster, Md., 1958. Rev.

Lubbock, Percy. *The Craft of Fiction* (c. 1921). New York, 1945.

Lynch, William F. *The Image Industries.* New York, 1959. Ins., 1959. Dj.: 15, 24, 27, 38, 40, 80, 126, 142.

--------. *The Integrating Mind: An Exploration into Western Thought.* New York, 1962. Rev.

Lynskey, Winifred C., ed. *Reading Modern Fiction: Thirty-One Stories with Critical Aids.* 3rd ed. New York, 1962. (Contains her "A Good Man Is Hard to Find").

McKenzie, John L. *The Bible in Current Catholic Thought.* New York, 1962. Ins., 1963.

--------. *The Two-Edged Sword: An Interpretation of the Old Testament.* Milwaukee, 1956. Ins., December, 1956. Rev.

McLuhan, Herbert Marshall. *The Mechanical Bride: Folklore of Industrial Man.* New York, 1951. Ins., 1954.

Maison, Margaret M. *The Victorian Vision: Studies in the Religious Novel.* New York, 1962. Ins., 1962. Rev.

Malamud, Bernard. *The Magic Barrel.* New York, 1958. Ins., 1959.

Malavez, L[éopold]. *The Christian Message and Myth: The Theology of Rudolph Bultmann.* Trans. Olive Wyon. Westminster, Md., 1958. Ins., April, 1960. Annot. Rev.

Malraux, André. *The Voices of Silence.* Trans. Stuart Gilbert. Garden City, N.Y., 1953.

Mann, Erika. *The Last Year of Thomas Mann: A Revealing Memoir by His Daughter.* Trans. Richard Graves. New York, 1958.

Mann, Thomas. *Death in Venice, and Seven Other Stories.* Trans. H. T. Lowe-Porter. New York, 1954.

Mansfield, Katherine. *The Garden Party.* New York, 1922.

Manzoni, Alessandro. *The Betrothed, "I promessi sposi": A Tale of Seventeenth Century Milan.* Trans. Archibald Colquhoun. New York, 1959. Ins.: Christmas, 1961. To Flannery with a promise of prayer, Father Dadwell.

Marcel, Gabriel. *Metaphysical Journal.* Trans. Bernard Wall. Chicago, 1952.

--------. *The Mystery of Being.* 2 vols. Chicago, 1950 and 1951. Trans. Vol. I, G. S. Fraser; Vol. II, René Hague. Ins., 1953 (Vol. I and II).

Maritain, Jacques. *Art and Scholasticism, with Other Essays.* Trans. J. F. Scanlan. New York, n.d. (c. 1930). Ins. Annot.

--------. *Creative Intuition in Art and Poetry.* New York, 1955. Annot.

--------. *A Preface to Metaphysics: Seven Lectures on Being* (1939). New York, 1962.

--------. *The Range of Reason.* New York, 1952; rpt. 1961. Rev.

--------. *The Sin of the Angel: An Essay on a Re-interpretation of Some Thomistic Positions.* Trans. William L. Rossner. Westminster, Md., 1959.

Matt, Leonard von, and Louis Cognet. *St. Vincent de Paul.* Trans. Emma Craufurd. Chicago, 1960. Rev.

Maugham, W[illiam] Somerset, ed. *Teller of Tales: One Hundred Short Stories from the United States, England, France, Russia and Germany.* New York, 1939.

Mauriac, François. *Flesh and Blood.* Trans. Gerard Hopkins. New York, 1955.

--------. *The Frontenacs.* Trans. Gerard Hopkins. New York, 1961.

--------. *Great Men.* Trans. Elsie Pell. London, 1949.

--------. *The Lamb.* Trans. Gerard Hopkins. New York, 1955.

--------. *Lines of Life.* Trans. Gerard Hopkins. New York, 1957. Rev.

--------. *The Loved and the Unloved.* Trans. Gerard Hopkins. New York, 1952.

--------. *Mémoires Intérieurs.* Trans. Gerard Hopkins. New York, 1960. Dj.: E. Bronte 61 ff. Annot.

--------. *Questions of Precedence.* Trans. Gerard Hopkins. New York, 1958.

--------. *The Son of Man.* Trans. Bernard Murchland. Cleveland, 1960. Rev.

--------. *Thérèse: A Portrait in Four Parts.* Trans. Gerard Hopkins. New York, 1947.

--------. *The Unknown Sea.* Trans. Gerard Hopkins. New York, 1948.

--------. *Viper's Tangle.* Trans. Warre B. Wells. Garden City, N.Y., 1957.

--------. *The Weakling, and The Enemy.* Trans. Gerard Hopkins. New York, 1952.

--------. *What I Believe.* Trans. Wallace Fowlie. New York, 1963. Ins., 1963.

--------. *Words of Faith.* Trans. Edward H. Flannery. New York, 1955.

Maxwell, William [Keepers]. *The Folded Leaf.* New York, 1959

Medley, Stanley, ed. *Some Postwar American Writers.* Sveriges radio, 1962. (Contains her "Good Country People").

Melville, Herman. *Moby Dick; or, The White Whale.* Boston, 1950.

Meredith, George. *Diana of the Crossways.* New York, n.d.

Meredith, William. *The Open Sea, and Other Poems.* New York, 1958.

Merton, Thomas. *The Sign of Jonas.* New York, 1953.

--------. *Thoughts in Solitude.* New York, 1958.

Meseguer, Pedro. *The Secret of Dreams.* Trans. Paul Burns. Westminster, Md., 1960. Ins., 1960.

Mitchell, Walter, and the Carisbrooke Dominicans, eds. *Christian Asceticism and Modern Man.* New York, 1955. Ins., January, 1959. Dj.: 191, 204, 259. Rev.

Molière, [Jean Baptiste Poquelin]. *Plays.* New York, 1950.

Montaigne, Michel [Eyquem] de. *Selected Essays.* Trans. Donald M. Frame. New York, 1943. Ins., M. F. O'Connor, 1943.

Montgomery, Marion. *Dry Lightning.* Lincoln, Nebr., 1960. Ins.: For Flannery O'Connor with admiration and best regards, Marion Montgomery, December 5, 1960.

Morley, Helena (pseud., i.e. Alice Dayrell Brant). *The Diary of "Helena Morley."* Trans. Elizabeth Bishop. New York, 1957. Ins. on card enclosed: This book is sent with the compliments of the author. Farrar, Straus and Cudahy, Inc., Publishers, New York.

Mounier, Emmanuel. *The Character of Man.* Trans. Cynthia Rowland. New York, 1956. Ins., 1957. Annot. Rev.

--------. *Personalism.* Trans. Philip Mairet. New York, 1952. Annot.

Mouroux, Jean. *The Christian Experience: An Introduction to a Theology.* Trans. George Lamb. New York, 1954.

Mumford, Lewis. *Man as Interpreter.* New York, 1950.

Murry, J[ohn] Middleton. *The Problem of Style.* London, 1960. Ins., 1961.

Nabakov, Vladimir [Vladimirovich]. *Nikolai Gogol.* Norfolk, Conn., 1944.

--------. *The Real Life of Sebastian Knight.* Norfolk, Conn., 1959.

Neumann, Erich. *The Origins and History of Consciousness.* New York, 1954. Ins., June, 1955.

*New Signatures I.* See Swallow, Alan, ed.

*New World Writing.* See Richardson, Stewart, and Corlies M. Smith, eds.

Newman, John Henry. *Apologia Pro Vita Sua* (c. 1846). New York, 1950. Annot.

————————. *An Essay on the Development of Christian Doctrine* (c. 1845). Ed. Charles Frederick Harrold. New York, 1949. Ins., 1949.

————————. *An Essay in Aid of a Grammar of Assent* (1870). Garden City, N.Y., 1955.

————————. *Letters.* Ed. Derek Stanford and Muriel Spark. Westminster, Md., 1957.

Niebuhr, Rienhold. *What the Christian Hopes for In Society.* New York, 1957.

Nin, Anaïs. *Seduction of the Minotaur.* London, 1961. Ins.: Dean Owens.

O'Brien, Conor Cruise. *Maria Cross: Imaginative Patterns in a Group of Modern Catholic Writers.* Fresno, Cal., 1963.

O'Connor, Flannery. *Everything That Rises Must Converge.* New York, 1965. (2 copies).

O'Connor, Frank (pseud., i.e. Michael O'Donovan). *Stories by Frank O'Connor.* New York, 1956.

O'Dwyer, David T. *Our Lady in Art.* Washington, 1934. Ins.: Mary Flannery O'Connor, Aug., 1934 [not in her handwriting].

Oesterreicher, John M., ed. *The Bridge: A Yearbook of Judaeo Christian Studies.* Vol. I. New York, 1955.

O'Faoláin, Seán. *Newman's Way: The Odyssey of John Henry New man.* New York, 1952. Dj.: 5, 7, 8, 15, 21.

O'Flaherty, Liam. *The Stories of Liam O'Flaherty.* New York, 1956.

O'Gorman, Ned. *The Night of the Hammer: Poems.* New York, 1959.

Ong, Walter J. *Frontiers in American Catholicism: Essays on Ideology and Culture.* New York, 1961. Rev.

Ortega y Gasset, José. *The Dehumanization of Art, and Other Writings on Art and Culture.* Trans. Willard R. Trask. Garden City, N.Y., 1956.

————————. *Revolt of the Masses* (c. 1932). New York, 1952.

Partridge, Eric. *Origins: A Short Etymological Dictionary of Modern English.* 2nd ed. New York, 1959.

Pascal, Blaise. *Penseés, and The Provincial Letters.* Trans. W. F. Trotter and Thomas M'Crie. New York, 1941.

Payne, John Howard. *John Howard Payne to His Countrymen.* Ed. Clemens de Baillou. Athens, Ga., 1961. Ins.: To Miss Flannery O'Connor in admiration, Clemens de Baillou.

Payne, [Pierre Stephen] Robert. *The Holy Fire: The Story of the Fathers of the Eastern Church.* New York, 1957. Rev.

Pegis, Anton C[harles], ed. *Introduction to Saint Thomas Aquinas.* New York, 1948. Ins., 1953.

Péguy, Charles [Pierre]. *Temporal and Eternal.* Trans. Alexander Dru. New York, 1958. Rev.

Pelton, Robert S., ed. *The Church as the Body of Christ.* Vol. I. Notre Dame, 1963.

Pepper, Stephen C[oburn]. *The Basis of Criticism in the Arts.* Cambridge, Mass., 1946. Ins., October, 1946.

Percy, William Alexander. *Sappho in Levkas, and Other Poems.* New Haven, 1925.

Picard, Max. *The Flight from God.* Trans. Marianne Kuschnitzky and J. M. Cameron. Chicago, 1957. Ins., 1957.

--------. *Hitler in Our Selves.* Trans. Heinrich Hausen. Hinsdale, Ill., 1947.

--------. *The World of Silence.* Trans. Stanley Godman. Chicago, 1952. Ins., 1952.

Pieper, Josef. *Belief and Faith: A Philosophical Tract.* Trans. Richard and Clara Winston. New York, 1963. Ins., 1963. Dj.: 6, 8, 20, 23, 55, 61, 62, 72, 88.

--------. *Leisure: The Basis of Culture.* Trans. Alexander Dru. New York, 1952.

Plato. *Apology, Crito, Phaedo, Symposium, Republic.* Ed. Louise Ropes Loomis. Trans. B. Jowett. New York, 1942. Ins.: M. F. O'Connor, 1943.

Poelman, Roger. *Times of Grace: The Sign of Forty in the Bible.* Trans. D. P. Farina. New York, 1964.

Poirier, Richard, ed. *Prize Stories: 1963 O. Henry Awards.* Garden City, N.Y., 1963. (Contains her "Everything That Rises Must Converge").

*Polish Short Stories.* Warsaw, 1960.

Porter, Katherine Anne. *A Defense of Circe.* New York, 1954.

--------. *Flowering Judas.* New York, 1935.

--------. *The Old Order: Stories of the South from Flowering Judas; Pale Horse, Pale Rider; and The Leaning Tower.* New York, 1944.

----------. *Pale Horse, Pale Rider: Three Short Novels.* New
    York, 1939.

Poulet, Georges. *Studies in Human Time.* Trans. Elliott
    Coleman. New York, 1959.

Pourrat, Pierre. *Christian Spirituality.* 4 vols. West-
    minster, Md., 1953-1955. Trans. Vol. I, W. H. Mitchell
    and S. P. Jacques; Vol. II, S. P. Jacques; Vol. III,
    W. H. Mitchell; and Vol. IV, Donald Attwater.

Powers, J[ames] F[arl]. *Morte d'Urban.* Garden City, N.Y.,
    1962. Rev.

Praz, Mario. *The Flaming Heart: Essays on Crashaw, Machia-
    velli and Other Studies in the Relations between Italian
    and English Literature from Chaucer to T. S. Eliot.* Gar
    den City, N.Y., 1958.

----------. *The Romantic Agony.* Trans. Angus Davidson. 2nd
    ed. New York, 1956.

Prescott, Orville, ed. *Mid-Century: An Anthology of Distin-
    guished Contemporary American Short Stories.* New York,
    1958. Ins.

Purdy, James. *Color of Darkness: Eleven Stories and a Novell*
    New York, 1957.

Putz, Louis J., ed. *The Kingdom of God: A Short Bible.* Notr
    Dame, 1962. Ins., 1962. Rev.

Rabut, Oliver A. *Teilhard de Chardin: A Critical Study.* New
    York, 1961. Rev.

Racine, Jean Baptiste. *Phaedra and Figaro: Racine's Phèdre,
    and Beaumarchais's Figaro's Marriage.* Trans. Robert
    Lowell and Jacques Barzun. New York, 1961.

Rahill, Peter J. *The Catholic in America: From Colonial Time
    to the Present Day.* Chicago, 1961. Rev.

Rahner, Karl. *On the Theology of Death.* Trans. Charles H.
    Henkey. New York, 1963. Ins., 1963.

Raven, Charles E[arle]. *Teilhard de Chardin: Scientist and
    Seer.* New York, 1962. Ins., 1963. Annot.

Raymond of Capua. *The Life of St. Catherine of Siena.* Trans
    George Lamb. New York, 1960. Rev.

Rehder, Jessie C., ed. *The Young Writer at Work: An Antholog*
    New York, 1962. Ins.

Rice, Edward E. *The Church: A Pictorial History.* New York,
    1961.

Richards, I[vor] A[rmstrong]. *Practical Criticism: A Study
    of Literary Judgment.* New York, 1961.

Richardson, Samuel. *Clarissa; or, The History of a Young Lady.* Ed. John Angus Burrell. New York, 1950.

Richardson, Stewart, and Corlies M. Smith, eds. *New World Writing.* Vol. I, VII and XIX. New York, 1952, 1955 and 1961. (Vol. I contains her "Enoch and the Gorilla"; Vol. VII contains her "You Can't Be Any Poorer than Dead"; Vol. XIX contains her "Everything That Rises Must Converge").

Riesman, David. *The Lonely Crowd: A Study of the Changing American Character.* Garden City, N.Y., 1953.

Robo, Etienne. *Two Portraits of St. Thérèse of Lisieux.* Rev. ed. Chicago, 1955. Ins., January, 1956. Rev.

Roehler, Klaus. *The Dignity of Night.* Trans. John and Necke Mander. Philadelphia, 1961.

Rougemont, Denis de. *The Christian Opportunity.* Trans. Donald M. Lehmkuhl. New York, 1963. Ins., 1964. Rev.

--------. *The Devil's Share: An Essay on the Diabolic in Modern Society.* Trans. Haakon Chevalier. New York, 1944; rpt. 1956. Ins., 1960.

Rowley, H[arold] H[enry], ed. *The Old Testament and Modern Study: A Generation of Discovery and Research.* London, 1961. Rev.

Rubin, Louis D[ecimus]. *The Golden Weather.* New York, 1961. Ins.: To Flannery O'Connor--the much better builder-- Louis Rubin. 4/3/63.

--------, and Robert D. Jacobs, eds. *South: Modern Southern Literature in Its Cultural Setting.* Garden City, N.Y., 1961. Ins. on card enclosed: With the compliments of the College Dept., Doubleday and Co., Inc.

Ryan, Abram J[oseph]. *Poems: Patriotic, Religious, Miscellaneous.* 15th ed. New York, 1896.

Rynne, Xavier (pseud.). *Letters from Vatican City: Vatican II, First Session: Background and Debates.* New York, 1963.

Sandburg, Carl. *A Lincoln Preface.* New York, 1953.

Santayana, George. *Persons and Places: The Background of My Life.* Vol. I. New York, 1944.

--------. *Three Philosophical Poets: Lucretius, Dante, and Goethe* (c. 1910). Cambridge, Mass., 1945.

Santos, Bienvenido N. *My Brother, My Brother: A Collection of Stories.* Manila, 1960. Ins.

Schamoni, Wilhelm. *The Face of the Saints.* Trans. Anne Fremantle. New York, 1947. Ins.

Schnabel, Ernst. *The Voyage Home.* Trans. Denver Lindley. New York, 1958.

*Sewanee Review,* 72, No. 2 (Spring, 1964). (Contains her "Revelation").

Sewell, Elizabeth. *Poems, 1947-61.* Chapel Hill, N.C., 1962.

Shrady, M. L., ed. *Come South Wind: A Collection of Contemplatives.* New York, 1957. Rev.

Simkins, Frances Butler. *The Everlasting South.* Baton Rouge, 1963. Ins., 1964.

Simon, Paul. *The Human Element in the Church of Christ.* Trans. Meyrick Booth. Westminster, Md., 1954.

Singer, Isaac Bashevis. *The Spinoza of Market Street.* New York, 1961.

Smedt, Emile-Joseph de. *The Priesthood of the Faithful.* Trans. Joseph F. M. Marique. New York, 1962.

Smith, George D[uncan], ed. *The Teaching of the Catholic Church: A Summary of Catholic Doctrine.* 2 vols. New York, 1948 and 1949. Ins., 1949 [Vol. I and II].

*Some Postwar American Writers.* See Medley, Stanley, ed.

Sophocles. *The Oedipus Cycle.* Trans. Dudley Fitts and Robert Fitzgerald. New York, 1949.

————————. *Oedipus Rex.* Trans. Dudley Fitts and Robert Fitzgerald. New York, 1949. Ins.: To Flannery from Robert, September, 1949.

Spark, Muriel. *The Ballad of Peckham Rye.* Philadelphia, 1960. Flyleaf stamped: Retreat House Library, Lake Dallas, Texas.

————————. *The Girls of Slender Means.* London, 1963.

Stegner, Wallace [Earle], ed. *Selected American Prose, 1841-1900: The Realistic Movement.* New York, 1958.

Stein, Edith. *The Science of the Cross: A Study of St. John of the Cross.* Ed. L. Gelber and Romaeus Leuven. Trans. Hilda Graef. Chicago, 1960. Ins., 1960. Rev.

————————. *Writings.* Trans. Hilda Graef. Westminster, Md., 1956. Rev.

Stendahl. See Beyle, Marie-Henri.

Stern, Karl. *The Third Revolution: A Study of Psychiatry and Religion.* New York, 1954. Ins., 1955.

Strunk, William. *Elements of Style.* Rev. ed. New York, 1959.

*Studi americani.* See Lombardo, Agostino.

Summers, Hollis [Spurgeon], and Edgar Whan. *Literature: An Introduction.* New York, 1960.

Swallow, Alan, ed. *New Signatures I: A Selection of College Writing.* Prairie City, Ill., 1947. (Contains her "The Barber").

Swift, Jonathan (Isaac Bickerstaff, pseud.). *Gulliver's Travels: An Account of the Four Voyages into Several Remote Regions of the World.* New York, 1947.

Sypher, Wylie. *Four Stages of Renaissance Style: Transformations in Art and Literature, 1400-1700.* Garden City, N.Y., 1955.

Tabor, Eithne. *The Cliff's Edge: Songs of a Psychotic.* New York, 1959. Ins.: Janet McHane. Flyleaf: Mary--schizophrenia, Others, Alter Christus.

Tacitus, [Cornelius]. *Complete Works: The Annals, The History, The Life of Cnaeus Julius Agricola, Germany and Its Tribes, and A Dialogue on Oratory.* Trans. Alfred John Church and William Brodribb. Ed. Moses Hadas. New York, 1942.

Tate, Allen. *The Forlorn Demon: Didactic and Critical Essays.* Chicago, 1953. Ins., 1953.

--------, ed. *A Southern Vanguard.* New York, 1947. Ins. Annot.

Tavard, George H[enry]. *Protestant Hopes and the Catholic Responsibility.* Notre Dame, 1960.

--------. *Transiency and Permanence: The Nature of Theology According to St. Bonaventure.* St. Bonaventure, N.Y., 1954.

Tawney, R[ichard] H[enry]. *Religion and the Rise of Capitalism: A Historical Study* (c. 1926). New York, 1952.

Taylor, Peter [Hillsman]. *Happy Families Are All Alike: A Collection of Short Stories.* New York, 1959. Ins., 1960.

--------. *A Long Fourth, and Other Stories.* New York, 1948. Ins.

Taylor, William C. *Pinnock's Improved Edition of Dr. Goldsmith's History of Greece for the Use of Schools.* Philadelphia, 1851.

Teilhard de Chardin, Pierre. *The Divine Milieu: An Essay on the Interior Life.* New York, 1960. Ins., 1960. Annot. Rev.

--------. *Letters from a Traveler.* New York, 1962. Ins., 1962. Rev.

————————. *The Phenomenon of Man.* Trans. Bernard Wall. New
   York, 1959. Ins., 1959. Annot. Rev.

Teresa of Jesus. *The Interior Castle; or, The Mansions.*
   Trans. Discalced Carmelites. Westminster, Md., 1945.
   Ins., 1949.

Thackeray, William Makepeace. *Vanity Fair: A Novel without*
   *a Hero.* New York, 1958.

Thomas Aquinas. *Philosophical Texts.* Ed. and trans. Thomas
   Gilby. New York, 1960.

————————. *Treatise on Law, Summa Theologica, Questions 90-97*
   *On Truth and Falsity, Summa Theologica, Part I, Question*
   *16-17; On Human Knowledge, Summa Theologica, Questions*
   *84-88.* Chicago, 1949.

————————. *Truth.* 3 vols. Chicago, 1952-1954. Trans. Vol. I
   Robert W. Mulligan; Vol. II, James V. McGlynn; Vol. III,
   Robert W. Schmidt. Ins., 1960 [Vol.I].

Thurston, Herbert. *The Physical Phenomena of Mysticism.* Ed.
   J. H. Crehan. London, 1952.

Tindall, William York. *Forces in Modern British Literature:*
   *1885-1956.* New York, 1956.

Toal, M[artin] F[rancis], ed. and trans. *From the First Sun-*
   *day of Advent to Quinquagesima.* Vol. I of his *Partistic*
   *Homilies on the Gospels.* Chicago, 1955.

Tocqueville, Alexis [Charles Henri Maurice Clérel] de. *Demo-*
   *cracy in America.* 2 vols. Ed. Phillips Bradley. New
   York, 1954. Ins., 1954 [Vol. I and II].

————————. *The Old Regime and the French Revolution.* Trans.
   Stuart Gilbert. Garden City, N.Y., 1955.

Tolstoy Leo. *Anna Karenina.* Trans. Constance Garnett. New
   York, 1950. Dj.: titles marked: Conrad, *Victory.* Crane
   *Red Badge of Courage.* Cummings, *The Enormous Room.*
   Hemingway, *The Sun Also Rises.* Hughes, *A High Wind in*
   *Jamaica.* Balzac, *Père Goriot, and Eugénie Grandet.*

————————. *The Death of Ivan Ilych.* New York, 1960. Flyleaf
   543.

————————. *War and Peace.* Trans. Constance Garnett. New Yor
   1950.

Toynbee, Arnold J[oseph]. *A Study of History.* Abridged ed.
   Ed. D. C. Somerville. New York, 1947. Ins., 1947.

Tresmontant, Claude. *Pierre Teilhard de Chardin: His Thought*
   Trans. Salvator Attanasio. Baltimore, 1959. Ins., 1960
   Annot. Rev.

————————. *A Study of Hebrew Thought.* Trans. Michael Francis
   Gibson. New York, 1960. Ins., 1960. Annot.

--------. *Toward the Knowledge of God*. Trans. Robert J. Olsen. Baltimore, 1961. Ins., Milledgeville, Ga., 1961. Rev.

Trilling, Lionel. *Matthew Arnold*. New York, 1955.

Troeltsch, Ernst. *Christian Thought: Its History and Application*. Ed. Friedrich von Hügel. New York, 1957.

Trollope, Anthony. *Barchester Towers, and The Warden*. New York, 1950.

Turgenev, Ivan [Sergíeevĭch]. *Fathers and Sons*. Trans. Constance Garnett. New York, 1942. Ins.: M. F. O'Connor, 1944.

--------. *Literary Reminiscences and Autobiographical Fragments*. Ed. and trans. David Magarshack. New York, 1958.

--------. *A Sportsman's Notebook*. Trans. Charles and Natasha Hepburn. New York, 1957.

--------. *Three Famous Plays: A Month in the Country, A Provincial Lady, A Poor Gentleman*. Trans. Constance Garnett. New York, 1959.

Turnell, Martin. *The Novel in France: Mme. de Lafayette, Laclos, Constant, Stendhal, Balzac, Flaubert, Proust*. New York, 1958.

Turner, Arlin, ed. *Southern Stories*. New York, 1960. (Contains her "Greenleaf").

Ulanov, Barry. *Sources and Resources: The Literary Traditions of Christian Humanism*. Westminster, Md., 1960.

Underhill, Evelyn. *Mysticism: A Study in the Nature and Development of Man's Spiritual Consciousness*. New York, 1955.

Updike, John. *The Same Door: Short Stories*. New York, 1959. Ins.

Van Doren, Mark. *Nathaniel Hawthorne*. New York, 1957. Ins., 1963.

Vann, Gerald (Simon Oke, pseud.). *The Heart of Man*. Garden City, N.Y., 1960.

van Zeller, Hubert (Claude). *The Outspoken Ones: Twelve Prophets of Israel and Juda*. New York, 1955.

Vawter, Bruce. *The Consciousness of Israel: Pre-Exilic Prophets and Prophecy*. New York, 1961. Ins., 1961. Annot. Rev.

--------. *A Path through Genesis*. New York, 1956. Ins., October, 1956. Dj.: 34, 35, 49. Rev.

Villon, François. *The Ballades and Lyrics*. Trans. John Payne, et al. Mount Vernon, N.Y., 1940. Ins., 1945.

Vivas, Eliseo. *Creation and Discovery: Essays in Criticism and Aesthetics.* New York, 1955.

Voegelin, Eric. *Israel and Revelation.* Vol. I of his *Order and History.* Baton Rouge, 1956. Ins., 1958. Annot. Rev.

--------. *Plato and Aristotle.* Vol. III of his *Order and History.* Baton Rouge, 1957. Ins., 1959. Dj.: 6, 28, 51, 72, 103, 126, 127, 156, 170, 241, 263, 181. Annot. Rev.

--------. *The World of the Polis.* Vol. II of his *Order and History.* Baton Rouge, 1957. Ins., 1958. Dj.: 34, 37, 63, 69, 92, 80, 116-128, 133, 161, 169 fol., 186, 203, 221, 261, 284, 290, 364, 335 play and leisure. Annot. Rev.

von Hildebrand, Dietrich. *The New Tower of Babel: Essays.* New York, 1953.

Ward, J[oseph] A[nthony]. *The Imagination of Disaster: Evil in the Fiction of Henry James.* Lincoln, Neb., 1961.

Warren, Robert Penn, and Albert Erskine, eds. *A New Southern Harvest: An Anthology.* New York, 1957. (Contains her "The Life You Save May Be Your Own").

*Water: The Yearbook of Agriculture, 1955.* Washington, 1955.

Watts, Alan W[ilson]. *Myth and Ritual in Christianity.* New York, 1960.

Waugh, Evelyn. *Men at Arms, and Officers and Gentlemen.* New York, 1961.

--------. *Monsignor Ronald Knox: Fellow of Trinity College, Oxford, and Protonotary Apostolic to His Holiness Pope Pius XII.* Boston, 1959.

--------. *Vile Bodies, and Black Mischief.* New York, 1960. Ins.

Weaver, Richard M. *Ideas Have Consequences.* Chicago, 1948.

*Webster's New International Dictionary of the English Language.* Ed. W. T. Harris. Springfield, Mass., 1925. Ins.: Property of T. J. Lyon.

Weigel, Gustave. *Catholic Theology in Dialogue.* New York, 1961. Ins.: May--1964. For Flannery, Only in penetrating into this great Shekinah, past and present, shall we see the back of God--G. Weigel--66 Light-- Joy Janet.

--------. *Faith and Understanding in America.* New York, 1959. Rev.

--------. *The Modern God: Faith in a Secular Culture.* New York, 1963. Dj.: 8, 17, 27, 31, 37, 63, 98, <u>107</u>, 165, 168. Rev.

Weiger, Josef. *Mary: Mother of Faith.* Trans. Ruth Mary Bethell. Chicago, 1959. Ins., 1959. Rev.

Weil, Simone. *Waiting for God.* Trans. Emma Craufurd. New York, 1951.

Welty, Eudora. *The Bride of the Innisfallen, and Other Stories.* New York, 1955. Ins., 1955.

West, Jessamyn. *The Reading Public.* New York, 1952.

West, Nathanael. *The Day of the Locust.* New York, 1950.

West, Ray B[enedict], ed. *American Short Stories.* New York, 1959. (Contains her "The Life You Save May Be Your Own").

Wharton, Edith. *The Age of Innocence.* New York, 1920.

White, T[erence] H[anbury], ed. *The Bestiary: A Book of Beasts.* New York, 1960.

White, Victor. *God and the Unconscious.* Chicago, 1953. Ins., 1954.

--------. *God and the Unconscious.* London, 1960.

--------. *God and the Unknown, and Other Essays.* New York, 1956. Ins., March, 1957.

--------. *Soul and Psyche: An Inquiry into the Relationship of Psychotherapy and Religion.* New York, 1960. Ins., 1960. Rev.

Whitehead, Alfred North. *Modes of Thought* (c. 1938). New York, 1958.

Wiesinger, Alois. *Occult Phenomena in the Light of Theology.* Trans. Brian Battershaw. Westminster, Md. Ins., March, 1957.

Wilson, Edmund. *Axel's Castle.* New York, 1947. Ins., September, 1947.

Winters, Yvor. *In Defense of Reason.* Denver, 1943. Ins., 1958.

Wiseman, [Nicholas Patrick Stephen]. *Fabiola; or, The Church of the Catacombs.* Ed. John R. and Alice C. Hagan. London, 1922. Ins.: For Sister Mary Alice, July, 1962. Duport Wright.

Wood, Ernest. *Zen Dictionary.* New York, 1962. Ins., 1963. Rev.

Woods, Ralph L[ouis], ed. *The Catholic Companion to the Bible.* Philadelphia, 1956. Ins., 1956. Rev.

Woodward, C[omer] Vann. *The Burden of Southern History*.
    Baton Rouge, 1960. Ins., 1963.

————————. *Origins of the New South, 1877-1913*. Vol. IX of
    *A History of the South*. Ed. Wendell Holmes Stephenson.
    Baton Rouge, 1962. Ins., 1964.

Woolf, Virginia (Stephen). *Hours in a Library*. New York,
    1957.

————————. *Jacob's Room, and The Waves*. New York, 1959.

————————. *Mrs. Dalloway*. New York, 1928. Ins., 1947.

Wright, Clifford. *Helten i den nye verden*. Copenhagen, 1963.
    Ins.: To Flannery with affectionate regards, Clifford,
    Oct. 29, 1963. (Pages uncut).

Wright, G[eorge] E[rnest]. *The Bible and the Ancient Near
    East: Essays in Honor of William Foxwell Albright*. Gar-
    den City, N.Y., 1961. Rev.

Yashuda, Kenneth. *Japanese Haiku: Two Hundred Twenty Examples
    of Seventeen Syllable Poems*. Mount Vernon, N.Y., 1961.

Yeats, W[illiam] B[utler]. *Collected Poems*. 2nd ed. New
    York, 1953. Ins., 1954.

————————. *Mythologies*. New York, 1959. Ins., 1959.

Yourcenar, Marguerite. *Memoirs of Hadrian*. Trans. Grace
    Frick. Garden City, N.Y., 1957. Ins.: George Haslam,
    New York, N.Y., April, 1960.

Zilboorg, Gregory. *Freud and Religion: A Restatement of an
    Old Controversy*. Westminster, Md., 1958. Rev.

## SUPPLEMENT TO PERSONAL LIBRARY HOLDINGS

The following volumes are listed by Kathleen Feeley[5] as part of the original holdings in the Andalusia Library, but they do not appear in the Flannery O'Connor Collection at Georgia College.

Burchett, George. *Memoir of a Tattooist*. Ed. Peter Leighton. London, n.d.

Lynch, William F. *Christ and Apollo: The Dimensions of the Literary Imagination*. New York, 1960. Rev.

---

[5]Feeley, pp. 188-191. It is not possible at present to determine whether these volumes have been lost, withheld or initially incorrectly included.

PART THREE
FLANNERY O'CONNOR'S BOOK REVIEWS

AN INTRODUCTION TO THE BOOK REVIEWS

An avid reader with eclectic tastes and an eye for truth, Flannery O'Connor served as a regular book reviewer for the local diocesan press. Her reviews appeared between 1956 and 1963 in *The Bulletin* and from 1963 until her death in 1964 in *The Southern Cross*.[1] In total she reviewed more than one hundred thirty works on a wide range of religious and literary topics, often including the best Catholic works of her age.[2] Since little more than half of her reviews were published, and even those were not widely circulated[3] and have until now remained uncollected, she has received little attention as a critic.[4]

Flannery O'Connor did not think of herself primarily as a non-fiction writer. She considered her book reviews and her essays to be of secondary importance to her art. Stylis-

---

[1]For further data on the publication of O'Connor's reviews, including several items in other periodicals, see the List of Book Reviews which follows.

[2]The List of Book Reviews gives a complete list of the known published and unpublished reviews.

[3]The only known exceptions are her reviews of *What Is the Bible?* by Henri Daniel-Rops, *Faith, Reason and the Gospels* by John Heaney and *Morte d'Urban* by J. F. Powers published in *The Catholic Week*, and *The Phenomenon of Man* by Teilhard de Chardin published in *The American Scholar*.

[4]To date, the O'Connor reviews have received only limited treatment by two scholars. These critiques suffer from internal restrictions: Orvell's deals only with selected published reviews; Woods', though seeking to be all-inclusive, errs on the side of over-simplification and the lack of documentation. (See Orvell, *The Invisible Parade*, pp. 18-23, and Woods, "The Heterodoxy of Flannery O'Connor's Book Reviews," pp. 3-29). Perhaps the present collection of the published reviews will stimulate further study of this area.

tically they lack the quality of her fiction, and are in
places poorly written, even ungrammatical. Nonetheless, she
functioned well as a critic of contemporary religious fiction
and theology. Her reviews are concise, limited by the newspapers' two-hundred-fifty-word maximum; sometimes insightful,
as in her close scrutiny and considered judgment of a work
as substantial as Voeglin's *Israel and Revelation*, and direct,
as in her unrestricted praise of Gordon's *The Malefactors* and
Vawter's *The Conscience of Israel*, and her equally unqualified
condemnation of Buehrle's *The Cardinal Stritch Story* and
Kiefer's *Leo XIII: A Light from Heaven*.

In many instances the reviews reveal a facet of Flannery
O'Connor little known to her critics, namely the socially conservative, culturally enlightened Catholic pedant. Developing
throughout the reviews what amounts to a guidebook to current
Catholic literature written in series for lay readers, O'Connor pursues a course close to the heart of orthodoxy. She
patently rejects what she takes to be the superficial position
of liberalism as well as the sentimentalism found among conservatives.[5] Calling for a return to the center of Catholicism, O'Connor suggests a wide-ranging program for the faithful Catholic reader: Bible reading undertaken in the security
of faith and with the critical intelligence of the best in
scholarship, the study of candid biographies of saints, particularly Teresa of Jesus, Catherine of Genoa, Catherine of
Siena and Thérèse of Lisieux, frequent reading of contemporary
Christian humanists such as Maritain and Guardini, subscription
to Catholic magazines such as *Jubilee*, *Cross Currents* and *The
Critic*, and, as an antidote to too much "religious" reading,
a healthy portion of good Catholic[6] fiction.

---

[5] See Review 6, *Beyond the Dreams of Avarice*, by Kirk.

[6] O'Connor uses the term "Catholic" within the context of
her reviews specifically to indicate relatedness to the Roman
Catholic Church, its history, traditions, teachings, member-
ship, etc. Almost never does she refer to the Church's

O'Connor decries the Church's excessive assertion of
its authority in the realms of thought and action: the Index
of Forbidden Books for creating the low level of Catholic
literary taste and the numerous intrusions of religious power
into the secular society.[7] It is apparent that whereas
O'Connor is able to recognize overextended Church authority,
she does not notice the extent of her own didacticism in her
negative judgment of the American layperson's intellectual
acumen. She rejoices in the potential for renewal within the
Church as promised by the forthcoming Second Vatican Council
and its attendant ecumenical dialogue, and suggests that if
the Church were equipped with a "reverse Index," Küng's work,
*The Council, Reform and Reunion* should be among the required
readings.[8]

An examination of the collected book reviews reveals certain constants. While an eclectic reader, O'Connor was not
an eclectic thinker, but one who read everything from her own
experience as a Catholic and a Southerner. While seemingly
eager to consider the teachings of Protestantism and other
world religions and admiring their zeal, she searches them
for traces of orthodoxy concerning the meaning of the Incarnation, Scripture and the Word of God, and authentic articula-
tion of the human condition. That God is active in the world
and seeks interaction with human beings is central for O'Connor. She raises questions in her reviews as to how individuals
come to know God, how the human interacts with the divine, and
how this central interaction might be depicted in art. However, O'Connor does not directly address these issues, at
least she does not systematically answer them.

---

hierarchy, clergy, or religious, since her focus and concern
resides here with lay Catholics.

[7]See Review 11, *Criticism and Censorship*, by Kerr.

[8]See Review 59.

One of the most obvious characteristics of O'Connor's
theological position as demonstrated in the reviews is her
tendency to correct opposite extremes, a tendency noted
in Orvell's *The Invisible Parade*.[9]  O'Connor's reviews ack-
nowledge the tension between reason and faith, and matter and
spirit which is typical in modern religious writing, and which
O'Connor explores in her fiction and in her personal reflec-
tions. Even a cursory reading of the reviews reveals that
O'Connor refuses to embrace either side of the faith-reason
or matter-spirit dichotomy in isolation from the other. Thus
if an author tends to emphasize reason or matter apart from
orthodox Faith, O'Connor insists on the need for true belief
in a time of materialism and doubt. But if an author presents
the more fideistic, irrational or sentimental aspects of religion, O'Connor counters with an insistence on reason, progress
the social sciences and a critical approach to Scripture. She
insists that the ascetic practices of the mystics must be respected as part of the authentic development of Christianity,
but that these practices ought not to be advanced as a valid
part of contemporary spirituality. She evinces both a modern
sense of tough-minded rationality in correcting the sentimenta
and often perverted excesses in some devotional writing, and
a consistent rejection of Enlightenment rationalism. Without
the use of detailed or systematic analysis, O'Connor embodies
in her reviews, more than in her fiction, the attempt at a
balance between polarities, at a grasp of the tension inherent
in such theological themes as nature and grace, matter and
spirit, God and humanity, reason and faith.

This attempt at balancing opposites is true to Catholic orthodoxy. Though these tensions have never been resolved
--the sense of mystery remains--Catholic theology has consistently maintained both poles of the axis in its official dogmatic decrees. Human beings possess free will, but their

---

[9]Orvell, p. 19.

freedom depends on God's grace, which always prevails yet respects the integrity of the free human act. O'Connor sensed this paradox. Her reviews reflect it in their tendency to moderate one extreme with the other. Her fiction, however, tends to push the limits and to explore the extremes.[10]

Some scholars have criticized O'Connor for departing from Catholic orthodoxy in her reviews. Woods labels the theological position reflected in the reviews "heterodox," based on his definition of "orthodoxy" as Thomistic humanism.[11]

> O'Connor had an abiding sympathy for this venerable tradition. But she seems finally to have regarded the modern secular world as spiritually too moribund a place ever to be rescued by an infusion of well-tempered Catholic humanism. Something more radical was required--a darker reading of human misery, a more startling revelation of transcendent hope.[12]

Wood is correct in his attribution of an emphasis of this sort to much of O'Connor's fiction. Her depiction of grace and nature there often abandons the tension and reflects a more Jansenistic view. But this is not true of her reviews. And even in the fiction, it must be noted that "orthodoxy" within Catholicism is inclusive of more than the one school of Thomistic humanism with which Wood wants to identify it. O'Connor's stark view of reality and the seriousness of sin, sometimes emphasized to extremes, is also present in much traditional writing which has found a consecrated place within Catholic orthodoxy. We have already noted examples of this in her annotated library holdings.

---

[10]For further discussion of the relationship between nature and grace in O'Connor's fiction, see Getz, "Types of Grace in Flannery O'Connor's Fiction."

[11]Wood, pp. 3-4.

[12]Wood, p. 4.

That Flannery O'Connor considered herself an orthodox
Catholic is clear from her lectures as well as her reviews.[13]
Her consistent efforts to defend Catholic teaching and practice in the reviews take on at times an oppressive air.  Thou
she is critical of what she judges to be sentimentality or
mediocrity within Catholic writings, and offers the kinds of
correctives we have discussed, she tends almost automatically
to defend the Church and its teaching from any attack mounted
from without.  Thus she will agree with internal criticisms
of the Catholic preoccupation with literary censorship, and
she will consistently criticize the lack of intellectualism
among Catholic laity.  But if a non-Catholic questions Catholic teaching, as on birth control or on Scriptural criticism,
she hastens to the defense.  This may be due, at least in
part, to the limitations of the review genre and to the restri
ed audience of the diocesan press--in one review she approves
the notion that Catholics probably ought never to read Church
papers and magazines--but this does not completely explain
it.[14]  Though O'Connor can be critical of her Church with co-
believers, she does not display any real openness to the poss
bility of a radical critique of the Faith itself.  In this
sense, her reviews are apologies for the Catholic Faith.

* * *

Flannery O'Connor's book reviews are limited by their
very form and nature.  They are first of all capsules of informed opinion judging the merits of another author's work.
They are occasional in tone and meant to be read in isolation
from one another.  They are designed to reveal an educated, i
somewhat personal opinion.  They are not systematic theology;

---

[13]See *Mystery and Manners*, especially pp. 32, 33 and 11

[14]See Review 5, *Letters from Baron Friedrich von Hügel
to a Niece.*

nor are they works of literature.  They are brief essays, inferior to O'Connor's fiction and deserving of collection and study only as sources for greater understanding of this unique literary artist.

FLANNERY O'CONNOR'S PUBLISHED BOOK REVIEWS

This section contains the texts of Flannery O'Connor's published book reviews. The reviews are given here as they were printed in *American Scholar, The Catholic Week, The Bulletin* and *The Southern Cross,* when these could be found, and are reproduced with permission. Reviews whose published copie cannot be found are taken from O'Connor's submitted typescript as graciously furnished by Gerald Becham, curator of the O'Con nor Collection at Georgia College, and Leo Zuber, O'Connor's book review editor; these reviews are marked with an asterisk at the end of the heading.

No attempt has been made to change the sometimes ungram matical prose of the reviews, but obvious spelling errors have been corrected, on the assumption that O'Connor expected that such an editing would be done by the periodical before publication.

The texts of two reviews are not available, and have been noted in their proper places. Reviews are ordered accor ding to date of publication. An alphabetical listing of all reviews, published and unpublished, according to the author of the book reviewed, is given following this section.

(1)               March 31, 1956, *The Bulletin*.

*The Malefactors*, Caroline Gordon, Harcourt, Brace and Co.,
312 pp. Reviewed by Flannery O'Connor.*

   In a critical essay called "Nature and Grace in Caroline
Gordon," Louise Cowan has written that "though the surface of
her novels . . . moves toward destruction and despair, the current in their depths moves in a strongly different direction."
In her latest novel, *The Malefactors*, this current comes
openly to the surface and is seen as the sudden emergence of
the underground rivers of the mind into the clear spring of
grace. The novel's protagonist, a poet who is not producing,
is provoked by a recurrent impulse to wonder where his years
are bound. After an involvement with a lady intellectual
poet, which takes him away from his wife, he comes to the conclusion that they are bound nowhere unless he can return to
his wife who, in the meantime and after an attempt at suicide,
has found her way to the Church. He comes to the knowledge
that it is for him, as Adam, to "interpret the voices Eve
hears."
   A novel dealing with conversion is the most difficult
the fiction writer can assign himself. Miss Gordon brings a
sure knowledge of the craft to bear upon a task that most
novelists today would have neither the desire nor the courage
to attempt. *The Malefactors* is profoundly Catholic in theme
but it is doubtful if it will receive the attention it deserves from the Catholic reader, who is liable to be shocked
by the kind of life portrayed in it, or from the reader whose
interests are purely secular, for he will regard its outcome
as unsound and incredible and look upon it merely as a *roman à
clef*. The fact that the conversion is elaborately prepared
for and underwritten by the force of Jungian psychology will
be overlooked by those who are not willing to accept the reality of supernatural grace. Making grace believable to the
contemporary reader is the almost insurmountable problem of the
novelist who writes from the standpoint of Christian orthodoxy.
*The Malefactors* is undoubtedly the most serious and successful
fiction statement of a conversion in this country to date.

(2)                      March 31, 1956, *The Bulletin*


*The Presence of Grace*, J. F. Powers, Doubleday, 1956, 191 pp.
Reviewed by Flannery O'Connor.*


        In this collection, Mr. Powers again shows himself to be
one of the country's finest story writers.  In addition to a
deadly accurate eye and ear, he has a sense of form which
controls what he sees and hears in such a way that the many
levels of meaning which exist in the literal one are all
brought successfully to operate in the story.  The region
which he deals with to greatest effect is the parish, with
its heart, the rectory.  Here one feels that he has not merely
seen the immovable pastor, the ambitious curate, the salesman
missionary, the gothic housekeeper, the Regulars of Altar and
Rosary, but that he has suffered them and has come through
with his Faith intact.
        According to Mr. Evelyn Waugh on the book jacket, Mr. Pow-
ers is almost unique in his country as a lay writer who is at
ease in the Church; whose whole art, moreover, is everywhere
infused and directed by his Faith.  Indeed, if it were not
directed by his Faith, Mr. Powers would not have been able to
survive what his eye and ear have revealed to him, but he is
equipped with an inner eye which can discern the good as well
as the evil which may lurk behind the surface which to ordinary eyes has long been dead of staleness, so that his work,
however much directed by his Faith, seems more directed by
his charity.  But the explanation for any good writer is first
that he knows how to write and that writing is his vocation.
This is eminently true of Mr. Powers and it is for this reason
that one may be allowed to wonder why in two stories in this
collection, he has seen fit to use a cat for the Central Intelligence.  The cat in question is admirable, in his way.  He
has Mr. Powers' wit and sensibility, his Faith and enough of
his charity to serve, but he is a cat notwithstanding and in
both cases he lowers the tone and restricts the scope of what
should otherwise have been a major story.  It is the hope of
the reviewer that this animal will prove to have only one life
left and that some Minneapolis motorist, wishing to serve
literature, will dispatch him as soon as possible.

(3)                    May 26, 1956, *The Bulletin.*

*Two Portraits of St. Thérèse of Lisieux,* Etienne Robo, Regnery, 205 pp.   Reviewed by Flannery O'Connor.*

        Those of us who have been repulsed by popular portraits
of the life of St. Theresa of Lisieux and at the same time
attracted by her iron will and heroism, which appear even
through the most treacly portraits, will be cheered to learn
from Fr. Robo's study that this reaction is not entirely per-
verse.  The author shows that the life of the saint, as it
has appeared in various books, has been manipulated in order
to make it more edifying.  Indeed, he doubts if we may be sure
that the manuscript to her autobiography has not likewise been
tampered with for the same pious reason.  It is by now admitted by Carmel that the saint's photographs have been touched
up.  Carmel justifies this on the grounds that it is an attempt to achieve a "better average resemblance."
        This practice of making the saint appear edifying accord-
ing to the popular convention of what is edifying is of long
standing in hagiography and is based on a different conception
of truth from the one we hold now.  It is a conception that
does not scruple to permit the rearranging of nature in order
to make it fit the ideal type; as such, it is more closely
related to fiction than to history.  That St. Theresa has been
fictionalized by convent sources is now apparent, but Fr. Robo,
in this study, has gone far to uncover the real saint in her
very human and terrible greatness, and in this process surely
to widen devotion to her.
        Many will be loth to part with the legend and particularly
loth to part with the face which has so long passed as the face
of St. Theresa.  This face, however, is the result of some re-
touching by the saint's sister, Celine, who was, in the fashion
of nuns, a painter.  Celine turned the round, comical, fiercely
determined face that God apparently gave St. Theresa into an
elongated sweetly characterless one that she thought did more
justice to sanctity.  Fr. Robo, comparing it with untouched
photographs, wonders charitably if she did not suffer from
astigmatism.

(4)               June 6, 1956, *The Bulletin*.


*Humble Powers* (Three Novelettes), Paul Horgan, Doubleday,
$.65.  Reviewed by Flannery O'Connor.*


     There is always a loud cry in the land for fiction about
people with affirmative values who triumph by the exercise of
virtue.  Along with the demand goes the implication that none
is to be found.  Such fiction is indeed rare because it is the
most difficult to write, but these three novelettes by Mr. Hor
gan should prove at least that it can be found, and in this
case for 65¢.  It only remains for those who have been calling
for it to assure Mr. Horgan and Image Books a large sale--a
highly unlikely possibility.
     Virtue can believably triumph only in completely drawn
characters and against a background whose roots are recognized
to be in original sin.  Where there is this knowledge and
a knowledge of the Redemption, on the part of both writer and
reader, the story can unfold without that strain attendant
upon the writer who assumes, and correctly, that he will be
read largely by readers who do not share his beliefs.  Part
of the calm classical quality of Mr. Horgan's stories can
possibly be laid to the fact that he seems able to assume an
audience which has not lost its belief in Christian doctrine.
The rest may be laid to the fact that he is by nature an artist.
     In the preface it is noted that none of the stories was
written for "the purpose of setting forth as in a tract an
exemplary course of behaviour.  They were all written because
the energetic individuality and empowering belief of their
central characters proposed each time an irresistible dramatic
pattern.  In other words, the story, each time, came first."
This is not to say that Mr. Horgan is writer first and Catholic second, but simply that, so far as can be judged from
these three stories, he is, as every Catholic writer must be
at least in desire, completely both.

(5)              June 23, 1956, *The Bulletin.*

*Letters from Baron Friedrich von Hügel to a Niece,* A Thomas
More Book, Regnery, 274 pp.   Reviewed by Flannery O'Connor.*

    A Protestant minister once remarked to the reviewer that
he had never met a Catholic priest who had read Baron von
Hügel.  Since Friedrich von Hügel is frequently considered,
along with Newman and Acton, as one of the great Catholic
scholars, it is to be hoped that the minister's acquaintance
with priests was limited.  With the publication of Baron von
Hügel's letters to his niece, this great man and his vigorous,
intelligent piety may become better known to Americans.
    The letters were written to Gwendolen Greene, then about
thirty and an Anglican.  Baron von Hügel's intention was to try
to strengthen her religious sense by guiding her reading,
largely in non-religious subjects.  He warns her against the
mentality that reads only religious literature, however good,
and allows the fascinations of Grace to deaden the expressions
of nature and thereby "lose the material for Grace to work on."
Warning her against this, he says, "how thin and abstract, or
how strained and unattractive, the religion of most women becomes, owing to this, their elimination of religion's materials
and divinely intended tensions."  He advises her also not to
be "churchy," to love Holy Communion but "tactfully, unironi-
cally, to escape from all Eucharistic Guilds . . . to care for
God's work in the world . . . and yet (again quite silently,
with full contrary encouragement to others who are helped by
such literature) never opening a Church paper or magazine."
This last piece of advice, so gallantly subversive to the or-
ganizational appetite, may explain handily why Baron von Hügel
has not been widely read in American Catholic circles, but the
reader who has been fed (to the gills) on Irish piety, may
find Baron von Hügel's letters a welcome relief.
    His niece became a Roman Catholic two years after his
death.

(6)              July 21, 1956, *The Bulletin.*


*Beyond the Dreams of Avarice,* Russell Kirk, Regnery, $4.50.
Reviewed by Flannery O'Connor.*


        Monsignor Guardini has written that "when a man accepts
divine truth in the obedience of faith, he is forced to rethin
human truth," and it is such a rethinking in the obedience to
divine truth which must be the mainspring of any enlightened
social thought, whether it tends to be liberal or conservative
Since the Enlightenment, liberalism in its extreme forms has
not accepted divine truth and the conservatism which has en-
joyed any popularity has shown no tendency to rethink human
truth or to reexamine human society.  Mr. Kirk has managed in
a succession of books which have proved both scholarly and
popular to do both and to make the voice of an intelligent
and vigorous conservative thought respected in this country.
        *Beyond the Dreams of Avarice* is a collection of his es-
says which have appeared during the last ten years in England
and America.  The title is a phrase of Dr. Johnson's and it
is high praise to say of Mr. Kirk's books that Dr. Johnson
would almost certainly admire them, both for their thought
and the vigor with which it is expressed; and Mr. Kirk con-
fesses himself happily to be "one of those scholars whom
John Dewey detested"--high praise also, although in this case
Mr. Kirk is bestowing it on himself.
        The essays range from a consideration of Orestes Brown-
son's ideas of a just society to a handy return of Dr. Kinsey
to the field of zoology; but in spite of the merits of the
contents, a better introduction to Mr. Kirk as a writer would
be any of his other books--*The Conservative Mind, A Program
for Conservatives,* or *Academic Freedom*--since a collection of
reviews and magazine articles is necessarily repetitious and
occasional.

(7)          September 1, 1956, *The Bulletin.*

*The Catholic Companion to the Bible*, R. L. Woods, ed., Lip-
pincott, $3.95. Reviewed by Flannery O'Connor.*

    In the introduction to this anthology, Bishop John Wright
suggests that the reason Catholics are "frequently less articulate about their love for the Bible than other Christian
peoples . . . may be the presence among Catholics of an awe,
reverential and profound, which makes them feel humble in the
presence of this mighty compendium of divine revelation and
sacred mysteries." This statement would seem to be the extreme example of looking at our sins through stained glass
windows. Catholics who are not articulate about their love
of the Bible are generally those who do not love it since
they read it as seldom as possible, and those who do not
read the Bible, do not read it because of laziness or indifference or the fear that reading it will endanger their faith,
not the Catholic faith but faith itself. It is the latter
difficulty which this book would help to alleviate.
    In the scientistic atmosphere of this century, the Bible
can be a stumbling block to the faith of those who are not
equipped with an adequate knowledge of the nature of inspi-
ration and prophecy, the dates of the books and gospels,
and the literary modes of the authors, their use of allegory,
metaphor, and history.
    The present volume contains articles and quotations by
Catholic writers from St. Jerome to Dom Van Zeller. These
seem generally too short to give the reader more than an interest in finding a longer and more comprehensive treatment
elsewhere, but the book has the value of any anthology, along
with its grab-bag character. It will be a stimulant, a good
beginning, a companion as the title suggests; but Catholic
residents of the Bible Belt will find it expedient to go
further.

(8)              November 24, 1956, *The Bulletin.*


*Meditations before Mass*, Romano Guardini, Westminster, Md.,
1955.

    [No copy of this review is available.]

(9)              January 5, 1957, *The Bulletin*.

*The Metamorphic Tradition in Modern Poetry*, Sr. Bernetta
Quinn, Rutgers, $4.50.  Reviewed by Flannery O'Connor.*

According to the introduction, "the principle aim of *The
Metamorphic Tradition in Modern Poetry* is to give a sense of
direction in the exploration of what to many readers is a New
World, the world of contemporary verse." Such a statement
might suggest that Sr. Bernetta's essays are for the uninformed or for those who are only now being introduced to
modern poetry; however, only the well-informed reader already
acquainted with the longer works of Pound, Stevens, Eliot,
Yeats, Crane, Jarrell and Williams will be interested in
these essays, behind or in which lurks the not very well laid
ghost of a doctoral dissertation. The newcomer to modern
verse will be frightened away.
    Sr. Bernetta considers these seven poets according to a
variety of metamorphic elements which appear in their work
and she does it with scholarship and thoroughness and with a
sympathy for the poetry for which we may be grateful. The
essays seem to be valuable ground work but to lack what would
stimulate an interest in these poets if one is not already
present. Remarking that the book does not have a definite-
enough underlying structure, R. W. B. Lewis, writing in the
*Kenyon Review*, says that the "difficulty is not at all any
'Catholic bias'; oddly enough it is rather the contrary.
Sr. Bernetta . . . does not by any means impose a Catholic
structure on her materials. In my opnion, she muzzles her
Thomism overmuch." This is interesting, particularly to the
reader who has often seen a 'Catholic structure' used like a
bulldozer to undermine the work. It may be an awareness of
this danger that has made Sr. Bernetta overcareful in avoiding
tools that she might otherwise have made good use of. In any
case, we may be grateful to find a Sister of Saint Francis
writing with sympathy about the poetry of Ezra Pound and Hart
Crane and hope that this foreshadows some happy metamorphosis
in the general state of literary appreciation by Catholics.

(10)              March 2, 1957, *The Bulletin*.

*Writings of Edith Stein*, Newman Press, $3.75.    Reviewed by
Flannery O'Connor.*


    This is a selection of the writings of Edith Stein, a
German Jewish philosopher who became a Catholic in 1922, sub-
sequently entered the Carmelite Order and died in the gas
chambers at Auschwitz in 1942.  The selections have been
made, translated and introduced by Hilda Graef whose biography of the author, *The Scholar and the Cross*, appeared a year
or two ago.  The selections have apparently been made in order
to show the range of Edith Stein's personality and scholarship; a sampling is given from her spiritual, mystical, educational, and philosophical writings, but in each case not a
large enough sample to do more than tantalize the reader who
has a real interest in the subject she is writing about.
    The spiritual writings, of which only three examples are
given, are very impressive, being the type of spirituality
that is based on thought rather than emotion.  The mystical
writings include an essay on the Pseudo-Dionysius which is
perhaps the most interesting piece in the book.  The educational writings reveal the author to have been a thorough-
going feminist, willing when the occasion demanded to wrestle
with the Apostle Paul.  The philosophical writings will probably be of interest only to those who have a background in
the phenomenological approach of Edmund Husserl whose student
and assistant Edith Stein was in her early days.
    This is a valuable book in as much as it is at present
all that is available to us of Edith Stein's work in translat

(11)              May 11, 1957, *The Bulletin*.


*Criticism and Censorship*, Walter F. Kerr, Bruce, $1.25.
Reviewed by Flannery O'Connor.*


     The present volume makes up the fifth Gabriel Richard
Lecture and was delivered by Mr. Kerr, the drama critic for
the *New York Herald Tribune*, at Trinity College in 1954.
Along with the recent address of Fr. John Courtney Murray on
the subject of censorship in a pluralistic society, this lecture probably exhibits the most intelligent approach to censorship that one is presently liable to get from Catholic
writers on the subject.  While admitting the necessity of censorship, Mr. Kerr deplores its practice by unauthorized groups
in what is called pre-censorship, a custom which has created
the tendency to make every man a censor with a "watchdog" attitude toward art.  Mr. Kerr says "the generally low taste of
the Catholic community in America has been a minor scandal for
quite some time now.  It stares at us from the pages of the
same diocesan newspapers that devote so much of their space
to censorial exhortation."  That is a sentence that would deserve prompt publication even if the rest of the lecture did
not.  Mr. Kerr goes on to say that "to inhibit taste one must
first kill love; after that, distinctions won't matter.  I
suspect then that the generally low level of Catholic taste is
not something that has simply happened . . . it is more likely
something that has been created, a kind of paralysis born
of inculcated fear."  Along with the low level of taste, Mr.
Kerr says, goes the confidence that it need not be improved.
"Fear has cut off that natural affection which might have produced natural taste; indifference has cut off that serious
study which might have produced knowledge.  The subject of
art, in all of its aspects, is conveniently kept at arm's
length."
     This book can be recommended as a study manual for all
NCCW decent-literature committees.

(12)                    May 3, 1958, *The Bulletin*.


*The Transgressor*, Julian Green, Pantheon, $3.50.  Reviewed
by Flannery O'Connor.*


        Spokesmen for the deliver-us-from-gloom school of Cathol
criticism have found that this novel commits the unpardonable
sin: it is depressing.  It presents the situation of a young
girl, innocent and lacking all spiritual resources, who con-
ceives a passion for a man who not only cannot love her but
who is, in addition, thoroughly evil.  It proceeds to detail
her gradual realization of evil until the point when, pene-
trated by what remains a purely mental knowledge of it, she
kills herself.  She is surrounded throughout by a cast of
characters of whom the best lack power to help her and the
worst contrive to force her situation.
        Some slight criticism can be made of the book on litera1
grounds.  The reader is asked to believe in a passion which,
while possible, is not adequately dramatized in its beginning
We are told, not shown, that in a matter of minutes such a
love is conceived by the girl.  In the rest of the novel we
are most adequately shown the results of it but the book wou1
have proceeded on a less shaky foundation had the scene in
which the girl's infatuation began been presented.  However,
Mr. Green is such an excellent writer that he manages to ove1
come most of the problems presented by his situation.  The
novel is written with great deftness and delicacy and with a
moral awareness that comes only with long contemplation on
the nature of charity.  It presents the kind of situation
which emphasizes the mystery of evil in its starkest aspects
and it offers no solutions by the author in the name of God;
nor does it offer the solutions of faith for those who do no1
believe.  It is completely lacking in false piety and is in
every sense a book which has derived from the best type of
Catholic imagination.

(13)              July 12, 1958, *The Bulletin.*


*Patterns in Comparative Religion*, Mircea Eliade,  Sheed and
Ward, $6.50.   Reviewed by Flannery O'Connor.*


      This book describes various religious hierophanies--rite,
myth, cosmogony, god--in relation to and as a manifestation
of the mental world of those who believed in them.   These
hierophanies are in general alien to the Judeo-Christian religious life and, as the author points out, largely appear
as aberrations to us; but one object of this study is to get
away from prejudices of the lecture-room and instead of con-
sidering these beliefs simply as pantheism, fetishism, infan-
tilism and so on, to help the reader understand the meaning
of the sacred in primitive cultures.   "That the dialectic of
hierophanies of the manifestation of the sacred in material
things should be an object for even such complex theology as
that of the Middle Ages serves to prove that it remains the
cardinal problem of any religion.   One might even say that all
hierophanies are simply prefigurations of the miracle of the
Incarnation, that every hierophany is an abortive attempt to
reveal the mystery of the coming together of God and man."
This is reason enough to make this kind of study valuable.

(14)                    November 1, 1958, *The Bulletin*.

*American Classics Reconsidered*, H.C. Gardiner, S.J., ed.,
Scribners.  Reviewed by Flannery O'Connor.*


     In this collection of essays by competent Catholic lit-
erary scholars the aim, loosely, has been to reconsider 19th
century American writers in the light of Catholic theology
and to discover the influence of this theology on their
writing.  With the exception of Poe, the writers considered--
Emerson, Cooper, Brownson, Hawthorne, Longfellow, Poe, Tho-
reau, Melville, Whitman, and the literary historians--were
largely in reaction from a rapidly decaying Calvinism.  They
swung widely away from this to Transcendentalism, and in this
process of going from one extreme to another, they touched
upon or veered toward a great many pre-Reformation attitudes,
residual pieties that had their roots in something deeper
than Puritanism.  This is not to say, as Fr. Gardiner, the
editor, points out, that any of the writers under consideration were conscious of deeper roots or "would not have repu-
diated any such cultural affinity if it had been pointed
out to them; it is to suggest, however, that their work can
be adequately appreciated only if it is considered against
an older theological and philosophical background."
     Of late there has been a certain amount of renewed atten-
tion given to Christian theology and its influence on literature, and this book is a notable contribution to reestablish-
ing a long neglected point-of-view.

(15)             November 15, 1958, *The Bulletin*.

*Israel and Revelation*, Eric Voegelin, LSU Press, Baton Rouge,
$7.50.   Reviewed by Flannery O'Connor.*

This is the first volume of a six volume study, *Order
and History*, which for both breadth of imagination and close
scholarship is perhaps unequaled today by any work of com-
parable scope on the philosophy of history.   *Israel and Revelation* begins with a consideration of the archaic cultures of
the ancient Near East and their cosmological order.   Voegelin
considers the beginning of history as that break in civiliza-
tional development which began with Abram's exodus from Ur,
continued when Israel was brought out of Egypt by Moses and
became a people under God, and finally with the breakdown of
the Davidic Kingdom, continued with the Prophet's movement
away from the concrete Israel itself into the vision of Israel as the Suffering Servant of God.   In the Hellenic world
man was seeking God, in the Hebrew world God was seeking man.
Real history begins when man accepts the God Who is, Who seeks
him.

This monumental study, of which three volumes have so
far been published, has been compared in importance to the
work of Vico, Hegel, Spengler, and Toynbee.   However, unlike
Spengler and Toynbee, Voegelin does not see history as civ-
ilizational cycles, but as a journey away from civilizations
by a people which has taken the "leap in being," and has
accepted existence under God.   The study is a further advance
over Toynbee in that it satisfactorily answers the compara-
tivism which sees all spiritual movements as fundamentally
the same and of equal importance.   "Without Israel there
would be no history, but only the eternal recurrence of so-
cieties in cosmological form."

Eric Voegelin has lately returned to the University of
Munich from which he was at one time expelled by the Nazis.

(16)                    November 29, 1958, *The Bulletin*.


*Late Dawn*, Elizabeth Vandon, Sheed and Ward, $3.00.   Reviewed
by Flannery O'Connor.*


        This is the spiritual autobiography of an artist, now
a member of the Catholic Evidence Guild, who was brought up
in a materialist atmosphere with only a few depressing religious encounters in her youth.  After unsuccessful psychoanalysis for recurrent depression and a near addiction to
morphia, she fell into the Church in one of those conversions
for which there is no logical explanation except grace.
        It is always exciting to read a book of this kind where
the reader knows the outcome from the beginning but must
wait to learn the means, so often slight or ridiculous, by
which the miracle is brought about.  This book is not particularly well written, its slanginess is frequently irritat-
ing; but it is a true account of the mysterious workings of
God in a soul.

(17)          January 10, 1959, *The Bulletin.*

*Freud and Religion*, Gregory Zilboorg, Newman, $.95.   Reviewed
by Flannery O'Connor.

   This, the third of the Woodstock papers edited by
Fr. John Courtney Murray, is a study of Freud's atheism and
its sources in his personal life.  It is a successful attempt
to show that Freud's atheism was not scientific and is not
a necessary condition for the practice of psychoanalysis,
that Freud's teachings are in fact less dangerous to religion than Jung's theories, which use belief in the practical
service of psychotherapy.
   Dr. Zilboorg shows that Freud was not a "natural unbeliever" as Dr. Ernest Jones, his friend and biographer, insists.  In his insecurity Freud constantly sought faith in
unbelief.  One of his most persistent interests was the problem and image of Moses, whom he wished to find fully human
and historical and Egyptian rather than Jewish, as such a
theory would fit in more closely with his unconscious attitude toward the Hebraic-Christian tradition.  Religion was
so disturbing emotionally to Freud that he wished to abolish
it, and in order to do so, he cut it down to a size "chosen
by himself."  He made the man in the street the measure of
religion.  Dr. Zilboorg points out that such a reduction, if
applied to science "would make science come off as an art of
making mechanical toys."
   This is a valuable study for anyone interested in Freud-
ian theories and their compatibility with Christian belief.

(18)           January 10, 1959, *The Bulletin*.


*Temporal and Eternal*, Charles Péguy, Harper, $3.50.   Re-
viewed by Flannery O'Connor.*


        Apparently it is a great accomplishment to translate
Péguy's prose into English.  Mauriac once remarked that it
was a pity someone didn't translate it into French.  The
translator in this case, M. Alexander Dru, has been remark-
ably successful in conveying Péguy's peculiar and powerful
rhetoric.  He has also contributed a valuable introduction
to these two Cahiers which deal with Christianity, or rather
with the lack of it, in the modern world, with the progressive transformation of a mystique into a politique, of founders into profiteers, of faith into power.
        The first Cahier, *Memories of Youth*, is a long essay on
the political issues involved in the Dreyfus Affair.  Péguy
was an ardent Dreyfusite.  The second, *Cleo I*, is a disquisi-
tion to the author by the Muse of History, who lays the lack
of Christianity in the modern world to the clergy.   "It is
no riddle.  It is no longer a secret, even in the schools,
and it can no longer be concealed, except perhaps in the
seminaries, that the de-Christianization stems from the clergy.  The shrinking, the withering of the trunk of the spiritu
al city, temporally founded, eternally promised, does not
come from the laity, it comes from the clerks."  Péguy was in
great measure instrumental in decreasing the opposition of
liberty and tradition in France.  His is a voice which has
been listened to to the great benefit of Catholic revival
everywhere.

(19)            March 7, 1959, *The Bulletin.*

*Harry Vernon at Prep,* Franc Smith.

   [No copy of this review is available.]

(20)                    February 6, 1960, *The Bulletin.*


*Jesus Christus*, Romano Guardini, Regnery, $2.75.
*Mary, Mother of Faith*, Josef Weiger, Regnery, $5.00.
Reviewed by Flannery O'Connor.


    *Jesus Christus* is a short book of meditations on the
life of Christ, originally delivered as sermons to the students at Berlin University when Monsignor Guardini was pre-
paring to write his major work, *The Lord.* This book is only
a sample of what is brought to fruition in *The Lord.* Perhaps it has been offered for those who would be frightened
of a larger book. Any sample of Monsignor Guardini's religious spirit can be gratefully received if it leads readers
to his major work.
    *Mary, Mother of Faith* is a longer book of meditations
on the life of the Virgin. Monsignor Guardini, who contri-
butes the introduction, points out that there is "a way of
speaking of Mary which presupposes that honour is propor-
tionate to the abandon with which one encomium is piled
upon another," and that this tendency is responsible for the
aversion that many feel at the mention of Mary. This book
avoids the treacly and exaggerated presentations that we are
accustomed to receive in sermons and considers the mother of
God largely in relation to the virtue of faith and its absolute necessity in her life. It is a quiet and simple work bu
repetitious and not as intellectually stimulating as Jean
Guitton's book on the Virgin.

(21)        April 16, 1960, *The Bulletin.*

*Sister Clare*, Loretta Burrough, Houghton, Mifflin, $3.00.
*The Pyx*, John Buell, Farrar, Straus and Cudahy, $3.50.
Reviewed by Flannery O'Connor.

   *Sister Clare* will possibly be admired by those who are
tired of novels in which nuns decide that convent life is not
for them. The nun in this novel does not question her vocation. Her trials are with commonplaces such as washing down
the belfry stairs and with a pride which is exhibited several
times and is considered by her superiors a great impediment
to Carmelite perfection. Most of the nuns in this book who
do not have lovably tart tongues speak with a pious coyness
which may, unfortunately, be authentic. The note of the
novel is authenticity to Carmelite life; it is not depth of
characterization. Any novel which seeks to do justice to a
religious vocation, and particularly one to the severe order
of Mt. Carmel, will have to go very deeply into the inner
life of its main character, and this is perhaps an impossi-
bility in the case of mystics of this kind. The book may
be of interest to girls from twelve to twenty who want to
know what life is like in such a convent, but the world of
near-perfection seldom makes good fiction.
   At the other extreme is *The Pyx*, which should be kept
away from children twelve to twenty, although it is the bet-
ter-written novel. It deals with a milieu almost entirely
evil in which, nevertheless, martyrs may be found. The
martyr in this case is a prostitute who, when she is about
to be forced into participation in something like a black
mass, . . . [The text here is illegible.] a mystery novel in
the sense of leaving the reader with a deeper mystery to pon-
der when the literal mystery has been solved. The evil in
this novel is as rarified as the good in *Sister Clare*. Both
books follow their own logic but neither quite get away with
it.

(22)                    May 14, 1960, *The Bulletin*.


*God's Frontier*, by J. L. M. Descalzo, S.J., Knopf, $3.97.
Reviewed by Flannery O'Connor.


        The most interesting part of *God's Frontier* is the short
introduction by its Jesuit author in which he reminds us that
edifying literature is made with heavy "blocks of stone and
painful blows of the pick." A translator's note informs the
reader that in Spanish the word edification has not lost the
meaning of "act of building, of raising an edifice." The
author reminds us that edifying literature can only be the
work of mature beings and asks if he shall be blamed if some
of the pages of his work bleed or sizzle.
        Unfortunately, none of them do bleed or sizzle. There
is an excellent mind behind this book but it is not the mind
of a novelist. The story is of a young man who finds that he
works miracles without wanting to--embarrassing miracles, such
as bringing a canary back to life when the miracle the community wants is rain to alleviate a persistent drought. This
makes good allegory but genuine edification in the sense defined is lacking because there are not enough blows of the
axe, very little even of the spade work required to make fiction. The characters remain too easily good or bad, too pup-
pet-like to sustain belief in them for long. Allegory is all
that remains and edification in the less interesting, diluted
and abstract sense.
        This novel won the Eugenio Nadal Prize in Spain, which
indicates that it must have had something in Spanish that it
lacks in English--perhaps a poetic quality--or that there was
no better novel to choose from, or that critical literary
values were not uppermost in the minds of the judges.

(23)             May 14, 1960, *The Bulletin.*

*The Modernity of St. Augustine*, by Jean Guitton, Helicon,
$2.50. Reviewed by Flannery O'Connor.

     This is a brief but illuminating essay on the relevance
of St. Augustine to the modern age, particularly as regards
his conception of existence in time.  Before Augustine the
sense of personal sin and its connection with time had had
no literary expression.  For the Greek, sin was error; for
the Stoic accident.  The Jews had experienced sin and its
relation to history collectively but St. Augustine is the
first man of the West to have attained in personal fashion
this Jewish experience and to have written it for the ages.
M. Guitton traces aspects of Augustinian thought in Freud,
Sartre, Proust, Gide and Hegel, indicating the further step
into profundity that the saint took which these modern thinkers stop short of.  This essay was delivered in Paris on the
16th centenary of St. Augustine's birth and in Geneva before
the Faculty of Protestant theology.  It is full of profound
suggestions which deserve extension into a longer book.

(24)                 July 23, 1960, *The Bulletin.*


*The Christian Message and Myth*, by L. Malavez, S.J., Newman,
$4.50.  Reviewed by Flannery O'Connor.


        This is a critique of the theory of Rudolph Bultmann,
one of the most interesting of the new Protestant theologians.  Bultmann's concern is to make a real Christianity
acceptable to the man of the modern world--real Christianity
as distinct from that purely liberal Protestantism that eventually ends in a system of ethical values, but not real
Christianity as the orthodox know it.  Bultmann wishes to
preserve the central Christian message of the cross but to
take away everything unacceptable to modern science, thus
discarding every intervention of the Divine into human life.
He calls this demythologization.  He would judge the Christian message as found in the gospels by its relevance to an
existential philosophy.
        Fr. Malavez throws considerable light on this attempt in
an appendix which compares the opposed conceptions of Biblica
exegesis and philosophy of Bultmann and Barth.  While he
favors the conception of Bultmann, he deplores the poverty
of his metaphysic.  This will be an enlightening and clarifying book for the growing number of Catholics who are interest
in knowing more about Protestant theology as it is today ratl
than as it was in the 15th century.

(25)          August 20, 1960, *The Bulletin.*

*Christ and Apollo*, by William F. Lynch, S.J., Sheed and Ward,
$3.00. Reviewed by Flannery O'Connor.

In *Christ and Apollo*, Fr. Lynch describes the true nature
of the literary imagination as founded on a penetration of the
finite and limited. The opposition here is between Christ,
Who stands for reality in all its definiteness, and Apollo
who stands for the indefinite, the romantic, the endless. It
is again the opposition between the Hebraic imagination, always concrete, and the agnostic imagination, which is dream-
like. In genuine tragedy and comedy, the definite is explored
to its extremity and man is shown to be the limited creature
he is, and it is at this point of greatest penetration of the
limited that the artist finds insight. Much modern so-called
tragedy avoids this penetration and makes a leap toward transcendence, resulting in an unearned and spacious resolution
of the work. The principle of this thorough penetration of
the limited is best exemplified in medieval scriptural exegesis, in which three kinds of meaning were found in the literal
level of the sacred text: the moral, the allegorical, and the
anagogical. This is the Catholic way of reading nature as
well as scripture, and it is a way which leaves open the most
possibilities to be found in the actual.
    If Fr. Lynch's book could have a wide Catholic audience
in this country, particularly in the colleges, it might ultimately help in the formidable task of raising our level of
literary appreciation.

(26)            September 3, 1960, *The Bulletin*.

*The Son of Man*, by François Mauriac, World, $3.00.   Reviewed
by Flannery O'Connor.


    M. Mauriac's meditation on Christ reveals, as might be
expected of any man's meditation on the Lord, a good deal
more about himself than about Christ.  One comes away from
this book impressed afresh with Mauriac's sense of Christ's
presence in the contemporary world, but remembering perhaps
longer certain pictures of Mauriac as a child, his feet
sweating in his cold shoes as he waits on a freezing morning
to go to school.  This is a novelist's meditation; Mauriac
is always able to impress the reader with a strong sense of
the flesh--all men's flesh that Christ takes on--and of the
anguish of the human situation.  In this book he provides
a specific answer for the Jansenism of which he has often
been accused.
    He proposes in the place of that anguish that Gide
called the Catholic's "cramp of salvation,"--obsession with
personal salvation--an anguish transmuted into charity, anguish for another.  Thus for Sartre, "hell is other people,"
but for the Christian with Mauriac's anguish others are
Christ.  We realize that this way of looking at life was so
completely left out of Mauriac's youthful Catholic education
that it has had to come to him as a discovery in later life.
This is a valuable book, one which will provide the reader
with unforeseen insights into the Incarnation.

(27)               October 1, 1960, *The Bulletin.*


*The Science of the Cross*, by Edith Stein, Regnery, $4.75.
Reviewed by Flannery O'Connor.


          This book is a presentation of the life and doctrine of
St. John of the Cross by Edith Stein, a Jewish Carmelite nun
who met her death in the gas chambers at Auschwitz.  It is
her last work and knowing the outcome of her life, one feels
in it the modern fulfillment of St. John's doctrine by herself.
As for St. John of the Cross, his life was lived so very near
eternal realities that it seems an impossible life to understand.  One must simply accept it on faith with no recourse
to psychology.  Edith Stein was at one time the disciple of
the phenomenologist, Edmund Husserl.  Her intellectual training was not in theology but in philosophy of the phenomenologist school.  Both the translator and the editor of this
book point out that this background makes a difference in
Edith Stein's approach to St. John, but the reader who looks
for the difference will perhaps find it in very few instances.
The book seems largely made up of quotations from St. John
which Edith Stein adds very little to.  It is a moving book
but less for what is in it than for Edith Stein's own back-
ground--for the modern crucifixion that the reader knows was
waiting for her as she wrote the book.

(28)                    October 1, 1960, *The Bulletin.*


*Beat on a Damask Drum,* by T. K. Martin, Dutton, $3.75.
Reviewed by Flannery O'Connor.


     This is a very well-written war novel with religious un-
dertones.  It traces the penetration into reality of a film
actress who insinuates herself into the hide-out of five sol-
diers of fortune in French Indo China.  Her intention is to
retrieve one of them, a childhood companion, and bring him
back to London to live her kind of life, a kind of life which
he and all those who have experienced the horror of modern
war and the precariousness of modern life have out-grown.  In
the process of trying to get him back, she learns the lesson
of Christ's final abandonment on the cross.  Occasionally
meaning in this book is lost in shadows and credibility
strained, but in general it is a novel well worth reading
once and possibly twice.

(29)          October 15, 1960, *The Bulletin.*

*Pierre Teilhard de Chardin*, Nicolas Corte, Macmillan, $3.25.
Reviewed by Flannery O'Connor.

        Until Claude Cuenot's definitive biography of Teilhard
is published in this country, this long essay on the noted
evolutionist's life and spirit will have to fill a place for
which it is an inadequate but interesting stop-gap. Nicolas
Corte is the pseudonym of a French Monsignor, a professor
emeritus at one of the French universities. The biographical
part of the book is hardly more than a matter of he-went-here,
then-he-went-there, and is considerably less interesting than
the even shorter biographical section in Claude Tresmontant's
book on Teilhard. In an introduction, the translator,
Martin Jarrett-Kerr, C.R., remarks that Corte hardly does
justice to Teilhard's loyalty to the Church, an aspect of
the Jesuit's life that his non-Catholic admirers find hard to
understand or take, though it is the fact about Teilhard that
is the key to his personality. Nicolas Corte, while admiring
it, takes it for granted as almost any Catholic would.
        The more interesting part of the book is taken up with
Corte's assembling and outlining the main critical objection
both from theologians and scientists on Teilhard's thought.
This too is inadequate but balanced. In an interesting
evaluation at the end of the book, Corte compares Teilhard--
whom some have compared to Aquinas since he wished to recon-
cile the new learning with the old--not to St. Thomas but to
Origen. This comparison, like the book as a whole, is sugges-
tive and in the end may prove to be just, but more thorough
study will be required to indicate the depth of Teilhard's
life and spirit.

(30)                    October 29, 1960, *The Bulletin*.


*Soul and Psyche*, by Victor White, O.P., Harper, 1960, 312
pp., $5.00. Reviewed by Flannery O'Connor.


        Subtitled, "An enquiry into the relationship of psychiat
and religion," this book explores more thoroughly some of the
same ground that Fr. White surveyed in *God and the Unconsciou*
His main object in this study is to show that the conception
of a separation of soul and psyche is untenable from the
standpoint of both pastor and psychiatrist. This is a propo-
sition hotly denied by a great many eminent psychiatrists and
theologians. Whether Fr. White convinces the reader of his
point or not, he will at least deepen his understanding of
the relationship between the two.
        Some of the most interesting parts of the book are hints
thrown off in passing which show that attention to the study
of archetypes could benefit the Church in some of the acute
pastoral problems she faces today. In discussing the prevalent lapse of Catholics brought up in Catholic homes and educated in Catholic schools, Fr. White observes that this is ve
likely a failure of our sacred images to sustain an adequate
idea of what they are supposed to represent. The images ab-
sorbed in childhood are retained by the soul throughout life.
In medieval times, the child viewed the same images as his
elders, and these were images adequate to the realities they
stood for. He formed his images of the Lord from, for exampl
the stern and majestic Pantacrator, not from a smiling Jesus
with a bleeding heart. When childhood was over, the image
was still valid and was able to hold up under the assaults
given to belief. Today the idea of religion of large numbers
of Catholics remain trapped at the magical stage by static
and superficial images which neither mind nor stomach can any
longer take.
        This discussion alone makes *Soul and Psyche* worth readin

(31)            November 12, 1960, *The Bulletin.*

*Christian Initiation,* Louis Bouyer, Macmillan, $3.50.   Re-
viewed by Flannery O'Connor.*

This very short book is a restatement of religious truth,
beginning with first perceptions of the spiritual and continuing through the discovery of God, of the Divine Word, of the
living Church and the Eucharist, and finally of eternal life.
It is intended to show the reader how faith takes root in the
intelligence, but it is perhaps too summary a book to do this
successfully.
Louis Bouyer is one of the most interesting theologians
writing today.   This particular work, however, has the quality
of an exercise.   It lacks the excitement of Fr. Bouyer's other
well-known works, *The Spirit and Forms of Protestantism,* and
his biography of Newman.   In a short introduction, the author
says that it is a book written not so much to read as to reread.
It is possibly a book best suited to furnish the basis of
meditations on the Christian mystery.

(32)            December 24, 1960, *The Bulletin.*


*Modern Catholic Thinkers,* ed. A. R. Caponigri, Harper, $15.
Reviewed by Flannery O'Connor.*


     To anyone who happens to be sceptical about the modern
Catholic's freedom and ability to contribute to the intellectual life of our times, this book should be presented.   In
his introduction, Fr. D'Arcy, S.J., notes that those who are
prejudiced against Catholic thinkers "count it against them
that their views are very old and musty.   The art of living
and thinking, they claim, is to be contemporary.   Furthermore,
not only are the ideas they follow out of date; they are bound
to accept an authorized version and therefore, to repeat a
lesson by heart.   The Catholic is as tied to a set of formu-
las as the Marxist; he is equally intransigent and with a mind
closed to other ideas.   Such critics are inclined to look upon
counter-arguments as special pleading."
     Dr. Caponigri, assuming that evidence to the contrary is
the only suitable method of persuading such dissenting critics
has brought together 38 essays by Catholics whose work leaves
no suspicion that any system of ideas has been imposed or true
liberty of thought curtailed.   Aside from the excellence of
Dr. Caponigri's choices, the anthology has the further advan-
tage of leading the reader to the original work from which
many of these essays have been taken, and in presenting him
with translations of significant chapters of books which have
not and may never be published in English.   The selections
range from a chapter, "Human and Divine," taken from the
well-known *Mind and Heart of Love* by Fr. D'Arcy to "Existentialism," from an original manuscript of Regis Jolivet.   This
anthology will make an excellent Christmas gift for any college student brighter than most or for any one else concerned
with intellectual matters.

(33)              February 4, 1961, *The Bulletin*.


*The Divine Milieu*, P. Teilhard de Chardin, Harpers, 1960,
139 pp., $3.   Reviewed by Flannery O'Connor.*


     "Where is the Catholic as passionately vowed by conviction
and not by convention to spreading the hopes of the Incarnation as are many humanitarians to spreading the dream of the
new city?" Teilhard asks this question toward the end of *The
Divine Milieu*, the second of his books to be published in
America.  It is a question depressing to answer today when
the sense of expectation has largely disappeared from our religion.  No writer of the last few centuries is more capable
of restoring that sense to the Christian world than Teilhard,
whose work is both scientific and profoundly Pauline.
     Teilhard, who was a Jesuit and a paleontologist, was not
allowed by his order to publish but was permitted to continue
his work and was sent to China, the best place for its con-
tinuance.  There he played a major role in the discovery of
Pekin man and wrote the books which are being published now
after his death and which will probably have the effect of
giving a new face to Christian spirituality.  The first of
Teilhard's books to be published here, *The Phenomenon of Man*,
is scientific and traces the development of man through the
chemical, biological and reflective stages of life.  This
second volume is religious and puts the first in proper focus.
They should be read together for the first volume is liable
to seem heretical without the second and the second insubstan-
tial without the first.  It is doubtful if any Christian of
this century can be fully aware of his religion until he has
reseen it in the cosmic light which Teilhard has cast upon it.

(34)                    March 18, 1961, *The Bulletin.*


*The Life of St. Catherine of Siena*, Bl. Raymond of Capua,
Kenedy, New York, 1960, 384 pp., $4.95.   Reviewed by Flan-
nery O'Connor.*


        The signs and wonders that increased the faith of the
14th century will very generally have the opposite effect on
that of the 20th, and this biography of St. Catherine, written by her confessor, Blessed Raymond of Capua, can very well
have the effect of inspiring the reader with a genuine repul-
sion for the saint.  For many of the miracles herein describe
we can find natural causes, others we can ascribe to the imagination, and some to the gullibility of the author, but when
the reader has cut down these things to managable proportions
there still remains the hard core of Catherine's sanctity to
be mined out of Blessed Raymond's tiresome platitudes and
preaching.
        Catherine was a non-conformist of a high order and had
all the stubbornness necessary to carry out her way of life.
The consternation of her family at finding themselves with a
visionary in the house, a daughter who scourged herself three
times a day until the blood ran, ate nothing but herbs, and
occasionally fell in the fire during her ecstasies (but was
never burned) is well detailed by Blessed Raymond.  What
emerges most profoundly is that all that saint's actions were
conformed to a Reality of which the ordinary man is not aware
If the reader can once realize the strength and power of
Catherine's vision, the scourgings and other self-punishments
become understandable.  Conversely, it is only from these
penances that the vision can be surmised and vouched for.  Al
together this is not a book to give anyone faith, but one whi
only faith can make understandable.

(35)          April 1, 1961, *The Southern Cross.*

*The Cardinal Stritch Story,* Marie Buehrle, Bruce, 1959,
197 pp., $3.95.
*Leo XIII: A Light from Heaven,* Br. Wm. Kiefer, S.M., Bruce,
1961, 210 pp., $3.95.
Reviewed by Flannery O'Connor.

Here are two mediocre biographies of two great men. The
biography of Cardinal Stritch, published only a year after his
death, reads as if it were put together at high speed. A
good biography of Cardinal Stritch or a memoir by someone who
had been close to him would do much toward improving the popular image of the Catholic Church in this country, for he
was one of the most distinguished, scholarly and charming of
American churchmen. Miss Buehrle gives the facts and enough
little antidotes to make the Cardinal come through but the
writing is tiresome and not what the subject deserves.

Brother Kiefer claims no more for his biography of Leo
XIII than that it is adequate and the only one published in
America since 1903. It does give a good and chilling picture
of the condition of the Church when Leo became pope in 1878
and of the highlights of the troubles and accomplishments of
the next twenty-five years. The persecution of the Church
in Italy at that time seems worse than her troubles in the
Communist controlled countries today. This book will leave
the reader looking for a more definitive treatment of its
subject and perhaps that is as much as Brother Kiefer intended it to do.

(36)                    April 1, 1961, *The Bulletin.*

*Cross Currents,* ed. Joseph E. Cunneen, West Nyack, New York,
quarterly, $3.50 per year, reprints available $.25 each.  Reviewed by Flannery O'Connor.


        Of the many magazines in America published through the
initiative of Catholics, the one which makes the most important contribution to Catholic intellectual life in this
country is unfortunately the one least known to a wide audience.  This is *Cross Currents,* a quarterly review which re-
prints articles from all over the world on theology, philosophy, the arts and social thought.  These articles are the
best that can be found on religious subjects as they impinge
on the modern world, or on modern discoveries as they impinge
on the Judeo-Christian tradition.  The articles serve to fer-
tilize Catholic life with currents of thought from other religions and from those of our own which the average communi-
cant is not apt to come by.  The magazine serves an ecumenical
purpose since it . . . [The text here is illegible.]
        The magazine was founded in 1950 by a group of Catholic
laymen, its aim to "explore the implications of Christianity
for our times."  None of its articles is abridged or popu-
larized, no one article is exhausted by a first or second
reading, but all are accessible to any reasonably active
mind.  The editors would like to see *Cross Currents* used as
a basis for discussions in small parish groups.  Since the
use of the mind is seldom encouraged in parish activities,
this seems unlikely of fulfillment, but for any individual
concerned to discover the deep currents of Christian thought,
this magazine is invaluable.

(37)              May 27, 1961, *The Bulletin.*

*The Conversion of Augustine*, Romano Guardini, Newman, Westminster, Maryland, 253 pp., $3.95.   Reviewed by Flannery
O'Connor.*

          In his introduction to this analysis of St. Augustine's
odyssey, Msgr. Guardini notes two approaches usual in dealing
with his subject, both of which he has tried to avoid.  One
of these sees the Confessions as a record of a conversion
from evil to good, the outcome only being of interest, the
hesitations along the way of no real significance.  This view
leaves out of account the living man, ignores his psychology
and ends with merely theoretical insights.  The other approach
goes to the opposite extreme and makes psychology and the
living process everything and ends seeing the subject as a
case history.  Msgr. Guardini has steered well in between
these two approaches and has produced a psychological study
well informed on spiritual realities.  He unfolds Augustine's
story on ethical levels and on the levels of mind and idea
as well.  The result is as penetrating a study of the saint
as we are liable to get.
          The book is divided into two parts, the first of which
is designed to elucidate some of the key Augustinian ideas.
It seems unfortunate that this more abstract material had to
be put by itself at the beginning.  The second part, which is
an interpretation of Augustine's spiritual drama, is the more
readable section.  In any case, it is good to have a book on
St. Augustine by Msgr. Guardini.

(38)          June 10, 1961, *The Bulletin*.


*The Critic*, A Catholic Review of Books and the Arts, The
Thomas More Association, 210 West Madison Street, Chicago 6,
$3.50 per year. Reviewed by Flannery O'Connor.*


    Since its beginning, the magazine of the Thomas More
Association has gone through a series of changes which, it
is to be hoped, parallel the American Catholic's attitude
toward books and the arts. The magazine began in 1942 as
*Books on Trial*, a name which reflected the Catholic preoccupation for grading and judging books in accordance with
their likelihood of dealing blows to the reader's Faith.
*Books on Trial* offered eleven possible verdicts of the books
reviewed; the legal atmosphere was thick. The magazine eventually dropped the verdicts and then dropped the name. It is
now called *The Critic*, A Catholic Review of Books and the
Arts. There is in the designation, Catholic Review of Books
and the Arts, the implied assumption that there is a brand of
criticism special to Catholics rather than that any good
criticism will reflect a Catholic view of reality. The ghost
of *Books on Trial* is hard to lay.
    *The Critic* has in each issue three or four articles on
cultural subjects and about fifty short reviews of current
books, fiction and non-fiction. The articles on music and
the arts are usually better than the articles on literature,
which too frequently are about minor Catholic literary figure
or when about non-Catholic writers tend to show that these ar
Catholic in spite of themselves and therefore acceptable. The
reviews of books on social thought, history and religion are
better than the fiction reviews. Fiction is considered by
most Catholic readers to be a waste of time, and *The Critic*,
which recently began publishing a story or two an issue, has
taken a step which may prove dangerous to its circulation.
Already letters have appeared in the letters column expressin
displeasure that this space should be, in effect, wasted.
This may well be true since one feels that the fiction which
the majority of Catholics will put up with will be, while not
commercial fiction, still an innocuous variety that could as
well be done without. *The Critic* also occasionally devotes
space to poetry and recently published a large selection of
the verse of living American Catholic poets. The poetry will
probably be tolerated, though not read, and the fiction read
but not tolerated.
    The metamorphosis of *The Critic*, however, is not yet com
plete. Beginning in the fall the magazine will publish nine
or ten articles in each issue, there will be fewer but longer
and more thorough reviews, and the subtitle will be changed
from "A Catholic Review of Books and the Arts" to "A Magazine

of Christian Culture." All these changes promise a better
magazine, one which will be less parochial and which will
lead as well as reflect the American Catholic's growing appetite for the arts.

*The Critic* is well worth the price of the subscription.

(39)                    June 10, 1961, *The Bulletin*.


*Stop Pushing*, Dan Herr, Hanover House, New York, 192 pp.,
$3.50.  Reviewed by Flannery O'Connor.*


     Mr. Dan Herr's chief talent is for the pursuit and ex-
posure of idiotic printed matter.  He is at his best when
bringing to public attention the advertising in the Catholic
press (although this entails no more than copying it out word
for word) or when he sets up a mirror before the lady's magazines, the horror of which is that it is in no measure a dis-
torting mirror.  When he confines himself to such public ser-
vices, Mr. Herr is at least endurable, sometimes enjoyable,
and always valuable.
     Columnists in general, however, and those with preten-
sions to humor in particular, would be well advised to let
the impact of their talents come to the public in well-regu-
lated dribbles, to scatter rather than to collect their piece
Embedded in the general earnestness of *The Critic*, these col-
umns manage to thrust themselves forward with a certain vitri
olic verve, which when collected, by some obscure law of accu
mulation, becomes bluster.  The humorist can not allow himsel
to see two sides of any question unless he is a very complica
ted humorist.  Mr. Herr does not sport an ounce of complicati
and he depends for his effects 95% of the time on exaggeratio
alone.  While his opinions are in general sound--witness his
disaffection for the teen-ager--there is a sameness about the
presentation that makes it advisable to let a long period of
time elapse between reading one piece and the next; anytime
from two months to a year.

(40)         June 24, 1961, *The Bulletin*.

*Life's Long Journey*, Kenneth Walker, Nelson, New York, 1961, $3.50, 185 pp. Reviewed by Flannery O'Connor.*

This is a book on evolution written for the general reader. Its author, a medical doctor, believes that the scientist who is a non-specialist has, because of his over-all view, a great deal to contribute to this subject. He traces the evolution of the human species up to the present where he sees man facing a crisis. Dr. Walker's contention is that man's future evolution will be along spiritual lines. Teilhard is never mentioned in this book, which is a peculiar oversight since he is one of the few modern evolutionists who believes in spiritual evolution and a much greater expo-nent of it than Dr. Walker.

This may be explained by the author's obvious distaste for the Church's stand on birth control which Dr. Walker be-lieves should be one of the chief factors in our effort to direct evolution. No attempt is made to do justice to or even to understand the Catholic position on this subject. It is dismissed as superstition and the fatuous observation is made that the Church sanctions death control but not birth control. Dr. Walker apparently sees this as a grave inconsis-tency.

There is much of value in this book. As long as the doc-tor sticks to his science, he has something to offer. When he becomes a philosopher and social planner he oversteps his limits.

(41)                    August 5, 1961, *The Bulletin.*


*Selected Letters of Stephen Vincent Benét*, ed. Charles
Fenton, Yale University Press, New Haven, 1960, $6, 416 pp.
Reviewed by Flannery O'Connor.


        The epithet "best-loved poet" usually speaks more for
the man than his poetry, and after his death it will lead mor
often to a collection of his letters than to a critical appraisal of his work.  Stephen Vincent Benét was known for his
gay spirit and warm friendships and a quality of both is appa
ent in his letters.  They also say a good deal about the lite
ary life in the twenties and thirties among Benét's circle an
they say even more about the taste of the fiction-reading
public, then as now.  Benét struggled to make a living by fre
lance writing for the popular magazines.  In 1926, he wrote t
his wife, "I wrote another story yesterday and am typing it
today.  It is called "Bon Voyage" and is a dear little candy-
laxative of a tale about a sweet little girl named Sally.  I
do not see how it can fail to sell--it is so cheap."  Whether
Benét could have written better poetry had he not had this
burden constantly upon him, the letters cannot tell us, but
they make sad reading since they suggest the possibility.

(42)     September 16, 1961, *The Bulletin*.

*The Resurrection*, F. X. Durrwell, C.SS.R., Sheed and Ward,
1950, 359 pp., $6. Reviewed by Flannery O'Connor.*

This detailed and excellent theological study seeks to
restore the Resurrection to its proper place in the theology
of the Redemption, which has been truncated by thought which
pays exclusive attention to Christ's death. This situation
came about in those centuries when the Redemption was seen
solely as a satisfaction for sin.
With the rise of Biblical scholarship, the Resurrection
is again taking its place as central to the Redemption. Père
Durrwell's study, which was first published in France in 1950,
has become the standard work on the subject. It presents a
synthesis of all the Bible says about the Resurrection as
part of the mystery of salvation and considers the life of
the Church in the risen Christ. In a Note to the Second Edition Père Durrwell draws the reader's attention to two vital
truths which emerge from a study of the Resurrection: "The
fact that the death and resurrection remain forever actual in
Christ in glory, and the identification of the Church with
Christ in glory, not merely in one body with him, but actually
in the act of his death and glorification."
The liturgical revival has sought to give Catholics a
new consciousness of the full splendor of the message of salvation and this requires a rediscovery of the resurrection
According to Charles Davis, who supplies an introduction to
Père Durrwell's study, this is the reason few books in recent
times are more important than this one.

(43)                    September 16, 1961, *The Bulletin*.


*Themes of the Bible*, J. Guillet, S.J., Fides, Notre Dame,
Ind., 1961, 272 pp., $6.95.  Reviewed by Flannery O'Connor.*


    *Themes of the Bible* is essentially a study of religious
language and its supernatural character.  It is not intended
to be an exhaustive study but is meant to open up new perspectives of meaning through the study of the words in sacred
scripture.  A selection of Biblical themes--the exodus, grace,
justice, sin, damnation--are used to highlight the progress
of Revelation and to show that the religious language of Israel is the work of the Spirit of God as well as its human
authors.  Père Guillet's thesis is that "in its most diverse
forms, whether in the great work of a Moses, in the vibrant
heart of a poet, in the wise man's daily effort at being
faithful to the Law, in the message of the prophets, God was
blazing his paths."  The histories of certain key words are
traced through the Old Testament where their supernatural
character remains obscure into the New where it is manifested
fully when Christ appears.  Here "Revelation bursts forth in
a definitive manner."
    The general reader will find this study illuminating as
well as the student of Biblical criticism.

(44)              September 30, 1961, *The Bulletin.*


*The Mediaeval Mystics of England*, Eric Colledge, Scribners,
1961, 304 pp., $4.95.   Reviewed by Flannery O'Connor.*


     This anthology contains selected writings from seven of
the best known mystics of mediaeval England: St. Aelred of
Rievaulx, St. Edmund Rich, Richard Rolle, Walter Hilton,
Juliana of Norwich, and the unknown author of the *Cloud of
Unknowing.*  The latter is prepresented here by the less well-
known, *Book of Privy Counsel*, which, of these selections,
seems to the reviewer by far the most interesting.  Both
Hilton and the author of *The Book of Privy Counsel* were concerned to dispel the indiscreet and enthusiastic ideas about
mysticism that had come about through the popularity of earlier writers such as Richard Rolle.  To cut across futile in-
tellectualizing in prayer, the author of *The Book of Privy
Counsel* advises his monks to come down to the lowest level
of their intelligence and think "not what you are, but that
you are."
     Eric Colledge, a lecturer in English literature at Liver-
pool University has supplied a scholarly introduction which
the newcomer to these writers will find beyond him but which
will be of value to students of the period and of mysticism.

(45)                October 28, 1961, *The Bulletin.*


*Freedom, Grace and Destiny*, Romano Guardini, Pantheon, New
York, $4, 251 pp.  Reviewed by Flannery O'Connor.*


Msgr. Guardini here explores the Christian understanding
of freedom, grace and destiny, three interrelated concepts
which in modern thought have been distorted, discarded, or
diluted in a fashion that suggests nothing less than Satanic
influence.  Msgr. Guardini treats each concept in a separate
chapter, asking first how it is presented in immediate experi
ence, what revelation has to say about it, and finally what
is its significance for the whole pattern of existence.   In
all his work Msgr. Guardini's directive is this attempt to
view the pattern of Christian existence as a whole, as it was
viewed in early and mediaeval Christian thought before philosophy became separated from theology, empirical science from
philosophy, and practical instruction from knowledge of reality.  He is concerned that this conscious unity of existence
has been lost to a large extent even by believing Christians.
"The believer no longer stands with his faith amid the concrete, actual world, and he no longer rediscovers that world
by his faith.  He has made a grim necessity of this dismem-
berment by constructing, if we may employ the term, a chemi-
cally pure faith in which he insists upon seeing the true
form of orthodoxy.  This orthodoxy has a somewhat austere
and very courageous quality, but we must not forget that it
is an emergency position."  This is an important book.  It
will give the reader the whole view of life and faith which
has been Msgr. Guardini's aim in writing it.

(46)            November 25, 1961, *The Bulletin*.

*The Range of Reason*, Jacques Maritain, Scribners, New York,
1961, $1.45, 226 pp.   Reviewed by Flannery O'Connor.*

      In this book made up of ten chapters from *Raison et*
*Raisons* and eight essays from other sources, Maritain covers
a variety of philosophical topics and their social extensions,
in which the range of reason can be illustrated.  The age of
Enlightenment substituted reason for revelation, with the result that confidence in reason has gradually decayed until in
the present age, which doubts also fact and value, reason
finds few supporters outside of Neo-Thomist philosophy.  Maritain's has been one of the major voices in modern philosophy
to reassert the primacy of reason.  All his work springs from
confidence in it.  He puts it in the proper perspective, where
it serves and not substitutes for revelation.
      This book contains abridged discussions of most of the
subjects that Maritain has devoted whole works to.  Most readers who have any interest in Maritain at all will prefer the
longer works on these various topics, but *The Range of Reason*
is good for introducing those new to Maritain to the wide
range of his thought.

(47)              December 9, 1961, *The Bulletin*.


*The Bible and the Ancient Near East,* ed. G. E. Wright, Double
day, New York, 1961, 409 pp., $7.50.

*The Old Testament and Modern Study,* ed. H. H. Rowley, Oxford
Paperbacks, London, 1961, 370 pp., 8/6 net.

Reviewed by Flannery O'Connor.*


     These two books are collections of essays written by
Ancient Near East scholars for other Ancient Near East scholars.  *The Bible and the Ancient Near East* is a memorial volume in honor of William Foxwell Albright, one of this country
foremost Oriental scholars, who retired as Professor of Semit
Languages and Chairman of the Oriental Seminary at Johns Hopkins University in 1958.  *The Old Testament and Modern Study*
is a volume issued by the Society for Old Testament Study.
Its aim is to survey the significant work that has been done
in the field in the last thirty years in order to bring out
the new trends that have appeared.
     Although these essays are for the professional scholar,
they offer the lay public some fascinating insights into what
is involved in discovering ancient civilizations and language
Ironically, as more material, through excavation and more accurate methods of dating, becomes available, interpretation
grows increasingly difficult.  Nineteenth century Biblical
scholarship, which wrecked the faith of so many, has been almost entirely discredited and the historical value of many
Biblical texts attested to by chronologies worked out by radi
carbon dating and the comparison of cultures.  There is a
healthy sense in these books that as our knowledge of the
past grows, the mystery of it grows likewise.

(48)          December 23, 1961, *The Bulletin.*

*The Novelist and the Passion Story*, F. W. Dillistone, Sheed
and Ward, 1960, 128 pp., $3. Reviewed by Flannery O'Connor.

    This is a study of an Episcopal theologian of four nov-
els consciously intended by their authors to suggest the passion of Christ and its redemptive power. The novels are
Mauriac's *The Lamb*, Melville's *Billy Budd*, Kazantzakis' *The
Great Passion*, and Faulkner's *A Fable*, representing respectively, Catholic, Calvinist, Greek and (roughly) Lutheran
theology.
    It is interesting to note as an indication of the dif-
ficulty of attempting the Christ-figure that Mauriac and
Faulkner are represented by what most critics agree are their
worst books. *Billy Budd* is considered a classic but there is
some doubt whether Melville actually intended its hero to be
a Christ figure, though Dean Dillistone makes a good case for
it. He goes through each novel thoroughly, tracing the pattern of the passion, and its redemptive effects and then in a
final chapter, discusses what Auden calls "the insolubility
of the religious paradox in aesthetic terms," and indicates
the point of failure in each book. He suggests that Mauriac's
weakness is to resolve the paradox by some miraculous event.
He considers this the weakness of Catholic theology generally.
To the reviewer it appears a strictly novelistic weakness. In
any case Dean Dillistone can accommodate a good deal of heresy
in his Christ figures.
    The book is an interesting study of attempts which by
their nature must fail.

(49)        December 23, 1961, *The Bulletin*.

*Teilhard de Chardin*, Oliver Rabut, O.P., Sheed and Ward,
1961, 247 pp., $3.95.  Reviewed by Flannery O'Connor.


This is the best critical evaluation of the work of
Pere Teilhard de Chardin to appear in this country.  Most
of the studies written on Teilhard's thought have been either uncritically enthusiastic or uncritically condemnatory.
Oliver Rabut understands Teilhard's greatness without accepting as proven or even likely many of his hypotheses
He believes that Teilhard yields to a temptation to overem-
phasize the element of psychism in nature and that he does
not distinguish adequately between the supernatural action
of Christ and the purely natural ascent of evolution.  He
also feels that one of Teilhard's mistakes lay in not realizing that, past a certain point, it was necessary for him
to change his discipline from science to philosophy and
then to theology.
On the positive side he believes that those who condemn
Teilhard never see what it is in him that makes him so at-
tractive nor "the means of justifying one's final capitula-
tion to him."  He was a scientist who saw deeply certain intellectual and spiritual needs of our times.  "The solutions
he proposes, imperfect though they may be, are already such
as can be used; at times they are excellent."  The discovery
that we owe to Teilhard is that vocation of spirit is visible,
concrete, and of absorbing interest.  If his method did not
achieve all he thought it did, he was still making an attempt
which it is necessary for scientists and theologians to take
over and carry further.
This is a brilliant book which will be of great value
to any one interested in Teilhard.

(50)          Fall, 1961, *The American Scholar.*

*The Phenomenon of Man,* P. Teilhard de Chardin.   Reviewed by
Flannery O'Connor.


     *The Phenomenon of Man* by P. Teilhard de Chardin is a work
that demands the attention of scientist, theologian and poet.
It is a search for human significance in the evolutionary
process.   Because Teilhard is both a man of science and a believer, the scientist and the theologian will require considerable time to sift and evaluate his thought, but the poet,
whose sight is essentially prophetic, will at once recognize
in Teilhard a kindred intelligence.   His is a scientific
expression of what the poet attempts to do: penetrate matter
until spirit is revealed in it.   Teilhard's vision sweeps
forward without detaching itself at any point from the earth.

(51)                    January 6, 1962, *The Bulletin*.


*Conversations with Cassandra,* Sr. M. Madeleva, Macmillan,
New York, 1961, $3.50, 133 pp.   Reviewed by Flannery O'Connor.


        This book consists largely of short talks which Sister
Madeleva has given to the students at St. Mary's College at
Notre Dame where she has been president for 27 years.   She
discusses Christian education for women, its goals, its
purpose and the kind of woman she hopes will be its end
result.
        There are two chapters included which apparently were
not talks to students.   One is called "Conversations with
Children."   In it Sister Madeleva recounts several conversations she has had with young children who make various wise
comments on life, art, and the world in general.   These children are very hard to take.   The other is about Dame Julian
of Norwich and is one of the best chapters in the book.
        For the reader not specifically interested in Catholic
education this book will seem repetitious and a trifle dull,
dull not by virtue of its intellectual content which is splen-
did, but by a rather high-blown style which soon exhausts the
reader.   For those parents who are debating whether to send
their daughter to a Catholic college, the book is a good one.
They will probably be convinced that she will get something
there that she wouldn't get elsewhere.

(52)          February 17, 1962, *The Bulletin*.

*Christian Faith and Man's Religion,* Marc C. Ebersole, Crom-
well, New York, 1961, $.65, 183 pp.
*Christianity Divided,* ed. Callahan, Oberman and O'Hanlon,
Sheed and Ward, New York, 1961, $6, 333 pp.
Reviewed by Flannery O'Connor.*

    *Christian Faith and Man's Religion,* a study of five non-
Catholic religious thinkers, is based on the distinction between religion thought of simply as man's deep involvement
with his own existence, not necessarily from a theistic point
of view, and the specific belief in Christ as the God who has
redeemed us.  Much of the thought of these men, with the exception of Barth and Fromm, is an effort to fit Christianity
into a frame of the 18th century Enlightenment.  Fromm rejects
Christianity entirely in favor of natural religion; Barth rejects religion entirely and sees the Christian faith as a judgment against it.  Bonhoeffer rejects religion on the grounds
that man has outgrown it but accepts the Christian faith;
Schleiermacher sees the Christian faith as the fulfillment of
religion but makes this faith dependent on feeling.  Niebuhr
emerges as the most balanced and most nearly orthodox of the
five.  He sees the Christian faith as both the judgment against
and the fulfillment of religion.
    Aside from several references to St. Augustine and one to
St. Thomas, it is nowhere suggested that any thought took
place before the time of Luther.  This is a fascinating book
for any Catholic who wants to understand better the problems
and achievements of Protestant theology.
    An equally fascinating and more profound book is *Chris-
tianity Divided,* a collection of theological essays by Protestant and Catholic scholars on the fundamental issues which
divide them--scripture and tradition, hermeneutics, the
Church, the sacraments, and justification.  The aim of the
book is to make available to a wider audience some of the significant works of important theologians in critical areas of
ecumenical discussion.  The selections will reveal new directions in Protestant and Catholic thought that are not as well
known as they deserve to be.

(53)                    March 2, 1962, *The Bulletin*.


*Evidence of Satan in the Modern World*, Léon Christiani,
Macmillan, New York City, $4, 205 pp.   Reviewed by Flannery
O'Connor.*


    It is ironical that in these evil times we should need
fresh evidence of the existence of Satan, but such is the
case.  According to Baudelaire the devil's greatest wile is
to persuade us he does not exist.  The Christian drama is
meaningless without Satan, but only recently there has been
considerable publicity about a dispute among Anglicans over
whether the devil should be allowed to remain in their cate-
chism.  Such is the trend of the times.
    In *Evidence of Satan in the Modern World*, Léon Christi-
ani traces demonic activity from New Testament times to the
20th century, concentrating heavily on cases of possession.
Although the modern reader will find his credulity strained
by some of the macabre instances of possession described, he
will be required by a strictly scientific attitude not to
dismiss this evidence out of hand.  The jacket tells us that
this book is well-documented and presented in an unsensationa
manner.  The documentation here has to be accepted on the wor
of the author and the subject is sensational *per se*.
    The author's discussions of the more generalized activi-
ties of Satan are less disturbing to the credulity although
their implications are a good deal more terrifying.  All in
all, the reader leaves this book with his belief in Satan
considerably fortified.

(54)        March 2, 1962, *The Bulletin*.

*The Georgia Review*, quarterly, University of Georgia, Athens,
$3 yearly.  Reviewed by Flannery O'Connor.*

    The word which might best characterize *The Georgia Re-*
*view* is "pleasant."  It is, apparently by design, one of the
least intellectually strenuous of the college quarterlies.
Critics do not criticize the criticism of other critic's critics in the pages of *The Georgia Review*.  There are no bat-
tles in the footnotes; in fact, no footnotes.  It is obviously
a magazine by Southerners for Southerners about Southerners.
Its manner is so relaxed as to suggest genial front-porch
monologues by local scholars whom it is not necessary to lis-
ten to very attentively.  Though occasionally an article about
a non-Southerner, such as Robert Frost, may make its way into
these pages, most of the articles are about little known or
forgotten Georgia literary or historical figures--Frances
Newman, William Harris Crawford.  These articles are invari-
ably well-written.  *The Georgia Review* also prints poems and
stories.  Its poems are well-turned and undemanding.  Its
fiction, with only an occasional exception, leaves the impression that it has travelled much and been rejected many
times before finding asylum here.  It is the magazine's worst
feature.  All in all, *The Georgia Review* is an unpretentious,
and by that much, refreshing quarterly, admirably suited to
the Georgia temper.

(55)              March 17, 1962, *The Bulletin.*


*The Conscience of Israel*, Bruce Vawter, C.M., Sheed and Ward,
1961, 295 pp., $5.00.   Reviewed by Flannery O'Connor.


        In *The Conscience of Israel*, Fr. Vawter analyses the pre-
exilic prophets of the eighth and seventh centuries B.C.,
Amos, Hosea, Micah, Isaiah and Jeremiah and the minor prophets, Nahum, Sephaniah and Habakkuk, and attempts to reset
their words in the concrete historical moment that brought
them forth.   Nineteenth century Biblical criticism was
largely that of liberal Protestantism.   The result of this
was that the prophets were seen in the light of liberal Protestantism.   They became Israelite Luthers and Wesleys, in-
novators opposing ritualism, or social reformers of advanced
views.   Twentieth century Biblical criticism has returned
the prophets to their genuine mission, which was not to in-
novate, but to recall the people to truths they were already
well aware of but chose to ignore.   Victorian commentators
appear sometimes to have thought of the prophets as "liberal
vicars or non-conformist chaplains . . . with the same bluff
piety that made the Empire great."   Fr. Vawter restores them
to their exotic Oriental culture where they were seen by
their contemporaries as inspired men, in communication with
"that otherness that men have always associated with the
divine."   In this setting alone it is possible to understand
an Isaiah walking naked as a warning to Egypt, an Hosea agon-
izing over his prostitute wife or an Ezekiel baking his bread
over dung to symbolize the destruction to come.
        Fr. Vawter warns against making Christians of the pro-
phets.   The prophets prepared for the revelation of the New
Testament; they did not anticipate it.   This excellent book
will give the reader a fuller understanding of both preparation and fulfillment.

(56)     March 31, 1962, *The Bulletin*.


*The Victorian Vision*, Margaret M. Maison, Sheed and Ward, New York, 1961, $4.50, 343 pp. Reviewed by Flannery O'Connor.*


The favorite subject of the Victorians was religion. From Tractarian to Dissenter to Latitudinarian, their preoccupation was with questions of man's right relationship to God. Even Agnosticism as it began to take over toward the end of the period took on the lineaments of a religion. Dr. Maison in *The Victorian Vision* analyzes Victorian religious opinion as it is seen in popular novels of the period. Most of the novels she discusses are unashamedly propagandistic, badly written, and to the modern reader sources of high comedy. One of the funniest aspects of these novels was the treatment of that villain of the Protestant imagination-- the Jesuit. He was "a spy, a secret agent, suave, supercilious and satanically unscrupulous, laying his cunning plots for the submission of England to 'Jesuitocracy', wheedling rich widows, forcing his converts to change their wills in favor of his order, to kneel in penitence for hours through chilly nights and to leave their families at a minute's notice."

Not all the religious novelists of the period were of this stamp. Both Newman and Manning wrote novels as well as Disraeli. Dr. Maison has read an incredible number of these books, both good and bad, and analyzed them with zest. The result is one of the most enjoyable and enlightening books that have been written about the Victorian temper.

(57)              May 12, 1962, *The Bulletin*.


*Toward the Knowledge of God*, Claude Tresmontant, Helicon
Press, Baltimore, 1961, 120 pp., $3.50.   Reviewed by Flan-
nery O'Connor.*


In this essay Père Tresmontant demonstrates three ways
of showing the possibility of knowing that God exists.   The
problem is first approached from the standpoint of human
thought attaining to the knowledge of the Absolute when it
has as its point of departure a consideration of reality.
In this section the phenomenon of Israel is not brought in.
In the second section the problem is approached by discussing Israel.   Tresmontant shows that such a local and particular phenomenon may nevertheless contain a lesson of universal import.   In this approach any consideration of Christ
is omitted.   In the last section the person of Jesus is considered for what He may teach about the Absolute.
Tresmontant is convinced that a knowledge of God is
really possible by a correct use of human reason, beginning
with the fact of creation and without asking the unbeliever
to make Kierkegaard's leap into the absurd.   He does not suggest that this quest for God could have reached its destina-
tion without the guidance of Judaism and Christianity or if
there had been no manifestation of the Absolute to man, but
this "only proves that the human mind is congenitally affected
by a weakness or difficulty in conceiving of reality, life,
the spiritual or the new."
This closely reasoned book will reward a careful reading

(58)        August 4, 1962, *The Bulletin*.

*The Cardinal Spellman Story*, Robert I. Gannon, S.J., Doubleday, New York, 1962, 423 pp., $5.95.   Reviewed by Flannery
O'Connor.*

To the Protestant, Cardinal Spellman is the image of
the Church in America.  It was therefore with consternation
that many Catholics read the condensed version of Fr.
Gannon's biography of the Cardinal in *Look Magazine*.  The image created
there was of an opportunistic individual, innocently aggres-
sive, who fitted well into a church where prelates were more
concerned with protocol than piety.  Fortunately the book itself mitigates this image, and leaves one wondering who produced the condensation and with what malice aforethought.
Cardinal Spellman moves through *The Cardinal Spellman
Story* round, smiling, efficient and indefatigable.  Largely
through a few letters written home from servicemen, which seem
absolutely trustworthy, the reader gets a picture of a very
humble and simple man, one gladly willing to say Mass in the
rain in Korea on Christmas day when he could more easily have
been elsewhere.  Such glimpses are stuck here and there in a
mass of official material, some of it fascinating, a good deal
of it tedious.  We are given many official letters and tele-
grams verbatim and sizable portions of the Cardinal's sermons.
Cardinal Spellman has apparently often given as many as seven
talks a day, a feat which would kill a lesser man, but which
must account for the ease with which he exercises the clerical
gift for bringing forth the sonorous familiar phrase of slowly
deadening effect.
If parts of the biography also tend to anaesthetize, the
reason may be that the book is one long encomium which nowhere
questions the wisdom of any of the Cardinal's actions.  This
tends to make the reader feel that the portrait is one-dimen-
sional and that a good man has been slighted by being given
less weighty treatment than he deserves, but the subjects of
biographies should properly be dead and the subject of this
one is still very much alive.  Fr. Gannon has had a difficult
job and has done it with as much grace as could be expected.

(59)                  August 4, 1962, *The Bulletin*.


*The Council, Reform and Reunion,* Hans Küng, Sheed and Ward,
New York, 1961, 201 pp.

*The Integrating Mind,* Wm. F. Lynch, S.J., Sheed and Ward,
New York, 181 pp., $3.95.

Reviewed by Flannery O'Connor.*


     If the Church were equipped with a reverse Index which
required that certain books be read, these two would deserve
a high place on the list.  The wide distribution of *The
Council, Reform and Reunion* at this time would engender a
realistic attitude toward the coming council and would perhaps stimulate the laity to participate in it through prayer.
It would seem that an event of this magnitude in the Church's
life would inspire more enthusiasm among Catholics, but the
majority, being uninformed, take it lightly.  Fr. Küng first
sets forth the need of constant renewal in the Church, which,
because she has the limitation of taking her earthly shape
from the age, is subject to constant deformation.  In the
present age, it is indispensable that we make a "painfully
critical dispassionate analysis, the kind of description
which will appear one-sided, of the weaknesses in the Church's
position."  Fr. Küng proceeds relentlessly to do this.  He
is careful to point out the difference between the kind of
restoration which took place during the last period of the
Council of Trent and a genuine reform which would imply creative growth through a real understanding of the Protestant
Reformer's demands.  Particularly interesting is his discussio
of the Petrine office and its relation to episcopal initiative
but on every point this book has something to offer.  No Catho
lic can read it without profit to himself and the Church.
     *The Integrating Mind* reemphasizes and reinforces themes
found in Fr. Lynch's two previous books, *The Image Industries*
and *Christ and Apollo*.  It is an essay against the totalistic
temptation--in history, politics and art--which rigidly sep-
arates categories into either/or choices.  Fr. Lynch makes
clear that he is writing here of contraries, not contradic-
tions.  The book, "in substance a plea that we keep things
together that belong together," is timely, though not topi-
cal, and should serve as an antidote to prevailing exaggera-
tions in American political and social thought.

(60)               August 18, 1962, *The Bulletin*.


*Mystics of Our Times*, Hilda Graef, Hanover House, 1962, 238
pp., $4.50.   Reviewed by Flannery O'Connor.


       *Mystics of Our Times* contains ten short biographies of
modern men and women who have lived the mystical life and concerned themselves with contemporary problems.  The subjects,
among which are both laymen and religious, are as diverse
in temperament and interests as the American convert, Isaac
Hecker, the Irish stenographer, Edel Quinn, and the French
scientist, Pierre Teilhard de Chardin, S.J., but they all
have in common that each was, in his way, ahead of his time,
some by as much as a century.  No stress is laid on mystical
phenomena.  The intention throughout has been to show that
" . . . because our world is so distracting, and at the same
time so desperately in need of God, He will give very special
graces to those who, whether as priests or laymen, have been
called to work for him in this world and who must use those
means contemporary society has put at their disposal."
       In spite of an undistinguished style, the book is enjoy-
able, easily read, and offers considerable food for reflection.

(61)              November 24, 1962, *The Bulletin*.


*The Catholic in America*, Peter J. Rahill, Franciscan Herald
Press, 156 pp., illus., $2.95.   Reviewed by Flannery O'Connor.


    *The Catholic in America* is a short history of anti-Catho-
licism in this country.  Fr. Rahill confines himself to brief
descriptions of the more obvious events that exemplify American anti-Catholicism and traces the gradual diminution of its
vigor from Colonial times to the present.  The book manages
to be interesting in spite of the fact that it is written in
a sloppy journalistic style (at one point the grammar is incorrect) and is not adequate to the complexity of the subject.  No mention is made of that Catholic parochialism which
often incited bitter feelings among non-Catholics.  A good
book can be written on anti-Catholicism in America but it
would have to penetrate the subject to a greater depth than
this one does.

(62)        March 2, 1963, *The Southern Cross.*

*The Bible: Word of God in Words of Men,* Jean Levie, Kenedy,
301 pp., $7.50.  Reviewed by Flannery O'Connor.


        One of the most interesting facets of Church history in
the last hundred years has been the strides made in Biblical
scholarship.  The purpose of this excellent book is to trace
certain stages in the exegetical, archaeological and historical research of those years and thereby to show how the human
aspect of Scripture appears today.  The first half of the book
is limited to the history of these new discoveries and the
Church's response to them.  The second part is designed to
explore and emphasize the great complexity of Scriptural
assertion.  In it Fr. Levie discusses the various literary
forms, the way sources are used and reproduced, the progressive character of the Old Testament and other related problems of historical exigency.  Since the divine mes- . . .
[line missing from text] of its human author and since the
individual exegete is not always able to determine between
interpretations, it remains for the Church to judge its meaning.  "God, who alone sees the ultimate connection between
the doctrinal passages scattered throughout Scripture, gives
to his Church, enlightened by the continual presence of the
Spirit, the privilege of progressively gaining a deeper insight into the dogmatic synthesis he intended and willed from
the beginning, and this as a result of the moral endeavors of
the saints, the religious needs of the mass of the faithful,
the scientific work of the exegetes, theologians and doctors,
and the directives of the Magisterium."  A knowledge of the
material covered in this book should be part of the equipment
of every Bible-reading Catholic.

(63)            March 9, 1963, *The Southern Cross.*


*Frontiers in American Catholicism*, Walter J. Ong, S.J., Macmillan, 1961, $1.25, 125 pp.  Reviewed by Flannery O'Connor.


     These six excellent essays, reissued here in paperback,
are concerned with some of the cultural and ideological problems which face American Catholicism today.  They are considered in the light of the American Catholic's attitude toward
Europe and his own history, his misconceptions about the
medieval period, and his attitude toward technology and scienc
They seem to be addressed as much to Europeans as to Americans
Fr. Ong believes that if Catholic thought in this country is
going to have any real contact with the American experience it
needs to envision "a real Christian mystique of technology and
science."  Ever since the bogus heresy of "Americanism"--
ended by Leo XIII's letter to Cardinal Gibbons--Americans have
been loth to explore the meaning of America for Catholicism.
Fr. Ong believes that our intellectual contribution may be the
of explaining the social surface of life in the United States-
sports, luncheons, clubs, optimism, advertising, merchandising
etc.--along the lines of phenomenological analysis.  He sees
signs that there are some American Catholic philosophers who
are becoming interested in phenomenology.  These are fine
essays and should not be missed now that they are available
at this low price.

(64)          March 16, 1963, *The Southern Cross*.

*New Men for New Times*, Beatrice Avalos, Sheed and Ward, 1962,
$3.75, 182 pp.
*Seeds of Hope in the Modern World*, Barry Ulanov, Kenedy, 1962,
201 pp.
Reviewed by Flannery O'Connor.


Both of these books are concerned with new times, one
with the education of the Christians who will live in them,
the other with educating Christians to value them.
After two chapters analyzing the educational systems of
Marx and Dewey and their inadequate ways of meeting the up-
rootedness of modern man, Dr. Beatrice Avalos in *New Men for
New Times* describes a Christian conception of education, the
fundamentals of which she takes [from] the principles and practices of a contemporary movement of Catholic action, the
Schoenstatt Apostolic Movement. Her general thesis is that
the sound exercise of activities on the natural level is the
way to lay a solid foundation for the action of grace. She
elucidates this in relation to person, home and school and
provides the philosophical background. This book is written
with intelligence and considerable learning but unfortunately
with a heavy reliance, particularly in the first chapters, on
the jargon held dear in educational circles. The rule is:
if one word will do, use four; thus "experience" becomes
"experiential contact with reality." Bastard words are either
borrowed or invented, e.g., "educand"--an "educand" is pre-
sumably the victim of an educator. A boneyard of dead or
abstract or unnecessary phrases is thrown up between the
reader and the thought. If this were not a better book than
most in this field, there would be no need to complain about
this, but there is genuine danger that the reader, unless he
is a student of education and thus habituated to such, will
quit the book half way through, with the thought: if they do
this to the language, what do they do to the child?
Dr. Ulanov's book, *Seeds of Hope in the Modern World*,
should serve as an antidote to a tendency of Catholics to
despise the modern world on principle and condemn out of hand
anything that does not have obvious roots in the Middle Ages.
The author points out that "Meditation and contemplation in
our time, like language and thought, do not often follow
familiar paths. They could not, for the remarkable meditative minds of our time have looked elsewhere than to the
familiar for their meditations. Or rather, they have looked
through the familiar to the unfamiliar, have looked with such
intensity and ingenuity and patience at the commonplace that

they have discovered once again, as the Greek and Latin Father
and the Renaissance humanists did before them, how very uncom-
mon it is." Dr. Ulanov follows some of these meditations as
they are found in modern literature, art, music and science.
The procedure is much too rapid to be satisfying, but the
book well achieves its purpose, which is to suggest the potential power of the modern world to lead a man closer to
God.

(65)           March 23, 1963, *The Southern Cross*.


*The Wide World, My Parish*, Yves Congar, O.P., Helicon, 1961,
$4.50, 188 pp. Reviewed by Flannery O'Connor.


  Fr. Congar's book is concerned with eschatological questions and the meaning of salvation, particularly as it in-
volves those outside the visible church. His intention is
to provide "some elements" of answers to thoughtful people
who ask questions about the salvation of "the others." This
was a question which hardly occurred to the medieval mind,
but which has grown in urgency as the world has been explored
and other cultures discovered. Understanding of the formula,
"Outside the Church, no salvation," has changed drastically
since the time of its originator, St. Cyprian, who understood
it in an exclusive sense. Today it is understood to mean
that the Church is the only institution to which universal
salvation is committed, that she is the only institution
able to ensure salvation for every person who does not refuse
it.
  There are equally good discussions here of the meaning
of hell and the nature of purgatory and of the resurrection
of the body. Altogether this is an admirable book. Significantly its title has been suggested by a quotation from
John Wesley, "I look upon the world as my parish."

(66)            April 27, 1963, *The Southern Cross*.


*Letters from a Traveler*, Père Pierre Teilhard de Chardin,
Harper, 1962, 380 pp., $4.   Reviewed by Flannery O'Connor.


     The American publishers of Père Teilhard de Chardin
are probably waiting with interest to see what effect the
recent Monitum issued by the Holy Office on his works will
have on the sale of his books in this country.   It is rea-
sonable to suppose that it will have little appreciable
effect, for the purpose of the warning is not to forbid the
reading of Teilhard's books, but to point out to the reader
what to beware of when he does read them.   In any case, it
should not affect the sale of *Letters from a Traveler,* a
collection of Teilhard's letters from China and Africa and
America, written to his cousin, various colleagues and
friends.   The picture these letters give is one of exile,
suffering and absolute loyalty to the Church on the part of
a scientist whose life's effort was an attempt to fit his
knowledge of evolution into the pattern of his faith in
Christ.   To do such a thing is the work of neither scientist
nor theologian, but of poet and mystic.   That Teilhard was
to some degree these also is evident and that his failure was
the failure of a great and saintly man is not to be questioned
The Monitum takes a most respectful tone toward the man himself, and these letters are further evidence that his life of
faith and work can be emulated even though his books remain
incomplete and dangerous.

(67)        July 11, 1963, *The Southern Cross.*

*Saint Vincent de Paul*, M. V. Woodgate, Newman, 1960, 136 pp., $2.75.
*The Holiness of Vincent de Paul*, Jacques Delarue, Kenedy, 1960, 132 pp., $3.50.
*St. Vincent de Paul*, von Matt and Cognet, Henry Regnery Company, 1960, 190 pp., illus., $7.

Reviewed by Flannery O'Connor.

The three hundredth anniversary of the death of Vincent de Paul occurred in 1960 and these three volumes are a result of interest in the saint stimulated by that anniversary. The Woodgate book is a popular biography, adequate but not exciting in spite of the sharply dramatic life led by this shrewd peasant saint who grappled with the social ills of his day.
The Delarue book is better. It contains a short essay on the saint's life which traces his spiritual development from an ambitious young man to a devoted server of the poor. The rest of the book is made up of excerpts from St. Vincent's own letters, which is the proper place to find the spirit of the man.
The von Matt and Cognet book is perhaps the most satisfying of the three. It contains a short but very realistic life of the saint, interspersed with 190 magnificent photographs which have some connection with his time and place and the people who figured in his life.
These three volumes are a good beginning for anyone interested in the life of St. Vincent de Paul. It is a life which invites meditation and which no biography can exhaust.

(68)        July 18, 1963, *The Southern Cross.*
            November 29, 1963, *The Catholic Week.*


*What is the Bible*, Henri Daniel-Rops, Guild Press, 1960,
188 pp., $.85.

*Faith, Reason and the Gospels*, ed. John J. Heaney, S.J.,
Newman Press, 1962, 309 pp., $4.95 cloth, $1.95 paper.

Reviewed by Flannery O'Connor.


     In these days of renewed interest among Catholics in the
Bible and of considerable ferment in the field of Biblical
criticism, it is essential that anyone interested in acquaint-
ing himself with Biblical literature, get started on the right
foot.   Henri Daniel-Rops' *What is the Bible?* is an adequate
short book for the beginner.   It is a volume of the *Twentieth
Century Encyclopedia of Catholicism* here reprinted in a hand-
size 85¢ edition.   It covers rapidly the history of the creation of the Bible, the times and places in which it was written and its authors.   It is extremely simplified and should
neither hold the student long nor satisfy his curiosity on
the subject.   Controversy is avoided.
     *Faith, Reason and the Gospels* on the other hand is for
the mature student who is perplexed by Biblical problems as
they relate to scientific method.   It is not designed for the
nonbeliever but is meant to aid the man of belief to a better
understanding of why he believes.   Eleven of the articles included are by Catholics, four by Protestants.   The collection
grew out of and fulfills a distinct need.   Although summaries
of modern Christian thinking [with] regard to the gospels are
available, they are for the most part confined to technical
journals.   This collection brings together in one volume such
authorities in the field of Biblical studies as fathers Jean
Levie and David Stanley and Messrs. Floyd Filson and Archibald Hunter.   It is a fine book, not easily exhausted.

(69)      September 26, 1963, *The Southern Cross.*

*Images of America,* Norman Foerster, University of Notre Dame
Press, 1962, 152 pp., $1.95.
*The Modern God,* Gustave Weigle, S.J., Macmillan, 1963, 168
pp., $.395.
Reviewed by Flannery O'Connor.


        These two books can be read together with considerable
profit.  Prof. Foerster's is a brief social and literary history of America from the Puritan Age through the deistic and
romantic periods to the rise of realism and on to the present
times of disillusion and search for something new worth believing in.  Behind each of these changes in outlook is a
different view of God and man's relation to him.  The essay
ends in a brief consideration of the historical imagination
as found in Southern literature, particularly Faulkner.
        Prof. Foerster sees Americans as "an idealistic people,
responsive to humanitarian impulses, believing in the dignity of man and the primacy of human rights, but confused,
insecure, and anxious amid the forces of a world in turbu-
lent revolution."  Fr. Weigle begins at this point and analyzes the instability of the modern religious condition.  He
sees that our roots are in religious faith which we have not
been able to throw off like the Russians but that in practical
philosophy, we are as materialistic as they.  Fr. Weigle discusses the place given God in the civic order, in the moral
values of American culture, and by intellectuals.  He ends
by discussing the witness of the Church and its impression,
or lack of impression, on the public conscience.  He finds
that our dilemma is too many weak secular faiths and suggests
that what is needed is a "great faith resting on a big
theology."
        Both Prof. Foerster's and Fr. Weigle's are valuable
essays which should add greatly to the Catholic's understanding of his country and his times.

(70)        October 24, 1963, *The Southern Cross.*


*Evangelical Theology: An Introduction*, Karl Barth, Holt,
Rinehart and Winston, Inc., New York, $4, 206 pp.  Reviewed
by Flannery O'Connor.


     *Evangelical Theology: An Introduction* contains the series
of lectures Karl Barth delivered in the Spring of 1962 at the
University of Chicago and Princeton Theological Seminary plus
twelve additional chapters on the nature of the evangelical
theologian's faith and work and the dangers which threaten
them.  Although the book is a description of his own beliefs
about the subject, Barth does not use the term "evangelical"
in the confessional sense.  He points out that all Protestant
theology is not evangelical whereas some Catholic and Eastern
theology is.  What the term designates is that theology which
treats of the God of the Gospel.  "Theology is science seeking the knowledge of the Word of God spoken in God's work--
science learning in the school of Holy Scripture, which wit-
nesses to the word of God; science laboring in the quest for
truth, which is inescapably required of the community that
is called by the Word of God.  In this way alone does theology
fulfill its definition as the human logic of the divine Logos.
In every other respect theology is really without support."
Again, God "exercises law and justice when he makes the theologians, the church, and the world realize that even the best
theology is in itself and, as such, a human work, sinful, imperfect, in fact corrupt and subject to the powers of destruction."  This will remind the Catholic of St. Thomas' dying
vision of the *Summa* as all straw.  There is little or nothing
in this book that the Catholic cannot recognize as his own.
In fact, Barth's description of the wonder, concern and commitment of the evangelical theologian could equally well be
a description of the wonder, concern and commitment of the
ideal Catholic life.

(71)           November 29, 1963, *Catholic Week*.


*Morte D'Urban*, J. F. Powers, Doubleday, 1962, 336 pp., $4.50.
Reviewed by Flannery O'Connor.


    Mr. Powers' novel, long awaited, has arrived and it is
a fine novel, altogether better than the chapters published
separately in *The New Yorker, The Critic,* and *Esquire* had led
one to expect. These chapters were marked by a certain sameness that brooded no good for the future book, but the whole
proves to be greater than the sum of its parts and moves forward without tedium to a profound conclusion.
    The hero, Father Urban, is a go-getting priest in a
non-go-getting order. His mission is to be the "better-type"
soul and, against fearful odds, he manages to promote the con-
struction of a golf course at his order's retreat house; but
Father Urban's soul is worth saving and Mr. Powers proceeds
to save it, even if ultimately at the expense of the golf
course and the order's material gain.
    In some circles this novel will be read as if it were an
essay entitled "The Priest in America." Some reviewers will
point out that Father Urban is not typical of the American
priest; some will imply that he is. This reviewer would like
to point out that Mr. Powers is a novelist; moreover a comic
novelist, moreover the best one we have, and that Father
Urban represents Father Urban. If you must look for anyone
in him, Reader, look for yourself.

(72)          January 9, 1964, *The Southern Cross.*


*The Kingdom of God, A Short Bible,* ed. Louis J. Putz, C.S.C.,
Fides, 1962, 383 pp., $4.95.  Reviewed by Flannery O'Connor.


     *The Kingdom of God* is an abridged Bible for school use,
prepared for the German school system in 1960, and now available in English.  There is no indication as to what grades
this text is suitable for, but, since German schools are
generally more advanced than ours, the German child would
probably come to it several years before the American.  The
explanations before each reading are brief, stated in simple
language, and designed to show the child what the ancient
writer's intention was; for example, the explanation pre-
ceeding Genesis I reads: "The Bible begins with a song of
praise to God who created heaven and earth.  God, through His
Word, created and sanctified all things.  The Bible gives its
account of the creation of the world in the picture-story
language of the ancients; consequently the work of creation
is presented in the seven-day week framework."  Old and New
Testaments are tied in together with quotations in such a
way as to assist the teacher to show the child that sacred
history is a continuous revelation with the seeds of the future contained in the past.
     It is doubtful if the illustrations in this text will
appeal to children.  In every face depicted, the sign for
spirituality is emaciation.  Otherwise, this is an admirable
book, to be recommended for the child's use at home as well
as in school.

(73)          January 9, 1964, *The Southern Cross.*

*Prince of Democracy: James Cardinal Gibbons,* Arline Boucher
and John Tehan, Hanover House, 1962, 295 pp., $4.95. Re-
viewed by Flannery O'Connor.

        Cardinal Gibbons' life was equivalent to a short history
of the Catholic Church in America during its most crucial
years. He lived from 1834 to 1921, saw the United States
in three wars, and was an active churchman in the pontificates
of four Popes, Pius IX, Leo XIII, Pius X--in whose election
he played a decisive part--and Benedict XV. During these
years in Europe the Church, shackled on every side by vio-
lently anti-clerical governments, was facing perhaps the
blackest time in her entire history; only in America was she
expanding. Cardinal Gibbons' great role was to recognize and
proclaim to the rest of the Church what in America the separation of church and state had meant to the welfare of Catholics. His voice usually prevailed, not only in Europe but
in this country as well, where Bishops were divided and charity among them was not conspicuous. He took a firm hand in
molding the Church's position on labor, he effectively prevented the establishment of different national hierarchies in
the United States, he founded the Catholic University in
Washington and nursed it through many bad times, and he wrote
the most popular book of apologetics of his age, *The Faith of
Our Fathers.*
        This biography by Arline Boucher and John Tehan is better
written than most popular biographies and will whet the appetite for the definitive treatment of Cardinal Gibbons and his
times.

LIST OF BOOKS REVIEWED BY FLANNERY O'CONNOR

This list includes both published and unpublished reviews in as much as they can be determined. The only previously published source is a partial list of Flannery O'Connor's published reviews.[1] The present compilation completes and corrects that work and includes known unpublished reviews.

Flannery O'Connor, working as a book critic from 1953 to 1964, wrote most of her reviews under the direction of the book review editor of *The Bulletin*. Eileen Hall served in this capacity until 1960, when Leo Zuber replaced her. When that paper ceased publication of reviews in 1963, Zuber began to have the work of his reviewers published in *The Southern Cross*. Flannery O'Connor also published three reviews in *Catholic Week* and one review in *American Scholar*. It is impossible to determine whether or not she also wrote other reviews for other journals or periodicals.

An abbreviated form is used to indicate place of publication: "*B*" for *The Bulletin*, "*SC*" for *The Southern Cross*, "*CW*" for *Catholic Week*, and "*AS*" for *American Scholar*. Each item contains all available data.[2] Those entries bearing publication place (*The Bulletin* of *The Southern Cross*), date, but no page number, have been verified by Leo Zuber. However, his files do not include pagination. The identification number after each entry refers to the chronological order of the reviews and is the order in which they are presented in this

---

[1]Orvell, pp. 196-99.

[2]Back copies of *The Bulletin* and *The Southern Cross*, both held by the Diocese of Savannah, are being added to the newly established Archives Department. They are not at present publicly available.

text. Entries without parenthetical dates are unpublished
reviews and cannot be accurately dated.

Copies of those reviews listed here were supplied for
this study by Leo Zuber from his files and by Gerald Becham
from the files of the Flannery O'Connor Collection. No copy
has been found for two published reviews: Guardini's *Medita-*
*tions Before Mass* and Franc Smith's *Harry Vernon at Prep.*

Reviews of volumes found in the Flannery O'Connor Collection are indicated by "Coll." which appears after the
item. "Annot." following an entry indicates a Collection
volume annotated by O'Connor.

Adam, Karl. *The Christ of Faith: The Christology of the*
    *Church.* Trans. Joyce Crick. New York, 1957. Coll.

--------. *The Roots of Reformation.* Trans. Cecily Hastings.
    New York, 1957.

Avalos, Beatrice. *New Men for New Times: A Christian Philo-*
    *sophy of Education.* New York, 1962. *SC* (March 16,
    1963), p. 2. Coll. (64).

Barth, Karl. *Evangelical Theology: An Introduction.* Trans.
    Grover Foley. New York, 1963. *SC* (October 24, 1963).
    Coll. Annot. (70).

Benét, Stephen Vincent. *Selected Letters.* Ed. Charles
    Fenton. New Haven, 1960. *B* (August 5, 1961). (41).

Boucher, Arline, and John Tehan. *Prince of Democracy: James*
    *Cardinal Gibbons.* Garden City, N. Y., 1962. *SC* (Janu-
    ary 9, 1964), p. 5. (73).

Bouyer, Louis. *Christian Initiation.* Trans. J. R. Foster.
    New York, 1960. *B* (November 12, 1960). Coll. (31).

--------. *The Spirit and Forms of Protestantism.* Trans.
    A. V. Littledale. Westminster, Md., 1956. Coll.

Bruns, J. Edgar. *Hear His Voice Today: A Guide to the Con-*
    *tent and Comprehension of the Bible.* New York, 1963.
    Coll.

Buehrle, Marie Cecilia. *The Cardinal Stritch Story.* Mil-
    waukee, 1959. *SC* (April 1, 1961). Coll. (35).

Buell, John. *The Pyx: A Novel.* New York, 1959. *B* (April 16,
    1960), p. 7. (21).

Burrough, Loretta. *Sister Clare: A Novel.* Boston, 1960. *B*
    (April 16, 1960), p. 7. (21).

Callahan, Daniel J., Heiko A. Oberman, and Daniel J. O'Hanlon,
    eds. *Christianity Divided: Protestant and Roman Catholic
    Theological Issues*. New York, 1961. *B* (February 17,
    1962). Coll. (52).

Caponigri, A[loysius] Robert, ed. *Modern Catholic Thinkers:
    An Anthology*. New York, 1960. *B* (December 24, 1960).
    Coll. (32).

Chaine, J[oseph]. *God's Heralds: A Guide to the Prophets of
    Israel*. Trans. Brendan McGrath. New York, 1954. Coll.

Clancy, William, et al. *Religion and the Free Society* (pam-
    phlet). New York, n.d.

College, Eric, ed. *The Mediaeval Mystics of England*. New
    York, 1961. *B* (September 30, 1961). Coll. (44).

Congar, [George] Yves (Marie Joseph). *The Wide World, My
    Parish: Salvation and Its Problems*. Trans. Donald Att-
    water. Baltimore, 1961. *SC* (March 23, 1963), p. 7.
    Coll. (65).

Corte, Nicholas (pseud., i.e. Léon Cristiani). *Pierre Teil-
    hard de Chardin: His Life and Spirit*. Trans. Martin
    Jarrett-Kerr. New York, 1960. *B* (October 15, 1960),
    p. 3. Coll. (29).

Cristiani, Léon (Nicolas Corte, pseud.). *Evidence of Satan
    in the Modern World*. Trans. Cynthia Rowland. New York,
    1962. *B* (March 2, 1962). (53).

*The Critic: A Catholic Review of Books and the Arts* (quar-
    terly).[3] Chicago. *B* (June 10, 1961), p. 7. (38).

*Cross Currents* (quarterly). Ed. Joseph E. Cunneen. West
    Nyak, New York. *B* (April 1, 1961), p. 7. (36).

Daly, Sister Emily Joseph, ed. *Joseph, Son of David*. Pat-
    terson, N. J., 1961.

Daniel-Rops, Henri. *What Is the Bible?* Trans. J. R. Foster.
    New York, 1958. *SC* (July 18, 1963), and *CW* (November 29,
    1963), p. 7. (68).

D'Arcy, Martin C. *The Meeting of Love and Knowledge: Peren-
    nial Wisdom*. New York, 1957. Coll. Annot.

de la Bedoyere, Michael. *The Archbishop and the Lady: The
    Story of Fénelon and Madam Guyon*. New York, 1956. Coll.

---

[3] In her reviews of journals Flannery O'Connor never indicated that she worked from a specific issue. She reviewed
each of the four journals listed in general, with a view toward its purpose, style, quality.

Delarue, Jacques. *The Holiness of Vincent de Paul.* Trans. Suzanne Chapman. New York, 1960. *SC* (July 11, 1963). Coll. (67).

Descalzo, J[ose] L[uis] M[artin]. *God's Frontier.* Trans. Harriet de Onís. New York, 1959. *B* (May 14, 1960), p. 7. (22).

Dillistone, F[rederick] W[illiam]. *The Novelist and the Passion Story: A Study of Christ Figures in Faulkner, Mauriac, Melville, Kazantzakis.* New York, 1960. *B* (December 23, 1961), p. 6. Coll. (48).

Durrwell, F[rancis] X[avier]. *The Resurrection: A Biblical Study.* Trans. Rosemary Sheed. New York, 1960. *B* (September 16, 1961). Coll. (42).

Ebersole, Marc C. *Christian Faith and Man's Religion.* New York, 1961. *B* (February 17, 1962). Coll. (52).

Eliade, Mircea. *Patterns in Comparative Religion.* Trans. Rosemary Sheed. New York, 1958. *B* (July 12, 1958). Coll. Annot. (13).

Emily Joseph, Sister. See Daly, Sister Emily Joseph.

Farrell, Walter, Bernard Leeming, et al. *The Devil.* New York, 1957.

Fénelon, François de Salignac de La Mothe. *Letters to Men and Women.* Ed. Derek Stanford. Westminster, Md., 1957. Coll. Annot.

Fenton, Charles, ed. *Selected Letters of Stephen Vincent Benét.* See Benét, Stephen Vincent.

Flood, Charles Bracelen. *Tell Me, Stranger.* Boston, 1959.

Foerster, Norman. *Image of America: Our Literature from Puritanism to the Space Age.* Notre Dame, Ind., 1962. *SC* (September 26, 1963). Coll. (69).

Gannon, Robert I[gnatius]. *The Cardinal Spellman Story.* Garden City, N. Y., 1962. *B* (August 4, 1962). Coll. (58).

Gardiner, Harold C[harles], ed. *American Classics Reconsidered: A Christian Appraisal.* New York, 1958. *B* (November 1, 1958). Coll. (14).

*The Georgia Review* (quarterly). Athens, Ga. *B* (March 2, 1962). (54).

Gilson, Etienne Henry. *Painting and Reality.* New York, 1957.

––––––––. *Reason and Revelation in the Middle Ages.* New York, 1961. Coll.

Gordon, Caroline. *How to Read a Novel.* New York, 1957.

————————. *The Malefactors.* New York, 1956. *B* (March 31, 1956). Coll. (1).

Graef, Hilda C. *Mystics of Our Times.* Garden City, N. Y., 1962. *B* (August 18, 1962). Coll. (60).

Graham, Aelred. *Zen Catholicism: A Suggestion.* New York, 1963. Coll.

Green, Julian. *The Transgressor.* Trans. Anne Green. New York, 1957. *B* (May 3, 1958). (12).

Gryst, Edward. *Talk Sense! A Pilgrimage Through Philosophy.* New York, 1961.

Guardini, Romano. *The Conversion of Augustine.* Trans. Elinor C. Briefs. Westminster, Md., 1960. *B* (May 27, 1961). Coll. (37).

————————. *Freedom, Grace and Destiny: Three Chapters in the Interpretation of Existence.* Trans. John Murray. New York, 1961. *B* (October 28, 1961). Coll. Annot. (45).

————————. *Jesus Christus: Meditations.* Trans. Peter White. Chicago, 1959. *B* (February 6, 1960), p. 5. Coll. (20).

————————. *Meditations before Mass.* Trans. Elinor C. Briefs. Westminster, Md., 1955. *B* (November 24, 1956). Coll. Annot. (8).

————————. *Prayer in Practice.* Trans. Leopold of Loewenstein-Wertheim. New York, 1957. Coll.

————————. *The Rosary of Our Lady.* Trans. H. von Schuecking. New York, 1955. Coll. Annot.

Guillet, Jacques. *Themes of the Bible.* Trans. Albert J. LaMothe. Notre Dame, Ind., 1960. *B* (September 16, 1961). Coll. (43).

Guitton, Jean. *The Modernity of St. Augustine.* Trans. A. V. Littledale. Baltimore, 1959. *B* (May 14, 1960), p. 7. Coll. (23).

Heaney, John J., ed. *Faith, Reason and the Gospels: A Selection of Modern Thought on Faith and the Gospels.* Westminster, Md., 1962. *SC* (July 18, 1963), and *CW* (November 29, 1963), p. 7. Coll. (68).

Heenan, John Carmel. *Confession.* New York, 1957.

Herr, Dan. *Stop Pushing!* Garden City, N. Y., 1961. *B* (June 10, 1961). (39).

Horgan, Paul. *Give Me Possession.* New York, 1957.

————————. *Humble Powers: Three Novelettes.* Garden City, N. Y 1956. *B* (June 6, 1956). (4).

Hostie, Raymond. *Religion and the Psychology of Jung.* Trans. G. R. Lamb. New York, 1957. Coll.

Hügel, Friedrich von. *Essays and Addresses on the Philosophy of Religion* (1921). 2 vols. London, 1949 and 1951. Coll.

————————. *Letters from Baron Friedrich von Hügel to a Niece* (1928). Ed. Gwendolen Greene. Chicago, 1955. *B* (June 23, 1956). Coll. Annot. (5).

Hughes, Philip. *A Popular History of the Reformation.* Garden City, N. Y., 1957. Coll.

Hughes, Riley, ed. *All Manner of Men: Representative Fiction from the American Catholic Press.* New York, 1956.

*Jubilee* (monthly). Ed. Edward Rice, New York.

Journet, Charles. *The Meaning of Grace.* Trans. A. V. Littledale. New York, 1960. Coll.

Kerr, Walter F. *Criticism and Censorship.* Milwaukee, 1954. *B* (May 11, 1957). Coll. (11).

Kiefer, William J. *Leo XIII: A Light from Heaven.* Milwaukee, 1961. *SC* (April 1, 1961). Coll. (35).

Kirk, Russell. *Beyond the Dreams of Avarice: Essays of a Social Critic.* Chicago, 1956. *B* (July 21, 1956). Coll. (6).

Knox, R[onald] A[rbuthnott]. *In Soft Garments: A Collection of Oxford Conferences.* 2nd ed. New York, 1953. Coll.

Küng, Hans. *The Council, Reform and Reunion.* Trans. Cecily Hastings. New York, 1962. *B* (August 4, 1962). (59).

Leetham, Claude. *Rosmini: Priest, Philosopher and Patriot.* Baltimore, 1958. Coll.

Levie, Jean. *The Bible: Word of God in Words of Men.* Trans. S. H. Treman. New York, 1962. *SC* (March 2, 1963), Coll. (62).

Lubac, Henri de. *Further Paradoxes.* Trans. Ernest Beaumont. Westminster, Md., 1958. Coll.

Lynch, William F. *Christ and Apollo: The Dimensions of the Literary Imagination.* New York, 1960. *B* (August 20, 1960), p. 3. Coll. Supplement.[4] (25).

————————. *The Integrating Mind: An Exploration into Western Thought.* New York, 1962. *B* (August 4, 1962). Coll. (59).

McDonald, Donald. *Catholics in Conversation: Seventeen Interviews with Teaching American Catholics.* Philadelphia, 1960.

McKenzie, John L. *The Two-Edged Sword: An Interpretation of the Old Testament.* Milwaukee, 1956. Coll.

---

[4]See Part Two.

Madeleva, M., Sister. See Wolff, Sister M. Madeleva.

Maison, Margaret M. *The Victorian Vision: Studies in the Religious Novel.* New York, 1962. *B* (March 31, 1962). Coll. (56).

Malavez, L[éopold]. *The Christian Message and Myth: The Theology of Rudolf Bultmann.* Trans. Olive Wyon. Westminster, Md., 1958. *B* (July 23, 1960), p. 3. Coll. Annot. (24).

Maritain, Jacques. *The Range of Reason.* New York, 1952; rpt. 1961. *B* (November 25, 1961). Coll. (46).

Martin, T[roy] K[ennedy]. *Beat on a Damask Drum.* New York, 1960. *B* (October 1, 1960), p. 6. (28).

Matt, Leonard von, and Louis Cognet. *St. Vincent de Paul.* Trans. Emma Craufurd. Chicago, 1960. *SC* (July 11, 1963). Coll. (67).

Mauriac, François. *Lines of Life.* Trans. Gerard Hopkins. New York, 1957. Coll.

————————. *The Son of Man.* Trans. Bernard Murchland. Cleveland, 1960. *B* (September 3, 1960), p. 7. Coll. (26).

Mitchell, Walter, and the Carisbrooke Dominicans, eds. *Christian Asceticism and Modern Man.* New York, 1955. Coll.

Mounier, Emmanuel. *The Character of Man.* Trans. Cynthia Rowland. New York, 1956. Coll. Annot.

Ong, Walter J. *Frontiers in American Catholicism: Essays on Ideology and Culture.* New York, 1961. *SC* (March 9, 1963). Coll. (63).

Payne, [Pierre Stephen] Robert. *The Holy Fire: The Story of the Fathers of the Eastern Church.* New York, 1957. Coll.

Péguy, Charles [Pierre]. *Temporal and Eternal.* Trans. Alexander Dru. New York, 1958. *B* (January 10, 1959). Coll. (18).

Powers, J[ames] F[arl]. *Morte d'Urban.* Garden City, N. Y., 1962. *CW* (November 29, 1963), p. 7. Coll. (71).

————————. *The Presence of Grace.* Garden City, N. Y., 1956. *B* (March 31, 1956). Reprinted in *Mystery and Manners,* pp. 232-33. (2).

Putz, Louis J., ed. *The Kingdom of God: A Short Bible.* Notre Dame, Ind., 1962. *SC* (January 9, 1964), p. 5. Coll. (72).

Quinn, Sister Bernetta. *The Metamorphic Tradition in Modern Poetry: Essays on the Work of Ezra Pound, Wallace Stevens, William Carlos Williams, T. S. Eliot, Hart Crane,*

*Randall Jarrell, and William Butler Yeats.* New Brunswick, N. J., 1955. *B* (January 5, 1957). (9).

Rabut, Oliver A. *Teilhard de Chardin: A Critical Study.* New York, 1961. *B* (December 23, 1961), p. 6. Coll. (49).

Rahill, Peter J. *The Catholic in America: From Colonial Times to the Present Day.* Chicago, 1961. *B* (November 24, 1962). Coll. (61).

Raymond of Capua. *The Life of St. Catherine of Siena.* Trans. George Lamb. New York, 1960. *B* (March 18, 1961). Coll. (34).

Robo, Etienne. *Two Portraits of St. Thérèse of Lisieux.* Rev. ed. Chicago, 1955. *B* (May 26, 1956). Coll. (3).

Rougemont, Denis de. *The Christian Opportunity.* Trans. Donald M. Lehmkuhl. New York, 1963. Coll.

Rowley, H[arold] H[enry], ed. *The Old Testament and Modern Study: A Generation of Discovery and Research.* London, 1961. *B* (December 9, 1961). Coll. (47).

Sheed, Francis Joseph. *Marriage and the Family.* New York, 1957.

Shrady, M. L., ed. *Come South Wind: A Collection of Contemplatives.* New York, 1957. Coll.

Smith, Franc. *Harry Vernon at Prep.* Boston, 1959. *B* (March 7, 1959). (19).

Stein, Edith. *The Science of the Cross: A Study of St. John of the Cross.* Ed. L. Gelber and Romaeus Leuven. Trans. Hilda Graef. Chicago, 1960. *B* (October 1, 1960), p. 6. Coll. (27).

--------. *Writings.* Trans. Hilda Graef. Westminster, Md., 1956. *B* (March 2, 1957). Coll. (10).

Suzuki, Daisetz Teitaro. *Zen and Japanese Culture.* 2nd ed. New York, 1959.

Teilhard de Chardin, Pierre. *The Divine Milieu: An Essay on the Interior Life.* New York, 1960. *B* (February 4, 1961). Coll. Annot. (33).

--------. *Letters from a Traveler.* New York, 1962. *SC* (April 27, 1963). Coll. (66).

--------. *The Phenomenon of Man.* Trans. Bernard Wall. New York, 1959. *AS*, 30 (Fall, 1961), 618. Coll. Annot. (50).

Tresmontant, Claude. *Pierre Teilhard de Chardin: His Thought.* Trans. Salvator Attanasio. Baltimore, 1959. Coll. Annot.

--------. *Toward the Knowledge of God.* Trans. Robert J. Olsen. Baltimore, 1961. *B* (May 12, 1962). Coll. (57).

Ulanov, Barry. *Seeds of Hope in the Modern World*. New York, 1962. *SC* (March 16, 1963), p. 2. (65).

Vandon, Elizabeth. *Late Dawn*. New York, 1958. *B* (November 29, 1958). (16).

Vawter, Bruce. *The Conscience of Israel: Pre-Exilic Prophets and Prophecy*. New York, 1961. *B* (March 17, 1962), p. 6. Coll. Annot. (55).

--------. *A Path Through Genesis*. New York, 1956. Coll.

Voegelin, Eric. *Israel and Revelation*. Vol. I of his *Order and History*. Baton Rouge, 1956. *B* (November 15, 1958). Coll. Annot. (15).

--------. *Plato and Aristotle*. Vol. III of his *Order and History*. Baton Rouge, 1957. Coll. Annot.

--------. *The World of the Polis*. Vol. II of his *Order and History*. Baton Rouge, 1957. Coll. Annot.

Walker, Kenneth Macfarlane. *Life's Long Journey*. New York, 1961. *B* (June 24, 1961). (40).

Ward, Maisie. *The Rosary*. New York, 1957.

Waugh, Evelyn. *The Ordeal of Gilbert Pinfold: A Conversation Piece*. Boston, 1957.

Weigel, Gustave. *Faith and Understanding in America*. New York, 1959. Coll.

--------. *The Modern God: Faith in a Secular Culture*. New York, 1963. *SC* (September 26, 1963). Coll. (69).

Weiger, Josef. *Mary: Mother of Faith*. Trans. Ruth Mary Bethell. Chicago, 1959. *B* (February 6, 1960), p. 5. Coll. (20).

West, Morris L. *The Devil's Advocate*. New York, 1959.

White, Victor. *Soul and Psyche: An Enquiry into the Relationship of Psychotherapy and Religion*. New York, 1960. *B* (October 29, 1960), p. 3. Coll. (30).

Wood, Ernest. *Zen Dictionary*. New York, 1962. Coll.

Woodgate M[ildred] V[iolet]. *Saint Vincent de Paul*. Westminster, Md., 1960. *SC* (July 11, 1963). (67).

Woods, Ralph L[ouis], ed. *The Catholic Companion to the Bible* Philadelphia, 1956. *B* (September 1, 1956). Coll. (7).

Wolff, Sister M. Madeleva. *Conversations with Cassandra: Who Believes in Education?* New York, 1961. *B* (January 6, 1962). (51).

Wright, G[eorge] E[rnest]. *The Bible and the Ancient Near Eas Essays in Honor of William Loxwell Albright*. Garden City N. Y., 1961. *B* (December 9, 1961). Coll. (47).

Zilboorg, Gregory. *Freud and Religion: A Restatement of an Old Controversy.* Westminster, Md., 1958. *B* (January 10, 1959). Coll. (17).

# BIBLIOGRAPHY

Abbot, Louise Hardeman. "Remembering Flannery O'Connor."
*The Southern Literary Journal*, 2, No. 2 (Spring, 1970),
3-25.

Asals, Frederick. "Review of Kathleen Feeley's *Flannery
O'Connor: Voice of the Peacock*." *The Flannery O'Connor
Bulletin*, 1 (1972), 55-65.

Becham, Gerald. "The Flannery O'Connor Collection." *The
Flannery O'Connor Bulletin*, 1 (1972), 66-71.

Bradbury, John M. *Renaissance in the South: A Critical History of the Literature, 1920-1960*. Chapel Hill: Univ.
of North Carolina Press, 1964.

Burns, Stuart L. "How Wide Did 'The Heathen' Range?" *The
Flannery O'Connor Bulletin*, 4 (1975), 25-41.

Dominican Sisters of Our Lady of Perpetual Help Cancer Home.
*A Memoir of Mary Ann*. Ed. Flannery O'Connor. New York:
Farrar, Straus and Cudahy, 1961.

Drake, Robert. *Flannery O'Connor: A Critical Essay*. Grand
Rapids: William B. Eerdmans, 1966.

Duhamel, P. Albert. "The Novelist as Prophet." In *The Added
Dimension: The Art and Mind of Flannery O'Connor*. Ed.
Melvin J. Friedman and Lewis A. Lawson. New York: Ford-
ham Univ. Press, 1966, pp. 88-107.

Ellis, John Tracy. *American Catholicism*. 2nd ed. Chicago:
Univ. of Chicago Press, 1969.

Feeley, Kathleen. *Flannery O'Connor: Voice of the Peacock*.
New Brunswick, N.J.: Rutgers Univ. Press, 1972.

--------. Unpublished lecture. Georgia College, Milledgeville, Georgia. July 12, 1975.

Fitzgerald, Robert S. "Introduction," in Flannery O'Connor,
*Everything That Rises Must Converge*. New York: Noonday
Press [1965].

--------, and Sally Fitzgerald, eds. *Mystery and Manners:
The Occasional Prose of Flannery O'Connor*. New York:
Farrar, Straus and Giroux, 1970.

Fitzgerald, Sally. "The Habit of Being." *The Flannery O'Connor Bulletin*, 6 (1977), 5-16.

--------. Unpublished lecture, Flannery O'Connor Symposium,
    Georgia College, Milledgeville, Georgia. April 3, 1977.

--------, ed. *The Habit of Being: Letters of Flannery O'Con-
    nor*. New York: Farrar, Straus and Giroux, 1979.

Georgia Department of Agriculture. *Georgia, Historical and
    Industrial*. Atlanta: G. W. Harrison, 1901.

Getz, Lorine M. "Types of Grace in Flannery O'Connor's Fic-
    tion." Diss. Univ. of St. Michael's College, Toronto,
    1979.

Gilman, Richard. "On Flannery O'Connor." *New York Review
    of Books*, Aug. 21, 1969, pp. 24-26.

Giroux, Robert. "Introduction," in Flannery O'Connor, *The
    Complete Stories*. New York: Farrar, Straus and Giroux,
    1971.

Gordon, Caroline. "Heresy in Dixie." *Sewanee Review*, 76
    (1968), 263-297.

--------. *How to Read a Novel*. New York: Viking Press,
    1953.

--------, and Allen Tate, eds. *The House of Fiction: An
    Anthology of the Short Story with Commentary*. 2nd ed.
    New York: Scribner's, 1960.

Gossett, Louise Y. "The Test by Fire: Flannery O'Connor," in
    her *Violence in Recent Southern Fiction*. Durham, N.C.:
    Duke Univ. Press, 1965, pp. 75-97.

--------. *Violence in Recent Southern Fiction*. Durham,
    N.C.: Duke Univ. Press, 1965.

Hansen, Harry. "The Iowa Writers' Workshop." *The Saturday
    Review of Literature*, Nov. 21, 1931, p. 315.

Harden, William. *A History of Savannah and Southern Georgia*.
    Chicago: Lewis, 1913.

Hawkes, John. "Flannery O'Connor's Devil." *Sewanee Review*,
    70 (1963), 395-407.

Heaney, John J. "Modernism." *New Catholic Encyclopedia*.
    Vol. 9, 1967.

Hendin, Josephine. *The World of Flannery O'Connor*. Bloom-
    ington: Indiana Univ. Press, 1970.

Hitchcock, James. "Postmortem on a Rebirth: The Catholic In-
    tellectual Renaissance." *The American Scholar*, Spring,
    1980, pp. 211-225.

Holman, C. Hugh. "Her Rue with a Difference: Flannery O'Con-
    nor and the Southern Literary Tradition." In *The Added
    Dimension: The Art and Mind of Flannery O'Connor*. Ed.

Melvin J. Friedman and Lewis A. Lawson. New York: Fordham Univ. Press, 1966, pp. 73-87.

"Life Visits Yaddo." *Life*, July 15, 1946, pp. 110-113.

Lockridge, Betsy. "An Afternoon with Flannery O'Connor." *Atlanta Journal and Atlanta Constitution*, Nov. 1, 1959, pp. 38-40.

Lytle, Andrew. "Flannery O'Connor: A Tribute." *Esprit*, 8 (1964), 33-34.

McDowell, Frederick P. W. *Caroline Gordon*. Minneapolis: Univ. of Minnesota Press, 1966.

Malin, Irving. *New American Gothic*. Carbondale: Southern Illinois Univ. Press, 1962.

Martin, Carter. *The True Country: Themes in the Fiction of Flannery O'Connor*. Nashville: Vanderbilt Univ. Press, 1969.

Meaders, Margaret Inman. "Flannery O'Connor: Literary Witch." *The Colorado Quarterly*, 10 (1962), 377-386.

Merton, Thomas. "Flannery O'Connor: A Prose Elegy," in his *Raids on the Unspeakable*. New York: New Directions, 1966, pp. 41-42.

Muller, Gilbert H. *Nightmares and Visions: Flannery O'Connor and the Catholic Grotesque*. Athens: Univ. of Georgia Press, 1972.

Mullins, C. Ross. "Flannery O'Connor: An Interview." *Jubilee*, 9, No. 2 (June, 1963), 33-35.

Murphy, Rosalie, ed. *Contemporary Poets of the English Language*. New York: St. Martin's Press, 1971.

O'Brien, John T. "The Un-Christianity of Flannery O'Connor." *Listening*, 6 (1971), 71-82.

O'Connor, Flannery. *The Complete Stories*. Ed. Robert Giroux. New York: Farrar, Straus and Giroux, 1971.
Includes:
"The Geranium," pp. 3-14.
"The Barber," pp. 15-25.
"Wildcat," pp. 26-32.
"The Crop," pp. 33-41.
"The Turkey," pp. 42-53.
"The Train," pp. 54-62.
"The Peeler," pp. 63-80.
"The Heart of the Park," pp. 81-94.
"A Stroke of Good Fortune," pp. 95-107.
"Enoch and the Gorilla," pp. 108-116.
"A Good Man Is Hard to Find," pp. 117-133.
"A Late Encounter with the Enemy," pp. 134-144.
"The Life You Save May Be Your Own," pp. 145-156.

"The River," pp. 157-174.
"A Circle in the Fire," pp. 175-193.
"The Displaced Person," pp. 194-235.
"A Temple of the Holy Ghost," pp. 236-248.
"The Artificial Nigger," pp. 249-270.
"Good Country People," pp. 271-291.
"You Can't Be Any Poorer Than Dead," pp. 292-310.
"Greenleaf," pp. 311-334.
"A View of the Woods," pp. 335-356.
"The Enduring Chill," pp. 357-382.
"The Comforts of Home," pp. 383-404.
"Everything That Rises Must Converge," pp. 405-420.
"The Partridge Festival," pp. 421-444.
"The Lame Shall Enter First," pp. 445-482.
"Why Do the Heathen Rage?" pp. 483-487.
"Revelation," pp. 488-509.
"Parker's Back," pp. 510-530.
"Judgement Day," pp. 531-550.

--------. *The Habit of Being: Letters of Flannery O'Connor.*
Ed. Sally Fitzgerald. New York: Farrar, Straus and
Giroux, 1979.

--------. "Introduction," in *A Memoir of Mary Ann*, by the
Dominican Sisters of our Lady of Perpetual Help Cancer
Home. New York: Farrar, Straus and Cudahy, 1961, pp.
3-21.

--------. *Mystery and Manners: Occasional Prose.* Ed. Sally
and Robert Fitzgerald. New York: Farrar, Straus and
Cudahy, 1961; rpt. New York: Noonday Press, 1970.

--------. *Three by Flannery O'Connor.* New York: New Ameri-
can Library [c. 1963].
Includes:
*Wise Blood*, pp. 7-126.
*A Good Man Is Hard to Find*, pp. 127-299.
*The Violent Bear It Away*, pp. 301-447.

--------. "Why do the Heathen Rage?" *Esquire*, July, 1963,
pp. 60-61.

O'Connor, William Van. "The Grotesque: An American Genre,"
in his *The Grotesque: An American Genre, and Other
Essays.* Carbondale: Southern Illinois Univ. Press,
1962, pp. 3-19.

Orvell, Miles. *Invisible Parade: The Fiction of Flannery
O'Connor.* Philadelphia: Temple Univ. Press, 1972.

Owsley, Frank Lawrence. "The Irrepressible Conflict." In
*I'll Take My Stand: The South and the Agrarian Tradi-
tion* (1930), by Twelve Southerners. New York: Harper
and Brothers, 1962, pp. 61-91.

Quinn, Bernetta. "Flannery O'Connor, a Realist of Distances."
In *The Added Dimension: The Art and Mind of Flannery
O'Connor*. Ed. Melvin J. Friedman and Lewis A. Lawson.
New York: Fordham Univ. Press, 1966, pp. 157-183.

Rubin, Louis D. "Flannery O'Connor and the Bible Belt." In
*The Added Dimension: The Art and Mind of Flannery O'Con-
nor*. Ed. Melvin J. Friedman and Lewis A. Lawson. New
York: Fordham Univ. Press, 1966, pp. 49-72.

Sessions, William. "A Correspondence." In *The Added Dimen-
sion: The Art and Mind of Flannery O'Connor*. Ed. Melvin
J. Friedman and Lewis A. Lawson. New York: Fordham
Univ. Press, 1966, pp. 209-225.

Shannon, Margaret. "The World of Flannery O'Connor." *The
Atlanta Journal and Constitution*, Feb. 20, 1975, pp.
8-9, 37, 39.

Tate, Allen. "Remarks on the Southern Religion." In *I'll
Take My Stand: The South and the Agrarian Tradition*
(1930), by Twelve Southerners. New York: Harper and
Brothers, 1962, pp. 155-175.

Tate, Mary Barbara. Interview. Milledgeville, Georgia.
June 23, 1975.

Thomson, Philip. *The Grotesque*. London: Methuen, 1972.

Turner, Margaret. "A Visit to Flannery O'Connor Proves a
Novel Experience." *The Atlanta Journal and Constitution*,
May 29, 1960, p. 2-G.

Twelve Southerners. "Introduction: A Statement of Principles," in their *I'll Take My Stand: The South and the
Agrarian Tradition* (1930). New York: Harper and Brothers, 1962.

Vivante, Arturo. "Yaddo." *Writer*, 77, No. 8 (Aug., 1964),
28-29.

Wakeman, John, ed. "Flannery O'Connor," in his *World
Authors*. New York: H. W. Wilson, 1975, pp. 1076-1078.

Walters, Dorothy. *Flannery O'Connor*. New York: Twayne, 1973.

Woods, Ralph C. "The Heterodoxy of Flannery O'Connor's Book
Reviews." *The Flannery O'Connor Bulletin*, 5 (1976),
3-29.

"Yaddo and Substance." *Time*, Sept. 5, 1938, p. 50.